DATE DUE

DEMCO 38-296

THE LIVING ORGANIZATION

ORGANIZATION
Transforming Teams into
Workplace Communities

WHAT OTHERS ARE SAYING ABOUT
THE LIVING ORGANIZATION

"This is a great book. We would recommend it to our colleagues and quote it in our work in human resources. The reading was so good, we really couldn't just skim this material. We had to read it because it struck a chord, sounding what the change in corporate America is about. We would recommend the book as a candidate for business book of the year.

Professional Readers

"A ground-breaking overview of business organizations in transition. *The Living Organization* illuminates managers' tasks with a brilliant analysis of broad social forces now restructuring all human institutions."

Hazel Henderson, Author of *Paradigms in Progress*

"The ideas in this book can help employee-owned companies as well as other companies create a workplace of communal interests so that we will walk abreast into the 21st century."

Karen Young, National Center for Employee Ownership

"*The Living Organization* presents a wealth of information and good advice. It is impressive in its thoroughness and its scholarship."

Willis Harman, Founding Trustee of the World Business Academy, President of the Institute of Noetic Sciences and author of *Global Mind Change*

"Today's workplace environment, so commonly felt as a spiritually empty, brain-numbing day-to-day experience, can come alive with the insight offered in this book. Building workplace community will enable us to recommit ourselves to the American dream. Dr. Nirenberg has made an important contribution to management and to society as a whole. Total quality work environments must succeed, and will, when organizations take the moral responsibility necessary to ensure this critical transformation to workplace community."

Nancy Diamanté Bonazzoli, Senior Human Resource Manager, Digital Equipment Corporation

THE LIVING ORGANIZATION

ORGANIZATION

Transforming Teams into Workplace Communities

John Nirenberg

BUSINESS ONE IRWIN
Homewood, Illinois 60430

PFEIFFER & COMPANY
San Diego/Toronto/Amsterdam/Sydney

Grateful acknowledgment is made for the use of the following:

From *The Farther Reaches of Human Nature* by Abraham Maslow. Copyright © 1971 by Bertha G. Maslow. Used by permission of Viking Penguin, a division of Penguin Books, USA Inc.

Douglas McGregor, *The Human Side of Enterprise*. Reprinted, by permission of publisher, from *Management Review*, November/1957 © 1957. American Management Association, New York. All rights reserved.

Copyright © 1987 by M. Scott Peck, M.D., P.C. Reprinted by permission of Simon & Schuster, Inc.

R. Likert, *New Patterns of Management Copyright* © 1961 by McGraw-Hill, Inc. Material is reproduced with permission of McGraw-Hill.

This publication is designed to provide accurate and authoritative information in regard to the subject matter covered. It is sold with the understanding that neither the author nor the publisher is engaged in rendering legal, accounting, or other professional service. If legal advice or other expert assistance is required, the services of a competent professional person should be sought.

From a Declaration of Principles jointly adopted by a Committee of the American Bar Association and a Committee of Publishers.

Sponsoring editor: Cynthia A. Zigmund
Project editor: Gladys True
Production manager: Bette K. Ittersagen
Compositor: Monotype Composition Company, Inc.
Typeface: 10.5/12 Palatino
Printer: Book Press, Inc.

Library of Congress Cataloging-in-Publication Data
Nirenberg, John.
    The living organization: transforming teams into workplace
communities / John Nirenberg.
        p.   cm.
    ISBN 1–55623–943–2
    1. Management.   2. Quality of work life.   I. Title.
HD31.N53   1993
656.4'036—dc20

                                                                        92—37515

Printed in the United States of America
1 2 3 4 5 6 7 8 9 0 BP 0 9 8 7 6 5 4 3

This work is dedicated to Jennifer and Hillary Nirenberg and to Jonathan Walker, Tai Pan of Mera Saga, the three of whom will change the world. May they act from wisdom, and kindness always. I also dedicate this book to Drs. Tull, Shibles, and Ladd who, beyond their knowledge, made a life-long impression about good teaching and were supportive in ways they couldn't have imagined.

I also dedicate this work to my former students. Make a difference! And to grandmother Milly, born before the Spanish American War and still very much at home in New York. To my mother who taught me to question authority but always to do the right thing. She the critic. To the memory of my father who insisted that I think for myself and take responsibility for my actions. He the inventor. To Don and Sandy for keeping the faith. To uncle Lou and aunt Sally who always demonstrated what it takes to make a decent life and to uncle Sid who remained a faithful and caring ally when times were hard. To uncle Stan for being a great sport (and making the best Belgian pancakes). To aunt Elaine for her sense of humor and sticking to her art.

Finally, this book is dedicated to the creation of a compassionate, forthright and democratic future that has been the intergenerational dream of all Americans since the beginning.

Preface

"We have it in our power to begin the world again."

—*Thomas Paine*, Common Sense, 1776[1]

Are you:

- frustrated because your potential isn't being used?
- stymied by the seemingly inexplicable behavior of colleagues?
- dissatisfied with the fleeting and faddish nature of management reforms?
- feeling things could be better but unable to make a difference?
- disheartened by your inability to behave authentically at work?
- disillusioned with the incessant stress of your job?
- curious about the next major changes likely to affect you at work?
- ready to develop more personal control over the changes ahead?

Then this book is for you.

The Living Organization is about organizational reform and it has very ambitious goals. The book lays out a blueprint for a set of reforms that will both make our organizations more effective by aligning them to changes that are now transforming our society and, simultaneously, make them more personally satisfying workplaces. In addition, it addresses the underlying reasons why the efforts of so many well intentioned management experts have not substantially altered our experience of work, and why life in our organizations has become dispiriting to so many people. After reading this book you will know what it will take to make a meaningful difference in improving your organization and your work life. I hope you will agree that this is a very exciting prospect, indeed.

This is a tall order and I am mindful of the experience of Robert Owen, considered the father of personnel management. It was over 150 years ago that Owen, the managing partner of a very successful

vii

Scottish cotton mill, remedied the Dickensian conditions of factory life. At the same time he reversed many popular notions of proper manager-employee relations which had been characterized by the general contempt employers held of their servants (employees). He believed, and practiced in his mill, that employee welfare was a responsibility of the firm, and as human beings, employees deserved to be treated with dignity.[2] "Owen was the man who showed England that industrialism need not be built on cheap and brutally abused labor; he paved the way for factory legislation by putting his principles into effect and proving they would work."[3]

Though he proved the wisdom and the profitability of his reforms, he watched with incredulity as they were ignored by other manufacturers. Yet, over the years some of his and other innovative ideas eventually did become commonplace. Eight-hour work days, five-day weeks, vacation pay, health insurance, retirement plans, and profit sharing were all examples of progressive ideas of the time. Owen showed, however, that as long as best practice remains an optional matter to be based on the benevolence of any one person, and not institutionalized by actions of the board of directors or the legislature, reforms will be short lived. The vicissitudes of acceptance will remain a random matter facing each organization as circumstances and personalities dictate. Throughout history, reforms not legislated had to be re-proven and implemented afresh in every organization. Each was simply considered a managerial option; something one might get around to doing when there was time and money to be benevolent.

But now it is time for change. "Some 43 percent of the American populace fit the profile of the cynic,"[4] and most of our workplaces are uncooperative, hypercompetitive, boring or hostile places. Is it any wonder that amidst all of the potential of the postindustrial world is a fragmented, disconnected individual experience of work life characterized by cynicism, anomie and social paralysis?

Fortune magazine reports there is a morale crisis in American business but most chief executive officers don't see it.[5] Morale is an umbrella concept for many feelings and attitudes about one's life at work. It serves as a barometer indicating the kind of climate in the workplace. When it's inclement, organizational performance is weak; mediocrity is the norm.

In many respects, unfortunately, nothing has changed since Owen, even though everything has changed. We no longer have Dickensian physical working conditions, but we face the abusive harassment and a psychological treadmill at work that seems to speed up daily. As *Newsweek* has reported "For all its action and glamour, today's business world has generated corrosive ways to wear down bodies and spirits. The buzz around the water cooler is full of anxiety and paranoia. *The company is downsizing. The bean counters are out to get us. The boss has programmed the computers to monitor our phone calls.* No one can be sure when the dreaded takeover will strike. *A corporate raider has his eye on the firm. Pretty soon we'll all be working for the Japanese.* As the tension mounts, energies flag, blood pressures rise and that extra drink or two at the end of the day becomes more tempting. Across the office floor, fed up workers hide behind closed doors, furtively updating their resumes. . . ."[6]

Apparently, we are not having fun yet.

There has been a roller-coaster ride of innovation and retreat and many of Owen's ideas for reform are still topical today. Tom Peters, W. Edwards Deming, Charles Garfield, and Robert Levering,[7] all latter-day Owenites, have been purveying similar messages. But they have not been any more successful in helping to institutionalize these proven notions of best practice than Owen.

Why haven't we been able to widely implement what we know to be best practice? Has the search for excellence been called off? We must now challenge the overwhelming propensity to do business as usual and strive for systemic change that builds in to the structure and behavior of our organizations what we have come to know as best practice. Fundamental reforms are needed now because to conduct business as usual is to conduct business in decline. The times call for doing business as unusual. It is for lasting fundamental reform that *The Living Organization* was written.

This is the first book to discuss the need, and describe a process, for transforming organizations into workplace communities. In preparing the way, it points out the necessity of overcoming the all too familiar dichotomy of management vs. labor and calls for a new interpretation of organizations as holistic systems wherein each person plays an integral part being fully accountable to the workplace community as well as to stakeholders. This book also recognizes that the practice of management includes building and maintaining good working relationships with everyone in the organization, and that everyone shares the responsibility for this. Moreover, the book calls for the transformation of our organizations into workplace communities with full gain- and pain-sharing where the fortunes of each member of the community, employee, and investor, rise and fall with the organization's performance in the marketplace.

We begin with the theoretical underpinnings of the emerging paradigmatic changes now taking place and end with what you can do "Monday morning" to initiate the changes. The reader will come to learn that major reform is necessary and that *we can't have total-quality products until we have total-quality work environments.* We discuss the first postmanagerial structure to replace bureaucracy and accommodate the new assumptions and processes of community. In addition, the barriers to reform and prescriptions for dealing with them are mentioned. The reader will be able to act immediately on many of the ideas in the book, rather than have to wait for someone else to take the first step.

The Reader

The Living Organization speaks to all people in organizations from a managerial perspective. It addresses a general audience and is the first to recognize the power of creating a workplace community as a way of repairing our organizational decay. Boards of directors, aspiring CEOs, strategic planners, management and human resource professionals, university students of management, sociologists, organizational development specialists, trainers, union organizers, and everyone wishing to make a difference by using the workplace community concept should benefit from reading this book. It speaks to the vast majority of professionals, skilled workers, and middle managers who instinctively know something is rotten at work but are at a loss for a framework with which to look at their particular situations. Finally, this book speaks to all who want to understand what building organizational community is about and want to help facilitate its development.

The Book

The major contribution of *The Living Organization* is to pull together the various aspects of the new paradigm now piercing our organizational consciousness and to construct a system that accommodates the many societal and technological changes now taking place. Building workplace community will create and harness the synergy of what we already know about effective organizations by bringing together all the necessary components of the system. We see these components throughout Corporate America, but they are scattered about and achieving less than their full potential. This book is organized around three purposes: first to describe what is happening; second, to explain why it is happening; and, third, to describe how to align one's self and one's organization to the changes.

Chapter 1, "Introduction," discusses five myths of management that have hindered our ability to meet the new realities. It spells out the need for systemic change.

In Chapter 2, "New World, New Organizations," the stage is set by illustrating the breakdown of bureaucracy and the inappropriateness of an industrial model of organizing in a postindustrial world. It is argued that we have been trapped in paradigm one, which is the model underlying the industrial form of organization. Even though paradigm one has evolved through four distinct systems giving the misleading appearance of fundamental change, the underlying structure of the paradigm hasn't changed. Reformers have also been trapped in this thinking and it has undermined their recommendations.

In Chapter 3, "On The Current Transformation of Business: An Introduction to System Five," a new organization and management system is outlined and shown to represent the emergence of a distinctly new paradigm. It breaks through the myths and barriers that have restrained management thinkers from recommending fundamental changes to the existing system. By aligning organizations with the changes in society, System Five management opens the way for building more effective organizations. Many readers will identify with the new paradigm since it represents the belief system being adopted by an increasing number of people in America today. Leading edge companies are adapting accordingly. They have perceived the shift and understand the implications of the new circumstances underlying paradigm two.

Chapter 4, "The New Accountability: Building Balanced Relationships in a Postmanagerial Era," dramatizes the impact of the democracy movement worldwide, and specifically shows the dissonance between America's historical imperative for democratizing our institutions and the actual quality of work life in large organizations.

Since the collapse of the Soviet Union and East European socialist states we are coming to realize that it is corporations and not nation-states that create our quality of life. Corporations have eclipsed governments in their influence over our lives and they now dominate society. Thus, given their importance and the emergence of the new paradigm, we are questioning the legitimacy of organizational structures and the right of managers to govern without accountability to the governed, namely, the employees that work in them. We are beginning to question the validity of working in an environment which is not participative and inclusive. Organizations will be challenged to redefine the concept of organization to include all employees (who become members or organizational citizens), as well as stockholders, as legitimate *stake*holders. The concept of management will also be redefined to become the process of relationship building, rather than simply getting people to perform their jobs for the good of the organization.

Chapter 5, "Beyond Teams: Creating Organizational Community," develops the idea that organizations will be transformed into communities. It also discusses what it will take for an organization to become a community, what model may be useful in building community, and some of the benefits of becoming one. In addition, there is a short discussion of the kinds of issues that might work against community and how this model differs from the concept of self managing work teams.

This is a vital component of the book, since the transformation into communities will enable organizations to become aligned with the emergent paradigm.

Chapter Six, "A New Structure for The New Organization: Introducing Solacracy," describes a new organizational structure suitable to both teams and networks. I have coined the term solacracy (so•LOCK•ra•see) to describe the dynamics of large postbureaucratic organizations. It is a conjunctive of the stem sol implying a solar entity such as the Sun as well as an individual person such as in sole with -cracy a suffix from Greek meaning a structure of governance. Solacracy is the result of transforming the bureaucratic chain of command. Instead of the cumulative power of each level in a supervisory pyramid rising to a pinnacle where a CEO retains ultimate control over the organization, in solacracy a network of multiple power centers exists based on task relevance. Solacracy is the successor to bureaucracy, a counterpoint to the conditional paternalism and authoritarian forces that dehumanize people by treating them as means to an end rather than ends in themselves. Solacracy is a structure that combines democratic governance including a division of powers, accountability, and personal responsibility. Solacratic organizations adhere to the same democratic principles of representation, shared decision making and universal accountability that have been built into national, state and local governments; professional associations; interests groups; and, volunteer organizations. Acknowledging that corporations will inevitably assume an even bigger role in our lives, solacracy is a structure designed to insure that organizations become responsive to all their stakeholders by accelerating the transformation of organizations into workplace communities. Forming a solacracy is also a means for organizations to cope appropriately with the societal forces that are causing the transformation.

It is my intention in choosing the term solacracy to convey a visual image of a system in constant motion much like the solar system. The associated symbolism of enlightenment, holism, empowerment, and movement are enveloped in the definition. At the core is the emanation of the central idea, the vision, the essential purpose of the organization much like the Sun's energy is the center of the solar system.

Chapter 7, "New Organization, New Skills: Working in Community," focuses on the new assumptions about managing people. We then discuss managerial skills for working in community. Community and the solacratic structure require managerial competence for one to be an effective part of the entire work process and so it is assumed that all individuals are to be considered as managers in the new workplace. It is the equivalent of establishing workers as organizational citizens, each needing to have the skills necessary to live up to one's community responsibilities. This chapter discusses the skills needed by each person.

Chapter 8, "The Barriers to Community," discusses obstacles to be overcome, from biological, psychological and personal sources as well as inhibitors derived from the cultural milieu.

Chapter 9, "An Agenda for Monday Morning," prepares the reader for the moment of truth. After taking the reader through societal changes, arguing for the transformation of organizations into communities, suggesting a structure for accomplishing the transformation, outlining the skills needed to manage (indeed, work), in this new organizational world and pointing out some of the barriers to be faced in doing all of this, the individual's role is addressed—specifically in terms of actions the reader can take immediately, "Monday morning"—to begin the process of making a real difference. Concrete steps are offered, and the reader is asked to begin accepting responsibility for creating community in her or his workplace.

Chapter 10 is a brief afterword. May you enjoy the journey.

Note: I would very much like to hear from readers who wish to comment on the ideas in this book and who would be interested in learning more about workplace community. I would also like to hear from representatives of organizations which are pursuing some of the ideas in this book. In particular I would like to receive copies of company mission statements or policy statements that address issues raised here. If you would send along an anecdote that expresses the ideas in practice, I would be very appreciative. Please address all correspondence to: John Nirenberg, The Center for Workplace Community, P.O. Box 1395, Los Gatos, CA 95031. Thank you very much.

[The author is also available to speak to groups interested in exploring the concept of workplace community and to conduct workshops with companies interested in transforming themselves into community. Training in the specific skills outlined in this book is also available through The Center for Workplace Community.]

John Nirenberg

NOTES

1 I. Kramnick, ed., *Thomas Paine: Common Sense* (New York: Penguin, 1979), p. 120.

2 V. A. C. Gatrell, ed., *Robert Owen: Report to the County of Lanark and A New View of Society* (Baltimore, MD: Penguin Books, 1969).

3 C. S. George, Jr., *The History of Management Thought* (Englewood Cliffs, NJ: Prentice Hall, 1972), p. 63.

4 D. Kanter and P. Mirvis, *The Cynical Americans* (San Francisco: Jossey Bass, 1989), p. 1.

5 *Fortune* (November 18, 1991).

6 "Stress on the Job," *Newsweek*, April 25, 1988.

7 T. Peters and R. Waterman, *In Search of Excellence* (New York: Harper, 1982); T. Peters and N. Austin, *A Passion for Excellence* (New York: Random House, 1985); T. Peters, *Thriving on Chaos* (New York: Knopf 1987), W. E. Deming, *Out of The Crisis* (Cambridge, MA: Institute of Technology Center for Advanced Engineering Study, 1986); C. Garfield, *Second to None* (Homewood, IL: Business One Irwin, 1992); R. Levering, *A Great Place to Work* (New York: Avon, 1988).

Acknowledgments

First and foremost I must thank Richard Ogle, who has been a remarkable writing coach and friend throughout this entire project. He is a master of constructive criticism while being encouraging. He has provided superb meta-editorial help. Thanks also to brother Lloyd for opening the clubhouse to me whenever I needed it, for providing some basic research support, and for being critical when it all looked so easy. Thanks also to Bond University for a great schedule and for the serendipitous series of events that enabled me to have the luxury of a sabbatical to write this book. Thanks to Margaret because she cared from the outset. Thanks to Dr. Klaus Schmidt who gave a painstakingly thorough and most constructive review of the first draft and who was an early booster for its publication. Hats off to the anonymous reviewers for their support. And, last but by no means least, thanks to Cynthia Zigmund who saw the promise of the project from the proposal and championed the book through Business One Irwin.

J. N.

Contents

Chapter One

Introduction: Five Myths of Management

"Ah, but a man's reach should exceed his grasp, or what's a heaven for?"

—Robert Browning[1]

Comprehensive reform is long overdue as the state of the economy and the low morale of American workers so dramatically indicates. Although we know something is very wrong with our organizations, we have been reluctant to tamper with the system that has, until fairly recently, been responsible for creating tremendous wealth; yet that same system is now breaking down. Some fundamental aspects of the system seem incapable of meeting the demands created by a new world economic order, massive complexity, and the need for instantaneous responsiveness to customers, investors and employees.

The need for change seems more pressing today because with each managerial attempt to spark motivation, inspire innovation, infuse a commitment to a vision of what organizations can become, we get ever smaller returns for our effort and breed yet more cynics who see such efforts as just more manipulative cheerleading, at best.

The reforms proposed here are based on the optimistic belief that we are at a turning point and willing to make a real difference. Thankfully, there is a concrete reason to be optimistic; a vast latent army of disillusioned individuals in our workplaces is ready to respond to the call for a renewed sense of purpose. This storehouse of employee intelligence and energy waiting to be tapped represents a new magnitude of human potential as dramatic as the energy released with the smashing of the atom almost 50 years ago. This power can be realized if we reorient our thinking to accommodate recent changes in values, technology and society, and align our workplaces with a newly emerging holistic view of the world called paradigm two.

1

This book provides the reader a rationale and a plan for the creation of a new organization that will accommodate this new reality. It follows the transformation of the organization into workplace community. As will be shown, the transformation will release human potential, make our organizations more competitive and profitable, and satisfy our basic human urge to play a meaningful and respected role at work.

A system change is a prodigious endeavor and I am aware of the power of the conventional wisdom and the difficulty in bringing about a new order of things. But unless we make these changes we will fall further behind. As Charles F. Kettering said, "My interest is in the future because I am going to spend the rest of my life there."[2] Therefore, I believe (and I hope you share my sense of urgency about this) that the effort to rebuild our organizations is essential for our personal and national well being.

FIVE MYTHS OF MANAGEMENT

Myth One

The Manager Controls the Organization (We Look for Managerial Solutions When the Problems Organizations Face Require a Systems Approach)

This book has as its point of departure a most unusual paradox. From the end of World War II through the 1970's American business focused on techniques derived from the military's use of operations research and the earlier successes of scientific management in industry. Those techniques brought tremendous results. However, in the eighties, with the dawn of the post-industrial era, a breakdown occurred. American business was dramatically out-managed by Japanese, German and other competitors. In response we shifted our focus to reinvigorating managerial command and control through the application of new management techniques. Unfortunately, just as we redoubled our efforts, inspired by books such as *In Search of Excellence, Theory Z, The One-Minute Manager,* and others, changing the fundamental structure of the workplace remained taboo. So, while these and other authors were encouraging managers to solve the productivity mess through the application of personal power, productivity hardly budged throughout the decade and individual managers found it more difficult to control their commands in the old fashioned way.

What went wrong? As we focused on the manager, believing that the traditional hierarchical bureaucracy was still operative, the world changed. Instead of responding to the individual power of a manager, the organization was becoming a network of power centers; it seemed to metamorphose into a network of teams in order to deal with the complexity and increasing demands of the marketplace. Conditions changed necessitating solutions to the productivity problem embracing a system-wide view of the enterprise, not just a managerial one. Business was even moving toward a postmanagerial world where computer assisted communications among professionally trained colleagues reduced the need for middle management and the control orientation they represented. Thus, the more we attempted a managerial solution to a system's problem, the worse the problem became.

Because of the managerial orientation, there has been a roller-coaster ride of innovation and retreat and previous well intentioned reformers have only achieved small, incremental, changes around the edges of the current system. Each reform that has been offered in recent years, regardless of its potential, and even its proven worth, has too often floundered as just another managerial option; something one might get around to doing when there was time, money and the inclination to improve. But that is part of the inappropriateness of applying a managerial solution to a system's problem where the initiative depends solely on the motivations of an individual manager, right or wrong, instead of the group or organization that is ultimately affected by the action. Over the last eighty years, since the invention of scientific management, we applied ever more sophisticated managerial methods to symptoms instead of addressing the underlying problems. Those solutions as we have seen time and time again proved to be very low grade and short term palliatives to a system that today is in need of a massive overhaul.

While reformers have come and gone, one wonders: Why, if they were right, haven't the principles been codified into a readily acceptable standard body of knowledge which is widely and routinely practiced?

I argue that one reason is that we have allowed organizations to maintain a feudal structure wherein managers are not accountable to the managed. Even boards of directors are mostly controlled by the CEO so there are few checks and balances on their decision making and policy execution. Given the comprehensiveness of their power and its apparent speed and efficiency, it is understandable that there is a lot of resistance among top managers to accepting democratic practices. They simply have little incentive to democratize their organizations. There is also the strong denial of the frequently proven relationship between democratic ideas used to stimulate significantly higher levels of productivity, market and customer responsiveness, and innovation.

As long as the system's effectiveness remains an optional matter to be based on the benevolence or wisdom of any one person, or small group of individuals at the "top" of an organization, and not based on a continuous change process built into the whole organization, reform initiatives will be short lived and only partially effective if useful at all. The vicissitudes of acceptance will remain a random matter facing each organization as managerial personalities and preferences dictate. Thus the need for systemic change should be obvious.

Myth Two

Messiahs Will Save Our Organizations (We Look for Scapegoats When Our Leaders Fail Us, Instead of Depending on Ourselves)

Over the last twenty years there has been a deluge of books on leadership. CEOs of successful companies became hero's. Lee Iacocca of Chrysler, was extremely visible for his role in the bailout of Chrysler. Becoming a media celebrity as he advertised Chrysler products and chaired the Statue of Liberty restoration committee; he was even talked about as a possible presidential candidate. So was Donald Trump. Ross Perot waged a credible third party presidential candidacy that looked as though it would force the 1992 election into the House of Representatives. Leadership was indeed thought to be a necessary ingredient of corporate success—for awhile. Where leadership failed, scapegoats were found: "Unfair protectionist trade barriers," "cheap overseas labor," "poor schools at home," "entitlements that demotivated the work force," "high taxes," and "burdensome regulations," were all excuses for the lack of American competitiveness. Even if the charges were true they couldn't help repair the organizational breakdown. Those problems were too far removed from the influence of individual leaders acting alone. The leadership myth depended on an extreme form of the managerial solution and proved illusory at best.

Once organizations began turning to all of their members and tapped the innate creative insights of people wanting to do their best, we rediscovered a long standing, almost forgotten uniquely American approach to building effective organizations: self-managing teams. As we will see these teams are now laying the foundation for an organizational breakthrough poised to unleash that enormous human potential mentioned earlier; it is called workplace community. The companies now struggling with this concept are indeed creating living organizations.

Myth Three

Technology Will Solve All Our Problems (We Apply Hardware Solutions to Software Problems)

We have always been an inventive people. Until this decade we out-patented everyone, inventing much of the technology and "stuff" of the later part of the industrial era. We have always been a practical, can-do people seeing in our inventiveness and technological capabilities a solution to every problem. It is quite natural then to turn to technology to solve organizational problems. The mistake, however, is that robots and computers, lasers and assembly lines address only the physical output of our endeavors and not the processes that guide all organized action; the way people work together. Thus we focus intently on one half of the effectiveness equation while virtually ignoring the other, more subtle, equally necessary, but "soft" half of the equation. What businesses are now discovering as they adopt the "total quality" philosophy is that only a few of the reasons, indeed maybe none, for organizational breakdown and ineffectiveness are centered in a problem that technology alone can solve. Rather they find that the processes of working together, developing an understanding of the flow of work, reaching commitments and accepting personal responsibility for thoughtfully performing one's role are often the determining factors of organizational success. Organizational problems are not discrete breakdowns. Symptoms, perhaps. Rather, problems are usually "invisibly" embedded in the way things are and require attention to the processes that lead to their manifestation.

Myth Four

We Lost The Magic (We Allow Imitative Thinking about Organizational Innovation to Replace Original Thinking)

Our post-World War II confidence was battered. Because Japan, Germany and others flourished as we floundered we were sorely tempted to imitate their managerial practices. They were paternalistic; we extolled the virtues of being one big family. They had quality circles, we had quality circles. They modernized plant and equipment, we modernized plant and equipment. They used just-in-time inventory systems, we used just-in-time inventory systems. Again, the answer wasn't found in another's' managerial approaches. In fact we discovered that many of their approaches were refinements of techniques Americans had invented. It was our compatriot, W. Edwards Deming that brought quality consciousness to Japan. Admittedly they listened when we didn't but at least we knew better. Paternalism was never an American strong suit and we only fooled ourselves claiming to be one big family one day and announcing layoffs the next. No, the search for more techniques from abroad to imitate wasn't the way to go.

Myth Five

There Is Only One Way to Manage (We Easily Accept Simple Solutions to Multidimensional Problems)

All of the foregoing traps are set by the inclination to embrace *either/or* thinking and its attendant search for a single answer to the complexities of an organizational breakdown. There is a long history of attempts to answer many of the problems that arise in organizations with one dimensional answers. "Motivation is down; it must be lazy workers." "Profits are down; it must be marketing's problem." "We don't have new products; what's wrong with R&D anyway?" The situations that tempt us into one dimensional thinking are virtually endless and we are all too frequently ready to fall into the trap. Compounding the error of living by these myths is the corporate eclipse of the polity.

THE ECLIPSE OF THE POLITY

The corporation has eclipsed the polity as the locus of our sense of place and purpose. Life and work have inextricably merged. Yes, many of us can separate home and work life and at 5 o'clock focus on family and friends while others take work home to complete in the evenings. In either case our connection to the workplace determines the quality of our lives. We spend more time at work than with our families. Most of our friendships radiate around our work related interests and experiences and the organization, through its compensation and benefits system, influences how we live, where our children go to school, how we vacation, and the level of health care and retirement we enjoy. The corporation, in the aggregate, determines the standard of living. It has surpassed neighborhoods, local and state government, the church, schools and even culture itself, to become the most dominant and influential institution in the nation.

Because of the corporation's dominant role, an increasing number of people are questioning the legitimacy of the organizational world that has consistently resisted the extension of democracy, participation and personal efficacy into business institutions.

Henry Steele Commager, one of America's foremost historians, has pointed out that: "In the eighteenth century we were incompara-

bly the most inventive people in the world in the realm of politics
and society. We invented practically every major political institution
which we have, and we have invented none since. We invented the
political party and democracy and representative government. We
invented the first politically independent judiciary in history. . . .
We invented judicial review. We invented the superiority of the civil
over the military power. We invented freedom of religion, freedom of
speech, the bill of rights . . ."[3] and virtually, nothing new since, while
we watched the once small and public corporation mutate into a private economic behemoth now set to become a stateless entity beyond
public control.[4] As the polity is eclipsed we will need to recreate the
corporation into a living organization that responds to its new stakeholder constituency.

The corporation has successfully escaped efforts at democratization because of our collective denial of the dangers its authoritarian
system posed while we enjoyed the seductive fruits of material gain
that it provided. Unlike in the eighteenth century when only a
minuscule portion of us worked for corporations, today our lives and
fortunes are indeed wholly interconnected with the organizational
world.

Not only is it important to extend our democratic practices and
progressive ideas into the workplace for its own sake, which is essential to align organizations with our cultural and historical traditions,
but we know that doing so dramatically increases organizational
effectiveness in a turbulent environment. Ideas for involvement,
democracy, open communication, and decency at work have become
tired clichés. Yet, relatively few organizations fully address these
issues, while the need to address them seems more urgent now than
ever.

Positive Politicization

The variance between our work lives and our personal lives is
becoming too great to ignore. As the dissonance between our civic
lives and our work lives continues to grow, we are increasingly
unwilling to accept public democracy and private authoritarianism;
particularly when the organizational world has become so influential
in creating our quality of life. As we begin to question the legitimacy
of current organizational behavior and act to align organizational
practice with our expectations for building community, the corporation will become even more politicized than it already is—not just in
terms of its usual budgetary and departmental power struggles but
over issues of governance, personal efficacy and constitutional rights.

But after an initial period of increased turbulence associated with getting comfortable with the change from bureaucracy to community, the politicization will lead to a healthy exchange of views among people creating the shared experience of community.

Caution: Danger Ahead

If business leaders ignore the societal changes now taking place and people continue to experience frustration and disappointment at work, we will face more than an economic downturn. We might experience a catastrophe on the magnitude of that which hit eastern Europe and the Soviet Union. Some people have begun active, private, disobedience which is, according to the Futurist, ". . . a growing phenomenon in the United States. Unlike civil disobedience, this new militancy is uncompromising, direct and frequently violent."5 It doesn't make the newspapers and television yet; no one incident is so dramatic. But there is undeniable evidence of a restlessness and anger among employees that will find expression in one unproductive way or another if we continue business as usual. Preferably the board of directors will take the initiative for the restructuring of organizations but outside pressure to create a workplace community, just as we created a political community in the eighteenth century, is in the current winds of change. Ultimately, intentional communities will be established on principles set forth in future workplace constitutions. Failure to address the issues of workplace governance along with the productivity and climate issues may eventually result in Congress, statehouses, or regulatory bodies getting involved to align organizations with the American democratic imperative.

THE SEEDS OF REFORM AND THE PROMISE OF OUR TRADITIONS

Though the picture looks bleak there is much hope. Ironically, we can identify several seeds of real reform from the very factors perpetuating the malaise.

Technology

Advancing telecommunications and computer technology is having a profound effect on Corporate America. This technology is empowering individuals and busting the bureaucracy. It empowers because it gives individuals personal access to information and to other people throughout the organization. It busts bureaucracy for the same reasons and because the computer can so much more efficiently and effectively be used as a control mechanism thereby replacing layers of middle management. Thus, the hierarchy mutates into a network of multiple power centers rather than the single power center atop a pyramidal organization. The new telecommunications and computer technologies can liberate human potential.

Emergence of Multidimensional Thinking

As the information age explodes with data, and complexity becomes harder to ignore, it forces us to recognize that we can't know enough as individuals to solve problems alone. The result is the need to collaborate with others and to work more in teams. Here individuals begin to take more responsibility for their work and as we have seen with Total Quality Management/Control (TQM/C) self-management is a way of extending democracy to the workplace albeit in a localized fashion. Inevitably democracy and collaboration will spread as the efficiencies of self-management become obvious and individuals establish their commitment to the workplace community.

Aligning Our Organizations: Building Workplace Community

Fortunately, many people are now ready to explore an exciting new democratic mechanism: intentional workplace communities. The timing is perfect for this. Unlike earlier managerial reforms, this one requires the institutionalization of a new way of organizing; one that addresses all of the symptoms of the current breakdown.

We have seen how potentially effective innovations get killed off because they either ignored the need for systems thinking or because they depended on a single manager, or small group of managers, for their implementation and continued support. Intentionality means that much like in our civic lives, we bring a measure of influence to the decision making process by virtue of our being a member of the workplace community. Intentionality means to deliberately create a system for the good of its stakeholders. It means empowering each member to participate meaningfully in the creation and maintenance of an effective organization.

This sounds somewhat like a self-managed team but it is quite different. Community adds attention to the process, the software if you will, of building an effective organization. Focus is on both task and process. Members learn to participate from the position of being accepting of others and taking responsibility for the larger whole. Community gives greater autonomy to the self-managing process whereas self-managing teams are still subject to upper management prerogatives to overrule their decisions. In some respects self-management is a delegated joint responsibility whereas community is full responsibility among people in relationships that are reciprocal and balanced. In community, self-managed work teams would operate autonomously within the organization much like a state does within the federal structure of the United States. Indeed, the widespread adoption of self-managing work teams, for example, is paving the way toward full scale workplace community.

The general idea of community is enjoying a renaissance. Rebuilding a sense of community is a traditional American response to societal problems and will be one of the most powerful antidotes to the current organizational crisis—particularly since it seems so suited to emergent conditions.

The transformation of organizations into communities is essential because the new technologies and contingencies of work themselves require these changes to enable organizations to compete globally. They are necessary to succeed in the pursuit of efficiencies as well as to become responsive to customer and employee needs. Thus, the time is ripe to take the initiative in creating the kinds of organizations most suited to our present circumstances and future needs.

The changing conditions also suggest that we are at the dawn of a postmanagerial era; each of us will become a manager bound to each other in work groups and tethered to computer supervision with all necessary information at our fingertips. Workplaces are now being restructured into networks of teams, so one's typical assignment will be team-based, characterized by shifting personal responsibilities and shared leadership. In this kind of workplace environment with a flattened hierarchy and a huge lateral base of networks, the community model of organizing, proposed herein, seems most appropriate. It is the community model that promises a rather elegant fit between our historical experience and current need. It provides a perfect structural base for collegial and peer groups that deal with complex problems and unique customer demands in a turbulent environment requiring the need for frequent and cooperative communication. To build workplace community is to transform organizations into environments that encourage individuals to demonstrate mutual concern for each other's welfare and effectiveness. It also means providing each individual with a meaningful and empowered role to participate fully in the governance of the organization.

THE FUTURE

We are at a crossroads. We can take the high road, reinvigorate our organizations, and renew the American cultural tradition of democratizing our institutions, align our organizational practices with the emerging paradigm or we can take the low road, continue to use our organizations as instruments for immediate profit for a small number of us, squander our human resources, and watch the nation deteriorate from a cancer of the spirit.

The main assumption of this book is that most of us are ready to choose the high road: we are ready to resume our commitment to America's historical democratic imperative and revitalize our organizations and work lives.

Obviously it won't be easy but there is reason to believe it is quite possible and what follows is an attempt to show how this can be done.

NOTES

[1] R. Browning. "Andrea del Sarto," line 97, quoted in J. Bartlett, *Bartlett's Familiar Quotations*, 14th Edition (Boston: Little Brown & Co., 1968), p. 664.

[2] L. J. Peter, *Peter's Quotations* (New York: Bantam, 1979), p. 387.

[3] B. Moyers, *A World of Ideas* (New York: Doubleday, 1989), p. 232.

[4] R. Reich, "Corporation and Nation," *The Atlantic*, May 1988 pp 76–81.

[5] R. Scheel, "Private Disobedience: The New Militancy," *The Futurist*, May–June 1986, pp. 16–18.

Chapter Two

New World, New Organization

Sooner or later, if human society is to evolve—indeed, if it is to survive— we must match our lives to our new knowledge.

Marilyn Ferguson[1]

United States industry faces a quality and productivity disaster that has been quite unfamiliar to our national psyche as we watch Japanese, German, and others produce superior goods. Even individual Americans are experiencing quiet personal disasters with record levels of physical and psychological pain, stress and depression; and all of this is happening amidst the highest material standard of living in the history of mankind. Undoubtedly, something is very wrong.

The reasons for concern are becoming increasingly obvious. America isn't working so well anymore. The dream of economic comfort and leisure time has been interrupted by stress levels at epidemic proportions and a workplace filled with intimidation, humiliation and an invisible treadmill that speeds up daily. Many of us seem to be missing a sense of purpose and vast numbers are becoming impatient with the betrayal of leaders who don't seem to care.

It appears that the business world has typically been unwilling or unable to deal with the societal changes that have led to these very disasters because of the prevailing laissez faire attitude. The dominant operational ethic is to focus on the bottom line and to abide by legal requirements of doing business in this country. However, employee alienation has resulted from management's head-in-the sand, "it's not my job" response to these societal problems. Is it any wonder that over 40 percent of the American populace ". . . sees selfishness and fakery at the core of human nature"?[2]

The good news is that we are also living amidst a transformation of consciousness brought about, in part, by these very circumstances and by a new awareness of the way life could be. This new consciousness will enable us to reach a higher level of societal and personal well-being.

Three realizations are leading us to this new level of awareness: (1) collectively and individually we must arrest the deterioration of our environment; (2) we must likewise care about the work we do on the planet—our goods and services should represent our full capabilities; and (3) we can no longer neglect our personal growth and emotional/spiritual health any more than we can neglect the environment or our work and family responsibilities. All of these realizations have arisen due to the incontrovertible fact of their visibility.

The confluence of these realizations is commencing a healthy societal transformation. This book is about developing both an understanding of the transformation as well as an attempt to provide an initial blueprint to help organizations and individuals ease the transition into the new era. Previously, when we were warned of these emerging forces we scoffed at them. The symptoms were invisible, beyond our personal experience. We could not see the effects of DDT or auto exhaust. We didn't believe carcinogens in everyday products and foodstuffs would eventually kill us. We accepted garbage and waste as the price someone else pays for our wealth and progress. After all, if you can cart away your garbage what remains out of sight remains out of mind. To continue to scoff at these ideas is in effect to watch the richest nation in the history of the world choose to self-destruct.

At the same time that the deterioration of the environment is becoming painfully obvious, we are discovering the bankruptcy of myths one and two because managers no longer control the system and messiahs will not save us. Our expertise in management and production was an illusion based on being the only post-World War II industrial nation capable of producing anything. When our products failed to match the quality of those of our former enemies and we began an economic slide into enormous indebtedness, we finally got the message that quality counts, that managers aren't omniscient and that employees have much to contribute to an organization's success. Obvious, yes. But it took impending economic catastrophe as a result of unrelenting foreign competition to make us see it.

The conventional wisdom also encouraged—even expected—sabotage in the workplace through carelessness, psychological withdrawal, or resistance to the boss. This may actually have been a sensible way of behaving in an organizational world artificially divided and made into a battleground between management and labor. Neither side realized that their well-being was thoroughly dependent on the well-being of the other. If management exploited labor, it would undermine the viability of the enterprise much like dumping waste in rivers poisoned the water supply for everyone, including those that dumped the waste. If labor sabotaged the workplace or produced shoddy goods, it too would undermine the viability of the enterprise. It was clearly a no-win situation, though each side fooled itself into thinking it was possible to win at the other's expense.

As the 1990s unfold we find ourselves on the verge of three thresholds: First, it will be a classic psychic turning point, one which has always been laden with the prophesy of major change. Have we not heard that the Second Coming and the day of reckoning takes place at the millennium?

Second, in the context of our organizational settings, it also means a time when managers become overwhelmed with their inadequacy in facing an onrush of complexity and uncertainty never before experienced. The challenge is alive with possibilities. To be among the vanguard, one must be willing to let go of many assumptions, pretenses, and ways of doing things that are becoming increasingly dysfunctional. We must let go of the five myths of management mentioned earlier. The necessity for doing this is driven by complexity, market competition, new information technology, the emergent holistic postindustrial-era paradigm, and rapid societal change.

Third, a vast number of people now sense the need for community renewal and believe it must take place in our work organizations (in which we spend half our waking hours) as well as in our neighborhoods.

As we approach the thresholds, one useful way of thinking about issues we face is to shift from dichotomous thinking characterized by a mindset that requires one person to win while others lose, to holistic thinking characterized by an attempt to work together for mutual satisfaction. This is a dramatic shift in thinking but one that is occurring more frequently as individuals come to understand the seriousness of our malaise and the necessity of making a personal effort to turn things around. In the social world this is as dramatic a shift in thinking as when Copernicus discovered that the earth wasn't the center of the universe but is a planet circling the sun. It is a much harder truth to act upon, however, since human volition is required. If, through hardship, emotional illness, stubbornness, greed, or another of the many reasons for self-centeredness or societal unconsciousness, individuals can't bring themselves to be holistic in thinking and acting, they retard society's progress; whereas if individuals choose to think of the earth as the center of the universe, it is only harmless evidence of their ignorance.

Our growing willingness to see the world differently today and to raise fundamental questions regarding the wisdom of pursuing business as usual is a harbinger of a paradigm change that holds out the promise of reversing the current malaise. That is good news. However, we are caught between two minds—the old mind, destructive of the environment and human potential while in the pursuit of a material way of life, and a new consciousness more concerned with the quality of life and the texture of human experience—and this creates its own discomfort as individuals and organizations adapt. The first task of operationalizing these new insights is to transform our own behavior. Millions of individuals are doing just that as support groups, advocacy organizations, and the burgeoning personal growth literature attest. The second task, as a society, is to transform our institutions to align them with the new consciousness and to protect them from the damage that can be wrought by the persistence of the old mind.

This chapter takes a look at the shift between the old and new consciousness and what it means for our business organizations. The following chart is a rough representation of the characteristics of the industrial-era paradigm and the emerging postindustrial-era paradigm.

EXHIBIT 2-1
Characteristics of the Industrial- and Postindustrial-Era Paradigms

Industrial-Era Paradigm		*Postindustrial-Era Paradigm*
Yesterday	*Today*	*Tomorrow*
Acceptance		Learning
Acquiring		Experiencing
Adaptive learning (coping)		Generative learning (creating)
Alienated		Committed
Autocracy		Informed consent
Bottom line thinking		Process/goal/person thinking
Bureaucracy/hierarchy		Solacracy/solararchy
Centralization		Decentralization
Centripitel tendencies		Centrifugal tendencies
Class centered		Lifestyle centered
Compartmentalization		Integration

EXHIBIT 2–1 (Continued)
Characteristics of the Industrial- and Postindustrial-Era Paradigms

Industrial-Era Paradigm		Postindustrial-Era Paradigm
Yesterday	Today	Tomorrow
Competitive		Cooperative
Concrete		Abstract
Conflict avoidance		Conflict confrontation
Dependency at work		Autonomy at work
Deterministic, reductionistic thinking		Holistic, synergistic thinking
Dispensability		Community membership
Economic person		Social person
Ego control orientation basis of power		Competence, knowledge and respect basis of power
Ego building		Community building
Exclusion		Inclusion
External feedback		Internal feedback
Extrapolates data to see future		Constructs "what if?'" scenarios
Extrinsic motivation (incentives)		Intrinsic motivation dominant
Focus on "hard" science and data		Includes indeterminancy, intuition, "soft" sciences
Formal/hierarchical authority		Self-team direction
Fragmentation		Wholeness
Hero worship		Love of ideas
Higher standard of living		Better quality of life
Identity defined by status		Identity is with the community
Impersonal/denial of feelings		Personal/expression of feelings
Individual/organization centered		Organization as community/part of society
Information/data		Knowledge
Interpersonal game playing		Authenticity
Job centered		Community/profession centered
Job specialization		Job enrichment
Labor serves capital		Capital serves human need
Left brain emphasis		Rational/intuitive balance
Lifeboat ethic		Spaceship earth ethic
Linear reasoning, reversible models exclusively used		Nonlinear reasoning; irreversible models, evolutionary thinking also used
Live to work		Work in balance
Macho modeling		Androgyny
Management development		Organization/personal development
Manipulation		Collaboration
Material		Ideational

EXHIBIT 2–1 (Continued)
Characteristics of the Industrial- and Postindustrial-Era Paradigms

Industrial-Era Paradigm		Postindustrial-Era Paradigm
Yesterday	*Today*	*Tomorrow*
Material progress sole measure of value		Material and spiritual in harmony/balance
Mechanistic organizations		Living/organic organizations
Nuclear family		Alternative family
Obedience to boss		Respect to associates
Organizational Imperative		Individual imperative
Ownership of resources		Custody of resources
Paternalism		Community/voluntarism
People as expendable resource/liability		People as renewable resource/asset
People as means to organization's ends		People as ends in themselves/partners
People master nature		People as a part of nature
Performance evaluation as control		Evaluation for growth/learning
Permanence		Transience
Pessimistic philosophy of life		Optimistic philosophy of life
Planned obsolescence		Conservation
Politics of deceit and secrecy		Openness and authenticity
Power over others		Empowerment of others
Private enterprise		Community enterprise
Problems as dangers		Problems as opportunities
Profit centered		Value centered
Property rights		Personal rights
Provincialism		Cosmopolitanism
Quantity mentality		Quality, aesthetic mentality
Reactive		Proactive
Return on investment		Return to community
Risk averse		Entrepreneurial
Rational		Also intuitive and holistic
Routine work		Creative work/diversity of work
Secrecy/need to know		Openness
Self control		Self expression
Self-centered behavior		Organization centered behavior
Self-denial ethic		Self-fulfillment ethic in context
Self interest		Personhood/community
Shareholder/manager focus		Stakeholder equity
Short term fragmented thinking		Long term holistic thinking
Single standard of success: ($)		Individual definition of success
Slow evolving social life		Instant intimacy
Social Darwinism		Emphasis on connectedness
Standardized procedures		Integrated supervisory & work role

EXHIBIT 2–1 (Concluded)
Characteristics of the Industrial- and Postindustrial-Era Paradigms

Industrial-Era Paradigm		Postindustrial-Era Paradigm
Yesterday	*Today*	*Tomorrow*
Sufficiency		Excellence
Theory "X"		Theory "Y"
Thing oriented		Idea oriented
Thinking about what is		Thinking about what could be
Total planning		Spontaneity/intuition allowed
Traditional gender roles		Blurred gender roles
Trickle down theory as means to growth		Innovation, creativity as basis to growth
Universal social norms		Pluralistic social norms
Unlimited growth		Tempered sustainable growth
Vertical relations		Collegial relations
Win/lose		Win/win
Work as drudgery		Work as fun/meaningful
Worker as automation		Worker as dynamic colleague

Compiled and Adapted from Davis, Ferguson, Lippitt, Maslow, Nirenberg, Plummer, Renesch, Satin, Tannenbaum, Yankelovich. Tannenbaum and Davis, "Values, Man and Organisations," *Industrial Management Review*, Winter 1969; J. Nirenberg, "On the Frontier of American Business: Eupsychian Management," *Malaysian Institute of Management Newsletter*, February 1978; Satin, *New Age Politics*, (New York: Delta, 1979); M. Ferguson, *The Aquarian Conspiracy* (Los Angeles: Tarcher, 1980); G. Lippit, *Organizational Renewal* 2nd ed. (Englewood Cliffs, NJ; Prentice Hall, 1982); D. Yankelovich, *New Rules* (New York: Bantam, 1982); J. Nirenberg, "25 Years of Eupsychian Management: A Re-introduction and a Re-commitment," *International Organization Development Association*, Annual Meeting, Caracas, Venezuela, November, 1990; and "Technological Change, Societal Transformation and the Future of Management," *1986 International Conference on Innovation and Management*, Carlsbad, Czechoslovakia, October 1986; Plummer, *The Futurist*, January/February 1989; J. Renesch, quoted in W. Harman and J. Hormann, *Creative Work* (Indianapolis, IN: Knowledge Systems, Inc. 1990); H. Henderson, *Paradigms in Progress* (Indianapolis, IN: Knowledge Systems, Inc., 1991).

SOCIETAL AND ORGANIZATIONAL PAIN

The symptoms and manifestation of societal pain are observable everywhere in widespread pathologies:

- An undeniable breakdown of community has occurred character-ized by a diminishing sense of connection with others. It follows that as a people we lack a shared goal or common sense of purpose.
- The ever-presence of crime and myriad forms of violence leads to a fear of strangers and a reluctance to participate in the larger cultural experience surrounding us.
- The inability of societal institutions to socialize new members: The family is fragmented, the schools are in disarray, the church is no

longer a unifying force, the police cannot guarantee public order or even handle most emergencies, the legal system can't resolve disputes in a timely or equitable manner, and there is rising illiteracy amidst the technological revolution.

- The immersion in a hyper-stimulated society wherein television as a purveyor of the desire for instant and total gratification increases the level of routine excitement necessary to sustain social life. It also creates a general anxiety about our ability to fulfill our needs through material acquisition and suggests that our self-esteem is only as good as the products we buy.

There is a widespread reaction to these pathologies but business has failed to deal appropriately with their effects or the changes in values, conventions, and behavior that have now thoroughly permeated the organizational world. This failure makes the experience of work itself a contributor to the process of inauthentic or incomplete relationships. As a result, the individual has mixed feelings about how much to contribute—to invest of oneself in the process of work—and what to expect of others and the organization as a whole when one is at work. This is especially so when the future is uncertain and one is prepared for mergers, acquisitions, and divestitures usually resulting in casual, dismissive, exploitative treatment by the organization.

By controlling and intimidating employees, organizations and their managers can pretend the larger issues do not affect the organization. They can simply insist that employees be "professional" and forget concerns that are important to them personally but are not directly relevant to the process of accomplishing their work. This results in the suppression of one's best effort—displaced anger and frustration resulting in a lack of respect for the organization and its managers, poor quality work, and increased interpersonal conflicts.

In response, those in authority resort to the further application and abuse of power when these issues arise. This creates a cycle leading to a continued degeneration of the working relationships and the absolute distrust of all authority in organizations.

Fear of, and insecurity with, organizational motives is exacerbated in employees due to the prevailing emphasis on financial indicators as a measure of organizational success. When coupled with a refusal to accept the purposes of business as solely being stockholders' welfare and short-term financial returns, the combined anger and resentment among individuals in business organizations reaches quietly dangerous proportions. The first symptoms are: silent withdrawal; the lack of care in doing work, getting promoted, cooperating with others; the failure of traditional incentives, and the need for ever larger doses to achieve their desired effect. At this stage, open conflict is rare. Employees mark time as they fear conflict would lead to dismissal or would be futile. They need their jobs and conditions aren't yet totally unacceptable to them. But their resentment and anger await ignition to action when circumstances are favorable, such as when productivity is so bad, or competitors so strong, that management is finally willing to listen and act on what is heard.

Rising alienation is becoming less tolerable at both the individual and organizational levels. One of the flash-points of this seething resentment and cause for alienation is based on the unfairly skewed distribution of organizational rewards and benefits. Even the business press is questioning executive compensation that is not only gargantuan in absolute dollar amounts but too frequently not related to productivity. As *Business Week* says, "Compensation at the top is out of control."[3] Average total compensation of executives responding to a *Forbes* poll of 800 of the largest corporations totaled $1,592,000.[4] Two hundred and fifty-eight of the 800 made more than $1 million. Reebok International's Paul Fireman, for example, made $14,800,000 in 1990. An employee such as a manager of a store selling Reebok shoes, paid 10 times the minimum wage ($3.35 an hour) earns $69,680 a year, but is making only 1/212 of what Fireman made. To put it another way, the CEO of this fashion sport shoe company made 74 times the salary of the President of the United States of America in 1990.[5] (Even average CEO's are making 75 times an average secretary's pay of $20,000.)

In addition, a carelessness with employees is endemic under a managerial ethos that allows, among other things, the layoffs and firings of people as a natural part of the way business is conducted. The fundamental disrespect and low regard for individuals is evident in the vast distinctions made between top managers and middle managers, and between middle managers and everyone else.

The lack of concern for the success of the organization on the part of labor and middle management stems in part from the disconnection of one's role in the organization with any of its outcomes and, of course, to the frequently disdainful way employees are blatantly treated as a necessary evil by their managers. Thus, we find organizations setting themselves up for long term defeat.

THE SELF-DEFEATING ORGANIZATION

One paradox of organizations that results in their dysfunction is their inherent design which deliberately limits their reliance on individuals. Jobs are thoroughly circumscribed. People are hired at the minimum skill level possible, and no one is considered irreplaceable, though the role one plays is essential. Thus, we can elect new people to office and organizations can survive the departure of individuals because the system survives by refilling the roles needed to make it work. While this sustainability minimizes dangers to the organization, it too often creates a mindset of seeing individuals as costs and in turn, the organization unwittingly expects minimum performance from them. This, in turn, creates an alienated work force. Yet, at the same time the organization is alienating its work force, it wants motivated workers who willingly contribute and take the initiative to act creatively for the good of the organization.

This paradox is in part also due to the lingering master-servant mindset that dominates conventional business relationships between "boss" and "subordinate" and the increasingly outmoded bureaucratic structure of our organizations that reinforces myth one, that managers control the system and are omnipotent. If this continues, our organizations risk crumbling from within like a termite-infested house as employees surrender to apathy, psychological withdrawal and subtle sabotage.

The effect of the paradox becomes evident as our competitiveness stagnates and declines in the global marketplace, and the search for curative panaceas feverishly heats up. At a national meeting of the American Society of Training and Development, for example, there were hundreds of booths in the exhibit hall; many with a package to meet a specific training need. Slick training packages have truly become fashionable and there seems to be a "What's New?" syndrome that underlies the fact that these very solutions have a short life span. Yet, the search continues annually. Packages of techniques, however, will not be able to overcome the natural barriers organizations establish between their managers and employees and the barriers between employees doing what is right in meeting customer needs and simply serving bureaucratic interests.

Obsessive managerialism and an all-pervasive control orientation retard adaptive change that is required to meet global competition. It is also crippling the potential of the individual employees and their work teams. It makes all efforts of group and team action difficult at best and impossible at worst.

The Problem of Bureaucracy

In addition to managerial egocenteredness, bureaucracy is stifling organizational potential. At one time the modern bureaucracy was a beautiful social technology. It elegantly solved several problems.

First, it codified in rules and procedures all aspects of government services. What individuals could expect from government became delightfully predictable. Before bureaucracy, an assortment of lackeys, princelings and war lords had their way with a rather disorganized, apolitical, mass of powerless, land starved peasants. Bureaucracy was a reform instituted to give confidence to the people that their government was fighting corruption and that all citizens would be treated equally.

The major tenets of bureaucracy include in addition to a set of standard operating procedures and rules, a clear job description for each job holder, a chain of command from the lowest clerk to the highest officer, a separation of the use of power so that individuals couldn't act simply on their own behalf, and assurances that each individual office holder would be fully qualified to exercise the duties of that office and would be appropriately trained to unerringly use his or her powers with the most judicious equanimity. Not bad. It was, and in many respects still is, an ideal form of organization. No doubt we hope that bureaus such as the IRS, a local redevelopment agency, the motor vehicle department, and the welfare department act with as much discipline as promised in the ideal bureaucratic model.

When modern bureaucracy was created it served a facilitative role in transforming an agricultural people into an industrial people. It perfectly aligned the needs of the emergent industrial era with the state of readiness of the people. An undereducated mass of "labor" was socialized into a time-driven mechanical system where bosses knew what had to be done, engineers designed the work-flow process, and hired hands performed the chores owners and managers couldn't do themselves. The employee was a necessary evil and those hired weren't expected to make much of a contribution other than to be obedient, dependable, and loyal. Little by little as the entire population of the West was educated to internalize notions of efficiency, productivity, obedience to a boss and discipline in the performance of one's work, the industrial system matured. Bureaucracy was a very effective method to execute the transformation. And in many respects it still serves a purpose as in the execution of public agencies in an equitable, predictable fashion.

Dysfunctions of Bureaucracy

The bureaucratic rationale can be appreciated if one considers the antecedent circumstances leading to its creation. When it was devised the environment in which it worked was riddled with arbitrary,

unfair, untimely, chaotic, corrupt, unpredictable nepotism and crony-
ism. Bureaucracy stabilized organizational performance and offered
apparent justice and fair treatment for all. It was a very democratic
instrument in its time. Conditions have changed, however.

Its strengths have become weaknesses: slowness (careful deliberation), over-control (in the guise of total financial responsibility),
adherence to rules (no exceptions), observance of inadequate assumptions about, and little responsiveness to, individuals have all con-
tributed to the failure of bureaucracy.

Professor Warren Bennis, in one of his first popular books on the
subject, listed many of the major ills of bureaucracy.[6] First, echoing
the work of Argyris,[7] he points out how the control orientation and
rigid hierarchical structure deny recognition to the natural, human
developmental process; it does not allow for the personal growth and
the development of mature personalities. Furthermore, human
resources are not fully used as people's skills are narrowly defined
and an atmosphere of fear and mistrust pervades the organization.
Second, as it is designed to do, hierarchy develops conformity and a
tendency for "group think" (collective unconscious agreement), people are molded into "organization men" (behaving uniformly in the
interests of the bureaucracy). Third, the hierarchical decisions inhibit
and dilute innovative ideas and full communications. Control, conformity and fear naturally result in the retardation of initiative and
make the organization slower to change and unable to adapt to both
the internal creative power of individuals and internal forces emanating from the market place, community and competitors. Fourth,
there is no adequate juridical process or other means to resolve differences between ranks and functional groups. Fifth, the system of controls and authority relationships are outdated particularly since they
do not reflect the reality of how people work together and accomplish
their assigned tasks.

The most formidable characteristic of bureaucracy leading to its
dysfunction today is the hierarchy and its chain of command. In an
earlier era in which succeeding levels of bosses were needed to check
and recheck the work of subordinates and utilize an ever wider
overview of the decision making situation, time was not a major concern. Today it is. To limit each person's communication to written
messages sent up through a line of bosses and then down the hierarchy
again to the intended recipient of the communication is a tedious and
time-consuming procedure unsuited to today's extremely demanding
and fast-paced business world. With the advent of computer technology that is enabling control to be in the hands of each individual and
decisions to be made instantaneously and independently of a succes-

sion of intermediate bosses, hierarchy obviously becomes the pistol
with which business shoots itself in the foot.

Bureaucracy is Inappropriate for Tomorrow's Business World

In important ways, bureaucracy is severely out of date and many
of its attributes are cause for its own destruction—particularly as
bureaucracy has been applied in the private sector and particularly in
commercial areas involving serious competition in the marketplace.
In a word it has simply failed to adapt. It is no longer necessary to
socialize the populace to the ways of the industrial era, we are all
inextricably entangled in it. Our schools, massive urbanization, and
communications media have made us quite conscious of the underlying
concepts of bureaucracy and life in the industrial era. So we enter the
workplace with a readiness to take our role and have an understanding of its rationale. The only trouble is that our world is shifting dramatically and quickly which is shattering the industrial model.

Two disasters mark the crest of the bureaucratic age and metaphor-
ically symbolize precisely what has been wrong with both the
bureaucratic mindset and the captains of American business. The first
was the sinking of the *Titanic*. At the risk of overusing this analogy, it
is nevertheless rich with symbolism. The biggest ship of its day, it
sailed from England on its maiden voyage with all the confidence of
the engineering marvel that it was. The most technologically
advanced ship, it was thought prepared to weather any condition. It
is a statement of caution to others who feel that technology and engineering alone will make the operation of any device as smooth in
human hands as it appears on paper.

But it symbolizes much more. It sank because of what it couldn't
see; the part of the iceberg below the surface. Much like the iceberg,
there are many aspects of organizations that remain invisible to the
average manager. In the same way, to continue to think that what you
can't see won't hurt you is to cut short organizational success, as
surely as the iceberg cut the voyage of the *Titanic*. We can see the
effects of poor quality. We can see it in parts that don't fit, poorly
painted assemblies, overheated electrical equipment, burned out
appliances, and in many other ways. We can see the benefits doled
out to some people and not to others; we can see the organizational
chart and the structure of the power flows. What we can't see is the
emotional aspects of working, how well our relationships are doing,
who is not communicating or communicating well, which problems
are not being dealt with, norms that prevail, values that are shared by

some and not others, the flows of influence and the assignments of duties, and how well people execute their roles.

The *Titanic* was a vessel that took up to a mile to maneuver, a long slow process not amenable to short notice or handling immediate dangerous encounters. It required notice and careful planning, characteristics possible only in a predictable environment. It suffered the penalties of being big, overconfident, and slow to maneuver. The *Titanic* was the epitome of bureaucratic thinking and there is a lesson here for our organizations.

The *Titanic* sailed at about the time that the work of Max Weber was being widely popularized beyond the German sociologist's native academe. He was the first student of modern bureaucracy and codified its basic principles. The designers of the *Titanic* were thought to have anticipated all circumstances. But, it couldn't deal with the unseen or the unpredictable; that iceberg simply wasn't supposed to be there. The promise of its ultimate seaworthiness and its hope to set a speed record on its trip to New York attracted many people to the maiden voyage. It had procedures, each crew member was expertly trained (except for the emergency use of the lifeboats), the captain was the highest authority and his word was virtual law.

Communication appeared to be smooth but ultimately proved inadequate because "The (one) message which described ice directly ahead of *Titanic*, never did get to the bridge."[8]

The worst part of the disaster occurred, much to the horror of all aboard the vessel, when it was discovered that there were fewer spaces in the lifeboats than there were passengers and crew. It is this last fact that seems to have earned the sinking a particularly nasty reputation among twentieth-century catastrophes. The engineers and designers were so confident of the ship's invulnerability, they were sure lifeboats were superfluous at best and that those they did provide would mollify people concerned with safety. The number of lifeboats aboard the *Titanic* actually exceeded the number required by law, but were still over 1,000 seats short even if each was used to its capacity, which they were not.

The fact that they didn't have enough lifeboats is symbolized today with the great land *Titanics* of American bureaucracies that only provide golden parachutes for the executive management team and protect some investors but not others.

Ironically, the ship was produced and met its fate at the height of the scientific management craze founded by Frederick Taylor, who was convinced that this form of management would totally rationalize the processes of work for the benefit of both business owners and workers. It was a reliance on the application of science and the belief in the ability to discover the one best way of doing things. It was the first major management panacea after bureaucracy itself. Efficiencies were to be had by the score and its easy, early, successes made the efficiency expert a magician of sorts. McDonald's is today's best known example of this efficiency expert mentality at work.

The second and more recent catastrophe symbolic of the failure of bureaucracy was the *Challenger* disaster. The fear of communicating bad news to one's boss; the fear of forcing another delay in the scheduled launch and disappointing the public; the reluctance to deal with a real danger (though not believed a certainty) was all due to bureaucratic pathology: the fear of open communication and displeasing one's boss.[9] *Titanic* redux. "And bad news never gets better with time . . . failure to act on safety warnings in the *Challenger* case (was) an example of succumbing to pressure to ignore unwanted messages."[10]

Today in a postindustrial model of organizing, different qualities are needed by both management and labor. In fact, the distinction between management and labor is no longer useful because everyone is developing a managerial outlook. The public has outgrown the bureaucratic model. Rather than being in need of control and managerial guidance, each person comes to the organization with abilities to be tapped that will add value to the products and services of the information age. In a world defined by the personal contributions and creative inputs of each person, the impetus for control shifts from the organization to the profession and ultimately to the individual. The most vital natural resource is no longer iron, or electricity, or oil; it is people creatively handling data and rearranging information to meet a variety of individual customers' needs. Since each customer wants to be treated as an individual and not as a bureaucratic case or just another unit in the mass market, an organization needs to fashion a unique package of resources to satisfy that customer. This is an entirely different mindset from bureaucracy. It is a change that is absolutely essential to bring our organizations into alignment with the changing society and individual needs.

The challenge today is to reverse the emphasis from making the individual conform to the organization to making the organization serve its members as they meet a customer or client's need. This is a very powerful mental shift.

We are now on the verge of unleashing the enormous energy of people in organizations when we let go of the outmoded notion that bureaucracy is a necessary element of organizing. As just one example, a computer conferencing system led to the dismantling of a layer of middle management bureaucracy but also led to the same number of people being hired to consider projects never considered before. It was a tradeoff of administrators for creators.[11]

A critical mass has almost been reached. When it occurs it will fundamentally alter the way we think about organizations and the way that we manage them. To be first to operationalize this way of thinking is to corner a competitive advantage.

Organizational symptoms of the self-defeating organization include: increasing difficulty recruiting top notch employees; high turnover, absenteeism, and grievances or silent on-the-job withdrawal among employees; frequent reorganizations; a sense that people don't care about the company or their work and are unwilling to cooperate with others; interest groups beginning, or relentlessly continuing, to target the organization for moral as well as legal transgressions (perhaps product liability issues frequently arise); getting middle managers to create successes in implementing new strategic plans seems to take longer than necessary; or there are frequent cycles of hirings and layoffs. A sign that a person is trapped in a self-defeating organization is his or her surprise that these kinds of symptoms are cause for concern.

The Conventional Future

Many popular management writers (Drucker, Peters, Kanter, Davis and Handy[14]) focus on the entity's future and see consumer-centeredness, or strategic choices for diversification, or international alliances, or even product quality, as a driving strategy. The point of view is always that of an omniscient and omnipotent CEO that happens to be attached to an organization—as if that single individual, and he alone, is the difference between appropriate action and failure. Organizational victories glorify an individual leader who single-handedly champions the success while others, if mentioned at all, are inferior creatures prone to ineptness, myopia, and the need to be managed. The foremost myth of management at work again: managerialism.

Whether the future is imagined as a sterile techno-utopia or a competitive global battle ground between multinational colossi, there is seldom a role for the individual other than as an effect of the environment. Either economics or technology drives the scenario. Human choice has little to do with it unless, of course, it's the CEO or a CEO-in-waiting who will make the choice and change the world.

In their view of the future the organizational forms likely to sprout on the corporate landscape include the flat organization, the network organization, the nuclear organization, the orchestra-style organization, the ad hoc organization, even the shamrock organization. These and many others are formulated to describe the impact of new technology and new patterns of work. But once again something is conspicuously missing in these and other scenarios of our organizational future: the inclusion of the members of these organizations in choosing and creating their future. Deliberate, collaborative human choice has been conspicuously absent from practically all scenarios, yet it is the one element that will be the deciding factor in the design and actualization of successful organizations in the future.

It is foolishness to perpetuate the myth that the system is fine if only the messiah within emerges to lead us to the elysian fields. The fact is that many popular management books still gloss over all underlying issues of the organizational breakdown and ignore the real strength of any enterprise: the contributions each person is capable of making. Though five million copies of *In Search of Excellence* were sold, people now wonder why organizations still aren't excellent.

The essence of so many of these books seems to be: develop a mission or vision for the organization and motivate all employees to become as enthusiastic about achieving it as you are (the CEO or aspiring CEO). They seem to convey the belief that there is an elegant solution to every problem; that a manager can soon become omniscient if only he or she considers the universe of factors identified in theory; and, that workers can be trained to perfection and stay in their place performing perfectly and executing the company's will. But in a world where hierarchies are collapsing and decision making is dispersed throughout the organization, a network point of view must replace the bureaucratic one.

What we haven't come to grips with is that no matter how much more we push people and try to activate, manipulate, or motivate them to work for the good of the company, they are simply not responding the way they once did. They have hit the wall. It is no longer acceptable to expect people to work hard and imaginatively for the good of the company while thinking of them as mere human resources to be dispensed with as the company sees fit. That was the old way of seeing things. The new way of conceptualizing human beings sees them as an integral part of the organization with rewards commensurate with their contribution, and opportunities for them to realize their personal vision. Competitiveness in the emergent service/information age demands nothing less. Until the system develops the moral responsibility to care for each organizational member and not just those at the top, success will be illusive. Which workers today can give their best to a system that rewards top executives with astronomical compensation and golden parachutes while justifying cyclical hiring and firing of the rank and file without notice?

The CEO-centric view is altered when the vision is transformed into a team-centered, consensus-seeking representation of the whole system—the workplace community. Thus, a motivating vision is the outcome of an ongoing process of focusing community activity rather than the imposed view of an individual or a small group of individuals. It is in this way that the organization optimizes the use of its human potential and stimulates each person's full contribution by helping people in the organization create and understand their purpose and fulfill their responsibilities.

It is important to recognize that organizations embody the aggregate behavior of members of the workplace community. Individuals function at the interpersonal frontier where the intangibles such as the ebb and flow of our behavior and emotions, our group's behavior, and what we are together trying to accomplish, converge with the client or a colleague involved in a long convoluted chain of many performance steps, to realize the vision.

THE EVOLVING TRANSFORMATION

Essentially, the second law of thermodynamics teaches us that "any complex structure, whether coccyx or the federal constitution, requires an input of energy to keep it operating. Without natural selection or human consciousness providing regular input, non-random structures tend to decay. . . ."[12]

In order to function effectively organizations need the input of conscious design and the willing participation of their members. An organization is the interaction of the combined consciousness of the group focused on the commonweal and the organization's objectives. An organization is simply the sum total of the thinking that goes into creating and transforming an idea into reality. The ability of an organization to survive and prosper is a direct consequence of being receptive to possibilities and the will of each person to devote oneself along with others in the organization to work toward the creation of some jointly imagined possibility. Computer networking between all individuals in the organization makes possible tremendous new opportunities to communicate and to coordinate their activities. Thus, the amount of coordination actually increases as the cost of doing so is dramatically reduced.[13]

As the public consciousness changes, so too will societal institutions. As we become more concerned with our personal health and fitness, we seek solutions to the problem of a noticeably deteriorating environment. As our faith in institutions declines and one scandal follows on the heals of another, we seek personal control for our own well-being and of course become more attuned to reforms that are needed. Eventually we will press for these reforms in the workplace and elsewhere.

One change that appears well under way is the alteration of what the public will accept as a legitimate way of doing business. A shift is occurring toward democratic workplace communities and it will require the same responsiveness and accountability that we demand of our governments and other organizations. The recent growth in ESOPs (Employee Stock Ownership Plans) is evidence of this. The rising tide of awareness stems from many years of self-development and consciousness raising among the post-World War II generation now poised to take over the reins of power in our organizations. For those that are not taking over control, a major choice looms. Because there are simply so many people in the demographic bulge known as the baby boom, an enormous number of them will realize at mid-life that since they aren't going to be (or want to be) CEOs, and their mortality has been reconfirmed close to home with the passing of their parents, perhaps their remaining healthy years should be spent creating a more meaningful, connected life.

Partially confirming this is a new phenomenon of mid-life retirements now taking place that threatens to rob many organizations of their most talented and experienced individuals. Having made careers in the city centers and living atop highly appreciated real estate many mid-lifers are in a position to enjoy financial independence albeit at a modest level. Add to that their inheritance and considering the fact that their kids have graduated from college and are no longer a financial responsibility, many mid-lifers are simply leaving the rat race. Off to a simpler, less expensive life in the hinterland where a nearby college, airport and teleport give them the ability to connect quickly to any information source, a huge number of healthy, talented individuals will be forming the basis of a contributor culture that accelerates the coming transformation.

Of course these mid-lifers won't be idly retired. In building a new life they will be the vanguard of the age of volunteerism pursuing healing and reform. Others will choose to build small businesses and showcase their philosophy by building into them a way of life that will attract still others and demonstrate the possibilities of a socially responsible attitude toward business.

And for those who don't retire and head for the hills? They still will have met their basic and security needs and will have surrounded themselves with all the material comforts they've wanted. Then what? They'll turn to intellectual, spiritual, emotional, and health consciousness, not continued materialism, as a means for personal growth.

How will corporations deal with the reluctant mid-lifer who is still productive but more realistic about his life's goals and chances of reaching them? Who, after asking himself if he is happy, simply says "no!" How will organizations motivate a group of people no longer impressed with promises that won't be fulfilled by a corporate career? What is the impact of second marriages and starting life anew at 40? Will these individuals settle for the same kinds of organizations they settled for at 20? Hardly.

It is quite possible that the impetus toward transformation will see political activism in the latter part of the 1990s move from city halls, statehouses, and the streets of Washington into the boardrooms and executive suites of this nation. This consciousness revolution will succeed in altering the fundamental structure of business organizations for the first time in 300 years.

A few years ago this was unimaginable. But the evidence of a mounting transformation is widespread and abundant; examples are everywhere. First, they can be found in the ubiquitous professional meetings and networking events where agendas are filled with speakers and workshops on "Raising the Corporate Consciousness;" "Bringing the New Age to Your Company;" "Leadership through Empowerment;" "Self Managing Work Teams;" "Helping Your Company Save the Environment: What You Can Do;" "Counting Your Own Hours; Creating Your Own Benefits," and so on. Even CEOs themselves are being bombarded from their traditionally conservative and reactionary business and trade organizations to re-examine the place of the corporation in the larger community and to acknowledge the legitimacy of stakeholders as well as stockholders in the corporate decision-making process.

Pressures from within these networks actually increase the likelihood of regulation becoming an acceptable way of changing the reluctant organization. Equal employment opportunity, workman's compensation, and safety issues have all been regulated into organizational life because of the commitment of external networks. It is only a short step to include issues of governance, participation in decision making, compensation, and myriad other issues facing the organizational community, on the regulators' agenda. For "regulator," read representatives of government agencies at national, state, and local levels, as well as legislatures and courts.

Where organizations fail to change and legislation is absent and the courts remain disinterested, the most talented and enlightened employees will simply leave to form their own organizations or find jobs within organizations that have learned to harness these forces for change. Likewise, organizations seeking a real competitive advantage will find that building community and empowering their members is a profitable road to take.

There are many forces leading to the transformation of our society and our organizations. First, a competitive advantage goes to the organization that best utilizes new technologies and new ways of building interpersonal effectiveness. Those organizations will drive a segment of the transformation as they achieve the breakthroughs others will emulate. Second, society is changing. It is reflective of a large diverse urbanized population with a creative richness that stimulates the imagination and with it the realization that an immense number of possibilities exists for us to fashion a personal as well as community life. Third, as individuals we are becoming capable lifelong learners with the ability to develop a vast repertoire of skills and the motivation to apply them in creative ways at our workplace. All of this underlies the emergence of new egalitarian, network organizations and the demise of bureaucratic hierarchies.

The Transformation Has Many Fronts

- A self-styled study group of middle managers is circulating underground white papers on reforming and redesigning organizations to become more responsive to individual needs and to honor our humanity in the workplace. Like East Europeans devouring inspirational underground works that both gave hope for reform and laid out plans to make it happen, American corporate employees, middle managers, white collar employees, and labor are becoming intolerably restive. They are no longer willing to suffer the numbness that comes from being part of the status quo when the future demands and promises so much more, when to continue business as usual is to defy one's own common sense that the times call for a change.

- Furthering the revolutionary impetus, computer workstations now provide individuals access to vast on-line networks throughout the nation and most of the industrialized world. Thousands of people are using time "stolen" from their employers to help one another devise methods of striking back against unfair, inhumane, or antisocial corporate behavior. Tune in to "The Well," an electronic network based in the San Francisco Bay area, for example, and you will become part of an endless conversation about many subjects including changing the nature of our organizations and the future of economic life on the planet. These discussions result in frequent informal meetings that raise the consciousness among individuals who then generate reform efforts within their companies.

- Others fed up with business as usual but unsure of how to act to stem the tide of organizational abuse have withdrawn their energy and have become virtually "retired on the job"—part of an army of employed going through the motions until they intellectually starve their organizations into reform or until the transformation enters the next phase and they can find a way to purposefully act to reform their organizations.

If you are like most people who already have a sense that a fundamental change is occurring in the way we think about our organizations, our communities, and our society you may welcome the transformation.

The choice isn't as simple as it appears, of course. So many people have grown accustomed to their own private world that in spite of the changes to come, many of us will chose to live in a state of denial, the virtual unconsciousness of believing that our lives can remain stable while all about us are buffeted by the winds of change. That is to live with the fantasy that the status quo will endure.

To try to live in the past, to pretend we can continue with business as usual, is to support current management models and their dysfunctional, perverse ethos of domination and control for the sake of a few managers at the top and absent stockholders. To embrace the transformation is to reinvigorate the organization and to harness its human energy, to rebuild, even to recreate, the planet. To do so through building workplace community fosters human growth and dignity in our organizations. This is the choice we must make in order to soothe the societal and organizational pain all around us.

The Lead Scenario: Workplace Communities

There are many potential futures for American organizations but one in particular promises to be very productive and exciting. It differs from the techno-future and CEO-utopias mentioned earlier because it involves the transformation of work organizations into workplace communities. A workplace community is as different from today's organization—even a so-called excellent organization—as a Boeing 747 is from a Wright Flyer. But unlike the Wright brothers who could only imagine commercial flight from the perspective of 1903, we have the distinct advantage of possessing all the technology we need to make our organizational transformation a success right now. As I will demonstrate, we won't have to wait long to see the creation of organizational communities because they are emerging now.

It is one scenario that aligns the compelling societal forces, individual desire, and corporate need into a workable organization capable of meeting the demands of the 21st century. It is a compelling scenario. Chapter 5 outlines the details.

Additional forces for community. There are three complementary forces that indicate that "community" in the workplace is evolving now. First, there are technological alterations to the way work is conducted, most notably through the computerization of the work flow, of information data bases, and of communications linking workers with one another. Second, as the market changes and competition increases for customers, quick decision making will be required at the lowest levels in the organization. Production workers, service providers, and salespeople will need to be equipped with the ability to make decisions on the spot. There will be no time to send requests up a bureaucratic chain of command and wait for an answer to trickle down sometime in the distant future. Everyone will need to be empowered to work the resources of the organization in order to fulfill a customer demand. Third, widely held values and expectations of the work force about the nature of its relationship to the organization will influence the changing definition of management and ultimately the very concept of organization.

Technology. Technology is changing so rapidly, it is extremely difficult to keep up with its implications for business. One thing is clear, however: Technology is speeding up our ability to handle data and communicate. In this respect it is causing a very dramatic change in the nature of work relationships. Where computer technology is introduced into the workplace, individuals have a tool that dramatically increases their access to information and requires that for them to add value to the work flow process, they must be prepared to use that information in creative ways.

Because the power of computer technology and the resultant speed of accessibility to information, the organization has the ability to customize its product or service at the same time that customers are demanding personalized treatment from organizations they patronize. Employees first in contact with customers are required to make on-the-spot decisions in order to meet the demands of the moment. This shifting of information down the hierarchy and the use of new technology as a way of facilitating decision making lower in the ranks requires a new way of organizing that respects the capabilities of those at all levels in the organization and empowers them to act in appropriate ways, given the pressures to act quickly and to satisfy customers needs immediately.

Due to the complexity of personalization and customization, members of organizations must be able to consult with others in the work flow process in order to ultimately satisfy customer needs and reach organizational objectives. The customer/organizational interface increasingly becomes a problem-solving situation, not just a matter of filling an order. That requires collaboration and openness in interpersonal relations to enable the free flow of information among people as they solve problems and meet customer needs. We see once again that the hierarchy is undermined as networks develop to facilitate the work of the organization and ease the individual's task.

In addition, while it is relatively easy to expand the capacity of computers to handle and transmit data, the same is not the case for individuals. People in traditional organizations must continuously filter, inhibit, and suppress complete communications of both thought and feelings, given the exigencies of political life in their companies. Because one's boss has such complete control over their work lives and career prospects, relating to the boss may be a tortuous prospect if he or she is not communicative or amenable to other individuals' authentic and full expression. Thus, as new technology facilitates the transformation from hierarchy to network forms of organization we need to attend to the consequences on the new form of interpersonal relationships. When we shift from the superordinate/subordinate mindset to a collegial mindset we must also be willing to attend to redefining our expectations of one another and the nature of our own roles in the workplace.

In working communities the inclination to distort or filter information is reduced or eliminated because the basis of those inhibitions, fear for one's economic security and place in the organization, are eliminated.

Societal influences.   Many managers and entrepreneurs are instinctively building working communities as a way of preparing for the future. They haven't yet realized that they are building community but each innovation they make to infuse their organizations with qualities that inspire their members to participate as equals, to produce quality products and services, is taking a step in that direction. This is particularly true when each person hired is considered an integral part of the organization and is directly affected by the performance of the organization. People see the value of community because it creates alignment between the individuals involved in the new venture and the diverse challenges that they face.

Another important dimension of the societal influences moving organizations toward community is the awareness that many corporations have reached a size and command an influence that rivals governments. In the aggregate they have become instruments of social policy and creators of the quality of life. Our attachment to an urban, organizational life is undisputed and the welfare of the citizenry is clearly subject to the vicissitudes of organizational decisions made on behalf of private interests. Whether we can, as a society, afford these private actions involving the welfare of millions of people and the environmental quality is perhaps the most volatile topic of the day. The role of organizations in our society is a matter of great debate. How much influence they should retain and how much control the government should exercise through regulation and taxation is very much a topic of concern. It is one contention of this book that because organizations are so influential in our lives and because they are generally the driving force creating our quality of life, that we need to shift our political attention from the civil arena to the corporate arena. To leave quality-of-life issues to private interests is an oversight with the most serious consequences, not the least of which is the spoliation of the environment and the fiscal abuse of individuals (witness contamination of the water table and the S&L debacle).

Individual influences.   There are also many managers deliberately pulling their organizations along the road toward community not because of necessity or as a response to particular forces but because of a conviction that building a working community is the right thing to do. The moral position is the most difficult to maintain in a society fundamentally built on materialism and the accumulation of money. Morality for its own sake does not pay in a material culture and therefore has little persuasive (read monetary) value. The champions of the moral position for building community are few in number but growing rapidly as the transformation proceeds. Nevertheless, as you will see in Chapter 9, committed individuals as well as CEOs can make a decisive contribution to convert their organizations into communities. Whether community can be sustained depends solely on how well entrenched the policies and mechanisms are. Clearly they need to be structurally reinforced to make their repeal extremely difficult if not impossible. ESOPs (employee stock ownership programs) can change the structure and operations of companies to reflect the interests of employees though even ESOPs in themselves don't guarantee that community will be created.

One of the strongest influences determining whether or not an organization will become a community is, of course, the readiness of the individuals themselves to become part of one. People have grown cynical, reluctantly accepting their tethers to the organizational world. Labor is willing to play a constructive role in the organizational world because as never before it is clear that everyone's well-being depends on the success of the organizational entity. But the cynicism derives from the lesson people have learned over the last 15 years: that authority and money can't be trusted to act responsibly for the good of society. From Vietnam and Watergate through Iran arms sales, and the junk bonds scandal, the one consistent lesson has been that without accountability, disaster strikes. Community insists on accountability through democratizing the processes of decision making. Community establishes mechanisms such as representative forums to decide policy matters in terms of the organizational good. Stockholders, while important comprise but one stakeholder. There is quite simply too much at risk to leave whole organizations entirely in the hands of a CEO-maneuvered board of directors acting alone.

Evolution of systems. The development of the work organization has been an evolutionary process reflecting changes in knowledge, technology, and values. As each generation alters these factors, organizations change as well.

It's profitable. Perhaps the best reason for this transformation, from the point of view of managers wanting to improve their financial performance, is that community can be very profitable. It has the potential of building synergies that no other form of organization has. Its primary advantage is in the acceleration of creative energy in a low resistance, communicative environment where the speed of actions increases to allow the organization to optimize response time in the marketplace. It is also a highly motivational environment since members see the consequences of their performance in their financial position. Gainsharing is a natural outgrowth of the reconceptualization of the organization and directly links individual performance to personal gain (and loss).

Gainsharing is a fast growing component of new motivational efforts. Employee stock ownership programs are a major part of the gainsharing strategy where employees own a piece of their companies. Thousands of companies have a variation on this theme, first encouraged by Congress through a series of favorable tax measures in 1974.

Offering employees stock options is a newer twist on the gainsharing principle. Its purpose is also to get employees to have a sense of ownership which is intended to heighten their interest in corporate performance. "For instance, PepsiCo grants new options to employees every year on July 1. Workers then have the right, five years later to buy stock equal to 10 percent of their pay. The price stays fixed, so stock that was worth, say $25 a share last July 1 could be had five years hence for just $25, even if the market price has doubled in the meantime."[16] Of course if the stock falls employees can forgo their options. The point is that companies like PepsiCo, Du Pont, Toys 'R' Us, and Wendy's are beginning to think in terms of providing gain-sharing opportunities to all employees and this step inches the organization closer to building workplace community.

Starting at the Beginning: Redefining Management and Organization

The most exciting development in the last few years, stimulating the transformation of organizations into communities, but completely overlooked by much of the popular business press and schools of business, is the redefinition of the concept of management itself. The definition used to be "working with and through people for organizational objectives." Now, leading edge organizations define management as "the act of relationship building in order to achieve mutual objectives for mutual gain." Max DePree, CEO of Herman Miller furniture makers in Michigan stated this beautifully when he said, in terms of his managers and leaders building a covenantal relationship with subordinates: "A covenantal relationship rests on shared commitment to ideas, to issues, to values, to goals, and to management processes. Words such as love, warmth, and personal chemistry are certainly pertinent. Covenantal relationships are open to influence. They fill deep needs and they enable work to have meaning and to be fulfilling. Covenantal relationships reflect unity and grace and poise. They are an expression of the sacred nature of relationships."[15] Ultimately, we can't think of total quality in the products we produce or the services we provide without thinking of the total quality of our work lives and the relationships that are the fundamental building blocks of the workplace experience.

This dramatic turn of events has many roots but is essentially due to the prevalence of complex and nonroutine problems and to workers needing to become versatile colleagues in response to immediate and varied demands. It is also due to the widely held belief among millions of people that a holistic world is generally defined by the quality of its relationships. When the hierarchy flattens, attention must be devoted to developing relationships among colleagues because without the familiar constraints of bureaucracy new understandings and new rules are needed to suit the new interpersonal environment. As we will see later, the new paradigm gives rise to new ways of relating and a new personal experiences of the workplace.

One profound implication of the new definition is that it stimulates the metamorphosis of organizations into communities. Thus, because we are no longer passive components in a bureaucratic world, we need to intentionally become active members in a workplace community. Companies that redefine management in this way will have the potential to reach warp speed in global competition but they will need to acquire new structures and processes to complement their new attitude about the nature of management and organization. These aspects of the transformation will be discussed in detail later.

As the community mindset develops it alters every aspect of organizational life. It involves nothing less than a paradigmatic shift in our thinking. No longer will being an employee mean being without a role in the governance of the organization. No longer will being a manager mean one can hire and fire at will or have an imbalanced power advantage over others by virtue of simply holding a "higher" position. The entity called an organization will be conceptualized as inclusive of all people who are part of it, and eventually will include all its stakeholders in a meaningful role in the determination of the organization's future. In short, organizations will be the new polity. Perhaps they will develop constitutions and by-laws setting out the various responsibilities and obligations of organizational citizenship much as states do with their own constitutions and laws.

Chapters 5, 6 and 7, based on an inclusive conception of organizations, will explain what is necessary to transform organizations into responsive working communities and the skills required to succeed in the new environment.

NOTES

[1] M. Ferguson., *The Aquarian Conspiracy: Personal and Social Transformation in the 1980's* (Los Angeles: J. P. Tarcher, 1980), p. 187.

[2] D. Kanter and P. Mirvis, *The Cynical Americans* (San Francisco: Jossey Bass, 1989), p. 1.

[3] "Executive Pay," *Business Week*, March 30, 1992, p. 52.

[4] "What 800 Companies Paid Their Bosses," *Forbes*, May 27, 1991, pp. 236–89.

[5] "The Flap Over Executive Pay," *Business Week*, May 6, 1991, p. 90.

[6] W. Bennis, *Beyond Bureaucracy* (New York: McGraw-Hill, 1973).

[7] C. Argyris, *Personality and Organization* (New York: Harper & Row, 1957).

[8] J. Eaton and C. Haas, *Titanic: Destination Disaster* (New York: Norton, 1987), p. 14.

[9] C. Peters, "From Ouagadougou to Cape Canaveral: Why The Bad News Doesn't Travel Up," *Washington Monthly*, April 1986.

[10] K. H. Roberts and D. M. Hunt, *Organizational Behavior* (Boston: PWS Kent Publishing, 1991), p. 238.

[11] T. W. Malone. and J. F. Rockart, "Computers, Networks and the Corporation," *Scientific American*, September 1991, pp. 128–36.

[12] D. Barash, *The Hare and the Tortoise* (New York: Viking, 1986), p. 80.

[13] T. W. Malone and J. F. Rockart, "Computers, Networks and the Corporation," *Scientific American*, September 1991, p. 128.

[14] P. Drucker, *The New Realities* (New York: Harper & Row, 1989); T. Peters, *Thriving on Chaos* (New York: Knopf, 1987); R. Kanter, *When Giants Learn to Dance* (London: Unwin, 1989); S. Davis, *Future Perfect* (Reading, MA: Addison Wesley, 1987); C. Handy, *The Age of Unreason* (Cambridge, MA: Harvard Business School Press, 1990).

[15] M. DePree, *Leadership is An Art* (New York: Doubleday, 1989), p. 51

[16] J. Weber, "Offering Employees Stock Options They Can't Refuse," *Business Week*, October 7, 1991, p. 34.

Chapter Three

On the Current Transformation of Business

"A challenge to legitimacy is probably the most powerful force for change to be found in history."

Willis Harman[1]

The industrial era spawned a management versus labor mentality that has been the most self-defeating notion of all. It is manifested in what has been termed the organizational imperative wherein two value propositions and four rules comprise the dominant paradigm of organizational behavior. The two values are: ". . . whatever is good for the individual can only come from the modern organization" and, ". . . all behavior must enhance the health of such organizations." The rules that buttress these two main propositions require employees " . . . (1) to be obedient to the decisions of superior managers, (2) to be technically rational, (3) to be good stewards of other people's property, and (4) to be pragmatic."[2] As the organizational imperative has matured it has come to mean much more. It assumes the willingness of the individual to sacrifice for the good of an organization in which he or she is not a stakeholder beyond wages received. Traditionally, it also assumed that property rights, as exercised by owners of organizations over their material wealth, extend to the ownership of the employees who work for them. This reduces individuals to a state of virtual wage slavery, stripping them of many of the qualities that make them unique human beings and their lives worth living.

Contrast that thinking with the individual imperative which states, "First, all individuals have the civic obligation to realize their full potentials, otherwise they diminish self. When self is diminished, the life of every individual in the community is correspondingly diminished. Second, all individuals have the civic obligation to promote human diversity, since pluralism is an essential precondition of self-actualization. Third, all individuals have the civic obligation to reject all forms of human instrumentalism: individuals are ends in themselves, not instruments for attaining other goals. Finally, all individuals have the civic obligation to dissent when any individual, institution or organization abridges the Founding Values."[3] (The Founding Values are: individual dignity, people as ends in themselves, full participation in the decision making process at all levels, either directly or through chosen representatives, gain/pain sharing, and equal protection of the laws.) The development of the individual imperative has been the strongest single driving force in American history since the Pilgrims landed. It was the basis for the revolution, partly the basis for the Civil War, the basis of the labor union movement in the first half of this century, the cultural revolution of the sixties, and is still at work in the struggle to keep abortion legal and in the formal extension of civil rights to women, homosexuals, minorities, children, and the handicapped.

The state of the individual imperative, when viewed in the panorama of history, is a compelling underlying reason for being concerned with the direction our organizations have taken toward hegemony over the body politic in influencing our lives. We have become an organizational world and have quietly slipped into a political coma finding ourselves at the mercy of bosses who exercise greater powers over individuals than did King George III and his minions before the American War for Independence.

It was never dreamed that private property would become organizational and have the influence we have grown accustomed to it having today. Corporations were usually created temporarily to serve the common good such as to build a road or canal or other public work. By encouraging virtually unrestricted corporate growth under the guise of free-market economic permissibility, our very way of life has finally become inextricably tied up in the privately held organizational domain. There is no escape. The western lands no longer serve as a refuge. The money economy and organized employment have replaced the agricultural options for all but a minuscule number of us. Large system-wide change is, however, quite daunting. As Jefferson reminded us in the Declaration of Independence, ". . . Mankind are more disposed to suffer, while Evils are sufferable, than to right themselves by abolishing the forms to which they are accustomed." Major system change has been discouraged because the tradeoff for a living wage with moderately good purchasing power makes life quite bearable—even materially enjoyable for many people. So, spending our lives subservient to an organization has rather quietly become our way of life. Today business and life have virtually merged much like life on the farm in the agricultural era was the representation of a way of life. Regardless of how we spend our personal time away from the facto- ry, office, or store we are finding we need a new model of organizing that includes a new structure to reflect our new values and a new social contract to reflect new organizational and societal realities. We slipped into an organizational complacency much like into old age, except today many people have wondered not only where the years have gone but what have we wrought?

EXHIBIT 3–1
Corporate Eclipse of the Polity: Growth of Corporate Influence on the Body Politic

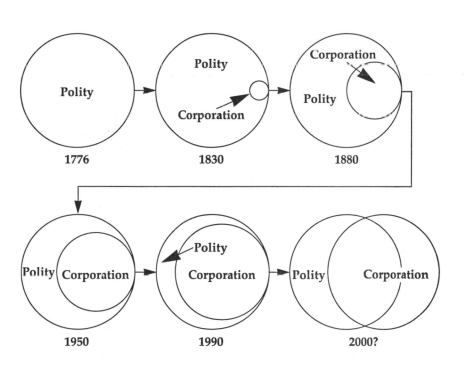

THE EMERGING PARADIGM: AT THE TRANSITION

A managerial system develops that aligns with the assumptions and prevailing values of the organizational paradigm. Over 30 years ago four general management systems were identified within the industrial era ethos.[4]

System One

System One, called Exploitive/Authoritative and was characterized by the efficiency expert mentality. Under this thinking, the owners and their managers could figure out the best way to handle virtually any contingency and labor was merely hired hands to obey instructions and put in a full days' work. In its pure form, people are virtually treated as physical machines. Sweat shops, mines, and assembly lines come to mind.

System Two

System Two, Benevolent/Authoritative, is a variation on the theme of System One. In fact you can draw gradations along a continuum where the four systems have evolved from an authoritarian extreme at the left side toward a more participative form at the right side. System Two recognized that people at work form, by their very presence, a social system that influences their performance since they are capable of thought and free will. This system responded to social science research that showed a modified, benevolent paternalism might result in greater productivity than a strictly authoritarian System One.

System Three

System Three, Consultative, is the first managerial system that recognizes the value of employee contributions and suggests that open communication to tap employee knowledge and point of view may be useful, particularly when circumstances are unpredictable or when the application of the efficiency expert's recommendations are subject to various interpretations when actually applied. This was further utilized when social science discovered that individual involvement leads to higher productivity through enhanced interest in one's work. The jobs that come to mind are perhaps more white collar such as research, marketing and sales, or possibly even craft work.

System Four

System Four, Participative, represents substantial employee involvement in their work. Quality circles come to mind as does the total quality movement where employees in their work teams actively make decisions and take responsibility for their work. You can imagine assemblers, quality engineers, packaging designers, and customer representatives getting together to solve product quality issues. You can also visualize a team of corporate buyers discussing strategies, quality of suppliers and analyzing the best way to approach materials acquisition for a new product, together in a self-managed team.

The conventional wisdom has cited Systems One through Four as representing different paradigms. The management literature is replete with contrasting organizational scenarios claiming the transformation of organizations from a System One mentality to a System Four mentality. The recent popularity of self-managing teams is an example of moving organizations into the participative style of System Four.

One very popular theory of managerial archetypes suggests that there are basically two underlying philosophical tendencies among managers that guide their ultimate behavior toward either System One or System Four. The first is a limited view of mankind that believes people are lazy, don't want to work, and don't want responsibility. This is called Theory X[5]. The other view sees mankind as wanting to take responsibility, capable of self direction, and able to make a contribution in the workplace. This is called Theory Y. Theory X managers are most comfortable in a System One environment and tend toward autocratic behavior while Theory Y managers feel most comfortable in a System Four environment. See the following chart for a summary of these attitudes.

EXHIBIT 3–2
The Authoritarian v. Participative Management Archtypes

Theory "X"	Theory "Y"
Management is responsible for organizing the elements of productive enterprise—money, materials, equipment, people—in the interest of economic ends.	Management is responsible for organizing the elements of productive enterprise—money, materials, equipment, people—in the interests of economic ends.
With respect to people, this is a process of directing their efforts, motivating them, controlling their actions, modifying their behavior to fit the needs of the organization.	People are *not* by nature passive or resistant to organizational needs. They have become so as a result of experience in organizations.

EXHIBIT 3–2 (Concluded)
The Authoritarian v. Participative Management Archtypes

Theory "X"	*Theory "Y"*
Without this active intervention by management, people would be passive—even resistant—to organizational needs. They must therefore be persuaded, rewarded punished, controlled—their activities must be directed. This is management's task.	The motivation, the potential for development, the capacity for assuming responsibility, the readiness to direct behavior toward organizational goals are all present in people. Management does not put them there. It is a responsibility of management to make it possible for people to recognize and develop these human characteristics for themselves.
The average man is by nature indolent—he works as little as possible.	The essential task of management is to arrange organizational conditons and methods of operation so that people can achieve their own goals *best* by directing *their own* efforts toward organizational objectives
He lacks ambition, dislikes responsibility, prefers to be led.	
He is inherently self-centered, indifferent to organizational needs.	
He is by nature resistant to change.	
He is gullible, not very bright, the ready dupe of the charlatan and the demagogue.	

From: D. McGregor, "The Human Side of Enterprise," *Management Review*, November 1957.

Today the challenge remains to move management from a position of fear and a limited behavioral repertoire to a position of confidence and the ability to act from "an instantaneous apprehension of the totality"[6] A Theory X individual can only act from his or her fear and limitations unable to imagine others without those fears influencing the relationship and unable to imagine the value of other people having different talents and abilities. It is the most limited world and inappropriate for the managerial challenges ahead. The increased sensitivity to issues of cultural diversity and gender issues in the workplace demonstrates the difficulty of acknowledging the legitimacy of managerial styles other than the dominant white male model that controls most large organizations. This is in part symptomatic of the rigidity accompanying a Theory X orientation.

The prevalence of Theory X types in conventional organizations is, in part, a happenstance of the era of their ascendancy. The new era demands the skills, openness and flexibility of the Theory Y individual in a Paradigm Two context. That person appears to be in ascendance as the transformation blossoms.

What many writers have missed is that each of these systems even though dramatically dichotomized into a simple System One/System Four comparison, is still embedded in the organizational form that has dominated western capitalism since the dawn of the industrial revolution—the Paradigm One organization.

In order to align organizations to accommodate our new knowledge and the emergent post-industrial paradigm, we must penetrate the self-imposed invisible wall at the edge of System Four and create System Five. Like trying something physically risky, many people will find moving into System Five a frightful experience—especially if they believe that the four systems of management truly constitute the realm of all management possibilities. But once the step is taken, no matter how tentative, one will find the fears quickly dispelled. System Five, is the organizational representation of the effects of Paradigm Two now driving a societal transformation. This then becomes a self-reinforcing process where the societal paradigm shift will facilitate the organizational changes required for the development of System Five.

To be sure, System Four represents a more enlightened model of management than previous Systems, but it hasn't adequately responded to the way society, the marketplace, the worker, and global competitiveness is changing. Certainly System Four recognizes the potential contribution each person can make to the organization's problem-solving process and does try to tap into that potential, but even System Four is still part of the manipulative, management versus labor, industrial era paradigm. Though it recognizes that to get the most from the members in an organization and to be flexible in meeting the contingencies of the marketplace, participation is essential, System Four still doesn't meet the needs of the individuals in the organization for a balanced reciprocal relationship. The basis for relationships in Systems One through Four remain essentially utilitarian and exclusionary. Many managers instinctively know this and have been at a loss regarding innovations to correct the disequilibrium between what the organization is demanding of the individual and what it is willing to return to the individual. System Five is posited as one major step toward a reconciliation of this divide.

System Five

System Five, Community. This is the first step in transcending the organizational imperative and the industrial era paradigm. Though one could point to the progress in moving from System One to System Four, the fact remains that the individual is not in control of his or her own destiny. Though it appears to be a more humane system, System Four is still a bifurcation between the owners and managers, and the employee who will always remain dependent, subordinate, and controlled.

The shift through the paradigmatic membrane at the limit of System Four into System Five necessitates a conceptual leap to develop a new mental construct. All employees will become organizational members and play a role in creating meaning for themselves in the workplace and for the organization. It is the first attempt to infuse organizations with the Founding Values. Eventually, written codes such as a constitution or bylaws will form the basis for a new social contract and will be developed by each organization. The worldwide democracy movement is the leading edge of this aspect of the transformation of our organizations. See the appendix* for a detailed summation of management systems one through five.

EXHIBIT 3-3:
Through the Wall: Toward a New Paradigm

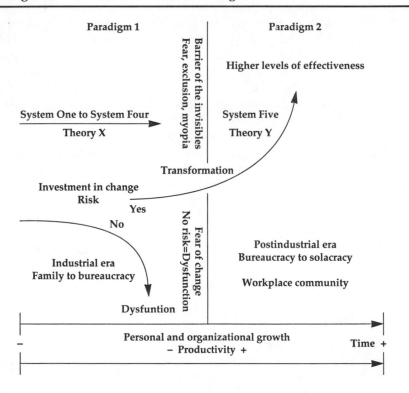

EXHIBIT 3-4
Archtypal Organizational Paradigms

Paradigm One	Paradigm Two
Industrial-Era Model *We/Them*	*Postindustrial/Community Model* *Us*
Incremental responses to environment as determined by dominant coalition.	Choice: The community consciously, intentionally chooses its future and creates the necessary processes to attain it.
Strategy is decided by a few at the top and dictated to entire entity; serial short term synthetic visions of a public relations nature.	Commitment to a jointly created vision forms the basis of a long-term strategy.
Responsibility in job holder according to either job description or results of delegated tasks; Accountability to one's boss sole criteria of performance; colleagues secondary.	Responsibility in each member according to tasks continuously determined in workflow process. Accountability to colleagues and others dependent on one's performance.
Exclusivity; entire status and reward structure based on limiting access to benefits and decision-making centers.	Inclusivity. Each member is a citizen of the workplace community and entitled to participate in the management of the community on an equal basis.
Decisions made by the few closest to the top without necessarily consulting others.	Representative or direct participation in all decision making.
Gain sharing for management; pain sharing for everyone else.	Gain/Pain sharing by everyone.
No individual rights beyond employment contract and those legally mandated.	Extensive individual rights with individual responsibilities as members of a workplace community.
People as means to others' ends; a necessary evil; a cost to the system.	People as ends in themselves; a valuable asset; increases the economic value and the quality of worklife of the community.
Financial criteria the only valid measures of the organization.	Multiple organizational outcomes validated; financial health an assumed requirement but social responsibilities of being part of a larger community acknowledged and individual satisfaction of each member a legitimate goal.

The Fits and Starts of a New Paradigm

Perceptual change leads to a fundamental shift in consciousness. When one sees the changes taking place it alters one's beliefs. Flight was not only thought impossible before the Wright brothers created the phenomenon and the industry, it was a heresy. When flight occurred and planes became commonplace, seeing was believing. We now expect that intergalactic travel will become just as routine some time in the future as air travel has become today. Changing one's consciousness, however, also changes what one sees. If you believe in the possibility of constructing a machine to enable mankind to fly like birds, you may just be able to realize it. And so the transformation of our organizations from the industrial-era mindset to the postindustrial-era mindset will occur on two fronts: among those who see the changing circumstances and will respond appropriately, and, among those who believe the change needs to occur and will likewise act accordingly.

When circumstances change for individuals and those circumstances influence an organization's competitiveness, change is much more rapid and can approach lightening speed. The personal computer (PC) was invented in the late 1970s. But imagine the biggest computer company of all, IBM, thinking there was no need to produce it![7] At the time the PC promised to reduce computational time and simplify certain jobs but no one seemed to see that it would change the world. That is except for Steven Jobs, Steve Wozniak, and Mike Markkula who founded Apple Computer with exactly that idea in mind. By the 1990s the computer's impact on organizations has been so dramatic that it has come to be one of the driving forces for the transformation of organizations. The personal computer so far has decimated middle management and the army of clerks once needed to tend to their informational needs. At the same time it provided an almost unforeseen tool to workers at the lowest levels of the hierarchy: the ability to freely communicate with others through in-house computer networks and to become self-managed because the computer's resources are far superior to, and infinitely faster, more accessible, and more accurate, than a supervisor.

Self-management is not only an ability but a necessity in a cost and time conscious business environment; it means that individuals need to be competent in more skills, in addition to computer literacy, and that the individual can take a more actively creative role in the performance of his or her job. The way these people are managed is fundamentally different from people doing routine work under the direction of a controlling supervisor or a middle manager using subordinates to simply process data.

This one innovation has caught on so fast throughout industry that it is changing the nature of virtually all management functions: recruitment, training, supervision, assessment, compensation, and job design, as well as the very structure of the organization. The hierarchy collapses with each departing level of middle management.

Thus, circumstances in the environment are propelling change at an accelerating rate that produces alterations of our organizational structures, relationships, and assumptions about the nature of doing business that indeed spell a paradigmatic shift in the way management will be conducted in the future.

The industrial paradigm taught people to work in factories and obey their managers. Now people must learn to think, to question, to work almost indistinguishably from managers in postindustrial organizations—and they may even be working from their homes! The alteration of the business environment is creating a set of circumstances that requires new societal software: a new set of values, lifelong education, and cooperative interpersonal processes just as it requires computers, fiber optics, biotechnology, and other technological hardware.

While Copernicus was scientifically right (though it is still more romantic to think of the sun rising and setting around the earth), a societal paradigm requires more than correctness and the force of circumstances, it requires the agreement of a preponderance of those in the system for it to be truly effectuated. The postindustrial paradigm does, however, have a certain apparent inevitability to it because the need for change is so impressive, but, like any societal construct, the new paradigm can only be sustained by the ability, and ultimately, the consent of the people.

It is unlike an "engineered system where the components are tangible, the variables controlled and the outputs identifiable. In the social sphere, the crucial elements often defy definition and control and do not behave according to a set of rules."[8] However, it appears that Paradigm Two consists of certain fundamental understandings that, when applied to our organizations, will move them toward community.

NINE ESSENTIALS OF PARADIGM TWO

1. Choice. The idea of choosing members for an organizational community and of individuals choosing to become members is the first powerful opportunity to reach agreement on the nature of the association to be formed and the purposes to be pursued. In the past we have taken the recruitment process for granted and simply thought we just advertise for workers and then fill jobs. The opportunity to more closely examine the personal fit of the applicant to the organization's needs as well as the organization's likelihood of meeting the individual's needs as part of developing a long-term relationship with one another has been overlooked. Further, by separating the decision to hire from the people ultimately faced with working with and responsible to the new person, we built in a higher probability that the match would be inappropriate and doomed to fail.

Choosing interested applicants for membership in the organization is an opportunity to consciously develop a new social contract of an entirely voluntary nature and free of hidden conventions, unspoken agendas and outdated orthodoxy. The new social contract, like an employment contract, spells out the duties and responsibilities and the nature of the relationship that the individuals will be entering into with the group. It's an attempt to fully understand the relationship to be formed in as explicit a manner as possible. Though obviously unable to predict the financial well being of the company, certainly the future can be discussed in terms of the role one plays in helping to create it and how the individual will pursue personal development throughout his or her association with the community. Companies such as Martin Marietta and Texas Instruments are beginning to make this happen. They have created self-managing work teams which is the prelude to fully empowering the work force. "Management at TI's Defense Systems and Electronics Group, one of this years Baldrige finalists, wants every employee to be in a 'self-directed work team'. . . ."[9] As work teams are established they frequently assume the responsibility for hiring and dismissing members. At first this might happen by the group choosing from a pool of existing employees and then if someone doesn't work out, returning him or her to a previous post in the company. But as self-managed work teams become the rule and not the exception they will select and dismiss members from the workplace community

There is another area of choice and that is in the strategic development of the community and how it will fulfill both its mission and social responsibilities. Thus, individuals help mold both their personal relationship to the community and the community's larger purpose. Chris Argyris described a frequently used process of getting top and middle management together to hash out strategy in an effort for them to begin "learning together about the problems of creating and implementing strategy." He "wanted the learning to occur as the participants were formulating and implementing actual strategies for the coming year(s)."[10] Specifically he wanted to help the group develop the company's strategy; to pinpoint the kinds of problems likely to occur during its implementation at various levels in the organization; and, develop an understanding of how the organization intended to deal with the problems the group identified. This employee involvement can radiate to any depth in the organization. The rule should be to strive to involve all appropriate and interested contributors. During the formulation of the strategic plan communications should ensure that the entire community is kept informed of the group's progress in an effort to elicit appropriate feedback from interested parties. This kind of involvement respects the individual/organizational compact established upon selection and deployment of new employees.

2. Commitment to a vision.   By virtue of establishing relationship and mission, one is intimately involved with setting the community's vision. It is the prelude to creating the strategic plan. It is what gives the community its uniqueness in serving the marketplace and in fulfilling the member's sense of purpose. It lays the foundation and rationale for all that follows. Establishing a vision is to establish a commitment, a bond between each of the members of a workplace community. It is not to be taken lightly. Most companies today make an effort to develop a vision. ARCO publishes a 100-page report entitled "To Make A Difference: ARCO and Society," which is an elaborate accounting of its involvement in public events. Its mission clearly demonstrates it sees itself in an interdependent relationship with the larger society. Pitney Bowes Business Systems announces its purpose is "to create superior and lasting economic and personal value for customers, employees, and stockholders," a position shared by many companies.

What many vision, mission, and strategic statements represent are not a community's perception of its purpose but the view of a small number of individuals at the top. Unless the thinking and actions of individual members of the community are aligned with the vision statement, progress toward it will be virtually accidental; hardly the declared daily purpose of workers on the shop floor. When a long standing sense of what the organization means to workers is abruptly changed by the declarations of a new CEO, as is their personal right in many companies, serious inefficiencies result. For example, at Procter & Gamble, the recent change-over at the top has resulted in a turnabout in corporate vision: Employees ". . . know that P&G's chairman doesn't play by the same genteel rules as his predecessors. . . . Artzt aims to build a tougher, faster, more global P&G. To do so, he is promoting individual accountability—turning back the clock from the 'team approach' of recent years."[11] This type of sudden change throws an organization into chaos. Unilaterally turning around a vision for an organization the size of P&G (77,000 employees) will have dramatic side effects. It is likely that after having built a team-based organization, reversing the mission will create a sense of betrayal, confusion, and high stress; and turnover will occur in key subordinate spots as has already happened at P&G.

3. Responsibility and accountability. Each person is responsible for both a role and specific tasks. He or she is also accountable to the community and to the work group and must meet agreed upon standards throughout the course of membership. The opportunities for review are frequent and within the context of job/membership performance. It is as close to a continuous process as is feasible. (Feasibilities will be decided by the individuals in their work group settings based upon need and available resources. The individuals will also consider intergroup issues to assure that there are smooth intergroup relationships.)

Ultimately the performance of the community is everyone's business and the way people execute their responsibilities is a matter for the community to decide. How this will be handled will be determined by each community but the principle is clear. Each person must eventually answer for his or her actions.

Individuals will be accountable to their colleagues and team members for their personal effectiveness in carrying out their responsibilities. Peer reviews will be common and held in real time as people work. These reviews will have established behavioral expectations and clear objectives spelled out in terms of how each person fits in to the work flow and the level of performance required. At Johnsonville Foods of Wisconsin, workers set performance standards for their teams and confront poor performers.[12]

It will be a two-way street. Everyone working with another person will be evaluated and will do evaluations. Because it is integral in the feedback process these occurrences will be frequent and focused on observable performance. Some jobs, such as team leader, representative, or liaison to other teams, will require the approval of their team members for a term of office. In effect the leaders serve with the consent of the teams. This is happening with self-managed work teams.

4. Inclusivity. All stakeholders are included in the relevant affairs of the organization. All stakeholders. All affairs. The hierarchy of job competence or position in the work flow does not carry over to the maintenance functions of the organization. All members are equals when it comes to matters of mutual interest to the community. Facilities utilization and design, the selection of benefits desired from those offered, workplace safety, social, cultural, educational, health, job design, and other issues should involve all employees or their representatives.

It's more than that, too. If you are building a community, the community needs to be involved in determining major strategic decisions that will affect it. Sound heretical? Unrealistic? Johnsonville Foods was faced with an enormous opportunity to partially merge with a competitor that would have greatly expanded its capacity. Management would have turned the decision down had they decided alone. In their view it was an overwhelming and risky project. Instead they put the question to the employees, created project teams to examine the pros and cons and then put it to a vote of the "members." The members voted almost unanimously to go ahead and prepared themselves for the changes needed to make the new business work. Results exceeded their most positive scenarios.[13]

5. Representative or direct participation used in decision making. In exercising one's role as a member of the community, each person is either directly involved in the decision making councils or they elect representatives. All issues of relevance will be open to community action or delegation by the community. Efficacy and empowerment mean nothing without this provision. There are issues of continuing interest to each member of the organization and each decision regarding the issue—such as compensation, overtime policy, distribution of benefits, job and role definitions, etc.—is really just a step down a long road of organizational improvement. These issues may require ongoing validation by the workplace community either directly by each member or through their representatives. Other matters, specifically tied to roles people play such as marketing manager, design coordinator, production planner, and so on, may require intermittent validation and feedback. In other words people may be selected to perform a job for a period of time and account to the membership for their performance at fixed intervals or at the completion of a designated assignment. These issues get worked out by each community as appropriate.

Teams of workers have been electing their leaders at A.O. Smith, an automotive company, since 1987. The leader takes ". . . managerial responsibility for scheduling production and overtime, ordering maintenance, and stopping the line to correct defects." In addition, "The teams can even revise work standards set by engineers."[14]

6. Gain/pain sharing with joint ownership. Responsibility means to partake in the outcome of one's action and those of others in the community. When success or defeat occurs it is everyone's business and each person will share in the good fortune, or pain, of being part of the community. Simply, one's compensation should be related to the company's performance. Given a base salary, the individual can earn a bonus or suffer a cut based on both a personal contribution to performance, one's team's contribution to the organization, and the organization's overall performance. Not unlike what salespeople already experience, the demarcation between one's base pay and credits for increased knowledge/skill that they develop on the job, and a variable company-based performance bonus will demonstrate the connection between the individual and the community that reflects the organization's performance in the marketplace.

Johnsonville Foods has a profit sharing program that depends on employee evaluations. ". . . the overall satisfaction with the system is very high, partly because fellow workers invented it, administer it, and constantly revise it in an effort to make it more equitable. The person currently in charge of the Johnsonville profit sharing team is an hourly worker from the shipping department."[15]

7. Individual rights with individual responsibility. In every case where an organization is transformed into a community both the group and the individual have undertaken a new social contract. Responsibilities and their explicit expectations of performance are discussed. Individuals frame their approach to their responsibilities and execute them on behalf of the organization. In return the organization accepts the fact that each person as a member is vested from the outset with certain rights and privileges that include being an integral part of the community. Rights safeguard the individual from group excesses, while clear responsibilities safeguard the community from individuals' apathy, withdrawal and nonreciprocity.

8. People treated as ends in themselves. The rights that accompany the individual's inclusion in the organizational community as a vested member include the constant vigilance that they and the processes attending to the assignment of responsibilities, always reflect the fact that individual's are ends in themselves and deserve the respect of the community. This is due each member in good standing regardless of their personal status. Thus, individuals are consulted or fully participate in decision-making situations that affect them.

9. Multiple organizational outcomes are validated. In addition to being successful financially, which is essential for a continuation of the community, other goals are equally worthy of attention, such as fulfilling the social responsibilities of an organizational citizen. Quality of life goals are as valid as financial goals. Personal goals are as valid as group goals. How the goals are incorporated into the action of the community is worked out in the decision-making bodies established for that purpose, as well as in each person's work teams.

FORCES FOR THE TRANSFORMATION

Power Shift

With telecommunications and computers driving the technological changes now taking place, there is a marked shift in power moving from the top of organizations toward the very lowest levels. Toffler, in his continuing prescience, has identified this force as one of the most momentous since the industrial revolution itself. The result will be the first major bloodless transfer of power in history.[16]

Speed

In every area of life, time has been compressed. What took days, now takes minutes, perhaps even seconds to accomplish. In communication and transportation there have been impressive changes in one life time.

The pace of life has likewise accelerated and in doing so has influenced the way we relate to one other. Many people are intimately exposed to more individuals in the course of a year than eighteenth-century Americans were in nearly a lifetime. Not only is life more complex but our penchant for moving every three or four years places us in either a new geographical community or workplace and maybe both, where we must cultivate an entirely new set of relationships with people. We are required to quickly overcome any hesitation in dealing with strangers and individual differences in order to get up to working speed with them. This influence accelerates the search for new ways of relating to people and for the acquisition of new skills to make those relationships work. It is a force for the transformation because of its concern for new relationships and because it breaks through traditions and cultural barriers that have inhibited change in the past.

Expertise and Professional Socialization

Complex technologies and widespread specialization and socialization into professions force an equalization of roles through establishing interdependence. Specialization has increased the value added by individuals in the course of their work. This supports a paradigm shift from the exploitation and consumption of human resources, to the husbanding and maintenance of those resources.

The socialization process, both into one's profession and into the corporation, leads to the internalization of a high standard and to the creation of systems to reinforce elaborate behavioral expectations of members so that the individual becomes self-managed. A new psychological community may be developing through the identification with one's profession. Professionalization also leads to their politicization as people look after their own career interests and make demands of the organization for empowerment, autonomy, and security—aspects of the new paradigm. This encourages the shift of many centralized corporate powers to individuals.

Teamwork and Self-Management

Increasingly complex work organizations are turning to teamwork at the lowest levels of the organization to increase communication, cross-functional cooperation, and joint problem solving. The effect is to increasingly depend on group autonomy to handle its own affairs both in terms of work flow and interpersonal relations.

Enlightenment

The personal growth movement has been one response to the disenchantment with the materialistic way of life. All of its manifestations, now loosely classified as "new age" thinking, focus on the spiritual, emotional, and physical well being of the individual. All means of personal growth, from meditation to formal education to holistic health, promise favorable emotional results for the individual. Another major reason for these personal growth efforts has been the dehumanizing effects of an alienating organizational life contributing to the loss of a sense of self.

Organizational pathologies are now coming to light because of the heightened awareness of all manner of abuses and dysfunctions at the individual and societal levels. New age sentiments are spreading among individuals who are becoming increasingly unwilling to work at a job that isn't fulfilling and part of something enduring. Nor do people want to work while sacrificing one's personal growth needs. Thus, personal change efforts will ultimately influence the organization in dramatic new ways as individuals share their concerns on the job.

Opportunities

As a result of technological change and its effect on institutions as well as individuals, we are beginning to be socialized differently. Common values and norms have given way to subcultures; institutional rigidity has given way to lifestyles and workstyles of choice. Cynicism and lack of faith in our institutions coupled with a refusal to recognize the legitimacy of anyone's right to "boss" have, in a healthy sense, led us to demand as much self-determination in our lives as possible.

Attempting to make organizations responsive, accountable, democratic, humane, and live up to our aspirations as a people, is the challenge we face as a society. It is a powerful force for the transformation.

THE CREATION OF THE LIVING ORGANIZATION

In social science, as opposed to physical science, there is a vast difference in the approach to theory and its application. In the physical sciences a theory is invalidated by a single exception and the elements, at least from the atomic level, have "fixed," predictable, properties. On the other hand social laws or theories are based on the interpretation of aggregates of experience roughly understood and roughly measured. Significantly, in social science, one successful case proves that something is possible and can therefore serve as a model for others to emulate or build upon. And since mankind has the ability to choose, to learn, to change, and to be intentional (identify and express wants and needs, be responsible, keep commitments) it can design a desirable future and in effect, create a new reality. It has happened before. Much of our own history is a testament to that fact; the very formation of the United States of America as the first nation created through popular choice at a constitutional convention is a dramatic case in point.

Cultural paradigms, unlike scientific paradigms are pliable. Each generation experiencing a unique mix of societal, technological and individual forces tempered by its particular history influences the design of interpersonal relationships. Furthermore, unlike scientific paradigms, each generation is able to choose a model of behavior that it feels is most suited to its circumstances.

The emergent paradigm shift represents the changing values of a large segment of the population to transcend self-centeredness and self-interest by deliberately choosing community and rejecting the organizational imperative. The community model, as will be seen later, is an innovative model for organizations but has deep roots in the American cultural tradition. Many people are now revisiting this concept and believe it is a sound response to current circumstances that will indeed alter our experience of work.

It begins with a fundamental shift away from the belief in the self-sufficiency of the lone individual, unlimited material progress based on financial pragmatism, and using people as means to that end. It is a shift toward a more holistic, ecological system's view of one's relationship to the larger society. Instead of being part of a huge deterministic societal machine that, in a great melting pot, deindividuates us and leads to great anxiety and disenchantment, psychic breakdown, and anomie, millions of people are choosing to reconnect with others to form community and view one another as ends in themselves.

The wisdom of the old social ethic of instant gratification, "looking out for number one" and the belief in material power and wealth as the primary basis of social life is being challenged. We have seen with the demise of the yuppie era that personal greed did not make life better for all of us. Internal competition destroys the teamwork and collaboration needed to create an effective organization. Many people now believe that we cannot separate our personal well-being from that of the society at large. The new managerial ethic claims that the bottom line is one and not the only viable measure of success and that how well we work together determines our organization's effectiveness. The utilitarian view of people characteristic of the passing industrial era is becoming less and less acceptable. Only focusing on the bottom line is increasingly being found to be dysfunctional; modern complex organizations are living human systems that require an understanding of, and attention to, the relationships and well-being of each participant. The organization of tomorrow indeed promises to be a living organization.

CAUTION: SOCIAL CHANGE ISN'T FOR EVERYONE

But just as one example may show the possibility for a new order of things and while many will gravitate toward the new system and embrace the possibilities they see, there are others who will not transcend their fears, who will not be able to adjust, who could lose their bearings. New paradigms may change the course of the world but organizations must be able to deal with everyone including resistors. In 1610 Galileo confirmed the Copernican view of the sun as the center of the solar system, not earth, but it wasn't until 1979 that the Catholic Church officially accepted this finding and exonerated Galileo.[17]

The new paradigm must be well-managed, alignment must be created between the individual and the organization and it must be recognized as an evolutionary process that varies in its degree of acceptance as it replaces the previous paradigm. The following aspects of Paradigm Two will, in their turn, evolve in varying degrees as each organization grapples with applying the principles in a manner best suited to its particular circumstances.

ARE WE WILLING TO CREATE THE FUTURE?

One premise of this book is that as individuals, if we have the will to make a difference, we can forge an intentional future, recreate our world, and build a responsive workplace community. We do not have to sit idly by and let the introduction of new technology, distant economic forces, demanding bosses, and other sources of organizational stress, control our lives. By bringing the societal transformation inside our organizations, with an activist orientation we can overcome the alienation and ennui that plagues much of modern life. So much of that alienation pivots around our organizational role. By asking the right questions and building alliances and networks of support we can begin to change organizations from within. At the same time we can help to accelerate a societal and technological change process already underway that indicates the coming of a completely new personal experience of organizations. But are we willing to create our own future?

Building workplace community is also an outcome that many people are actively advocating for today's organizations. The alienation and anomie of the twentieth century has reached a point that for many people, only corporations actually hold the promise of reinvigorating their lives with both a sense of purpose and a feeling of belonging to a community doing something worthwhile.

This pincer-like movement of forces to change organizations will be realized around the turn of the century, and leading edge companies today are taking steps to meet that challenge.

Another purpose of this book is to stimulate discussion and action about a future that honors the individuals' efficacy in participating in community and how we might establish this new organizational type based on the changing consciousness.

Transforming work organizations into workplace communities will reap rewards unmatched even in the post-war 1950s because community is likely to build enduring synergies, while conducting business-as-usual in this country is to conduct business-in-decline.

RENEWAL/RE-CREATION/TRANSFORMATION

Will organizational community bring a renewal of individual liberty, creativity, personal growth, real community? By creating workplace community the United States will once again lead the world in creating a model that returns to individuals control over their lives and recreates a democratic environment in that area of their lives heretofore untouched by the democratic impulse.

This message is getting through to those that can make a difference now. As *Fortune* magazine said, "A handful of visionary leaders—General Electric Chairman Jack Welch chief among them—are going beyond training seminars to a fundamental reordering of managerial priorities . . . (this movement recognizes) that reality is not absolute but a by-product of human consciousness . . . even the primacy of the profit motive (is) being questioned by those who argue that the real goal of enterprise is the mental and spiritual enrichment of those who take part in it."[18]

According to Ret Lt. Col. Jim Channon of Task Force Delta, "Three things are missing from almost every organization . . . a sincere desire to love each other in a brotherly way, an ability to incorporate spiritual values in their work, and an ability to do something physical together."[19] If we assume that man is good and that failure to nurture that goodness and growth may result in either decay of the goodness, stifling the growth need, or atrophy of the natural process of growth toward maturity, then organizations need to devote attention to these issues of fostering the right climate. The coming transformation is a natural representation of this desire.

Reality ultimately is what you think it is. There is no absolute when it comes to social constructs. More often than not, the reality we create works if we believe in it. Though we may not fly like our favorite fictional super heroes, certainly it is still easy to get on an airplane.

Mary Parker Follett put it this way: "Progress implies the respect for the creative process not the created thing; the created thing is forever and forever being left behind us."[20] It is important to focus on the process in order that we may be satisfied with the products of our workplaces and our lives within them.

The era of things is passing. The era of intangibles is on the rise—the use of information, the creation of knowledge, attention to work flow and interpersonal processes, and the creation of the right organizational environment. These intangibles are becoming more important than the product itself since they result from attention to the processes that creates the product. Investment also is moving from things to ideas, from material to creativity in its use and in the application of knowledge. People are invested, not money. Just as food is needed for the survival of the individual, money is needed to sustain the organizational context. But as one does not live to eat but eats to live, we will begin to see the quality of work life improve as our attention shifts from profit to the process of work and our relationships.

NOTES

[*] For a detailed descriptive supplement outlining the characteristics of systems one through five, write to: The Center for Workplace Community, P.O. Box 1395, Los Gatos, CA 95031.

[1] W. Harman, *Global Mind Change* (New York: Warner Books, 1988), p.1.

[2] W. Scott and D. Hart, *Organizational Values in America* (New Brunswick, NJ: Transaction Publishers, 1990), pp. 30–31.

[3] Ibid., p. 163.

[4] R. Likert, *New Patterns of Management* (New York: McGraw-Hill, 1961).

[5] D. McGregor, "The Human Side of Enterprise," *Management Review*, November 1957.

[6] R.G.H. Siu, *The Master Manager* (New York: Mentor, 1980).

[7] M. Moskowitz, R. Levering, and M. Katz; *Everybody's Business* (New York: Doubleday, 1990), p. 412.

[8] S. Lipset (Ed.), *The Third Century: America as a Postindustrial Society* (Chicago: University of Chicago Press, 1979), p 13.

[9] P. Burrows, "Power to the Workers," *Electronic Business*, October, 7, 1991, p. 97.

[10] C. Argyris, "Strategy Implementation: An Experience in Learning," *Organizational Dynamics* 18, no. 2 (Autumn 1989), p. 5.

[11] Z. Schiller, "No More Mr. Nice Guy at P&G—Not By A Long Shot," *Business Week*, February 3, 1992, p. 54.

[12] R. Stayer, "How I learned to Let My Workers Lead," *Harvard Business Review*, November–December 1990, p. 66.

[13] Ibid., p. 83.

[14] Reported in D. Mills, *Rebirth of the Corporation* (New York: John Wiley & Sons, 1991), p. 86.

[15] R. Stayer, "How I learned to Let My Workers Lead," p. 74.

[16] A. Toffler, *Power Shift* (New York: Bantam, 1990).

[17] See: Galileo, *Encyclopedia of Religion* (New York: Macmillan and Free Press, 1987), V. 5, p. 466

[18] "A New Age For Business," *Fortune,* October 8, 1990.

[19] Ibid.

[20] M. P. Follett, *The New State* (New York: Longmans Green, 1923), p. 98.

Chapter Four

The New Accountability:
Building Balanced Relationships in a Postmanagerial Era

". . . there is nothing more difficult to carry out, nor more doubtful of success, nor more dangerous to handle, than to initiate a new order of things."

Machiavelli[1]

In a world where democracy is breaking out in some of the unlikeliest places and in a world now committed to the idea of liberty, it is sadly ironic that Americans have so thoroughly surrendered themselves to corporate tyranny.

How have we come to accept so thoroughly the sacrifice of over half of our waking consciousness to the god of earning a living without the slightest thought to the propriety of the relationships in the workplace and the fact that we must surrender ourselves to an impersonal bureaucracy that defies our influence? How have we so completely surrendered ourselves to the rule of the dollar and the powers of an unelected, often unaccountable boss?

This chapter looks at our organizations from the conviction that they are the major institutions that shape our day-to-day experience of community and that the issues we face in the workplace greatly influence not only the quality of our work lives but the overall quality of our lives. Thus, as we turn our attention to the workplace as polity, as the locale for building a meaningful sense of community, a new political frontier will emerge where the same kinds of powerful interests that direct community life as we have known it in our neighborhoods will materialize in our organizations. One of the first items on the community-building agenda will be to level the playing field so that each employee, as a participant in a shared community, enjoys the same egalitarian role as an organizational citizen forging one's organizational destiny—as one has enjoyed in the larger geographical communities of city, state, and nation.

With this new realization that organizations are indeed arbiters of our way of life and that individual employees must have the right to influence their destiny at work, a new era of corporate governance dawns.

AN IMPERIAL MANAGEMENT

"All delegated power is trust, and all assumed power is usurpation."

Thomas Paine

In 1915, Louis Brandeis, later to become a U.S. Supreme Court Justice, foretold the impact of large corporations. He said, that they tended "to develop a benevolent absolutism, but it is an absolutism all the same; and it is that which makes the great corporation so dangerous. There develops within the state a state so powerful that the ordinary social and industrial forces existing are insufficient to cope with it."[2]

Today, a mere one-lifetime later, as Parenti has pointed out, "By controlling society's capital and labor, corporate conglomerates are able to build and demolish whole communities, preempt vast acreages of land, plunder and pollute the natural environment, manipulate entire technologies, shape the development of whole regions, obliterate fragile ancient environments, map the lines of national and international trade and transportation, control media content, create new wants and markets, destroy old skills, values, and tastes, and control the destinies of people throughout the world. The multinationals exercise a coercive power of a magnitude difficult to comprehend, impinging upon our lives in a multitude of ways, often without our knowing it. How then can anyone speak of the corporation as a 'private' organization, as if its decisions and actions had no effect on our collective destiny?"[3]

The rise of corporate power and its tendency toward totalitarian control over those who must work in them, as well as the society at large, was criticized shortly after World War II by the former chairman of the board of General Electric. Theodore Quinn declared in 1948, that these "brute economic monsters" are "leading our country just as surely as the sun sets to a brand of totalitarianism which is a perversion as far from individualism, civil liberties, and the democratic process as Russian Communism."[4]

But even in 1948, when the post war economic boom was just beginning (later fueled by the Korean War), corporate power and influence was a mere fraction of the globe-girdling strength of today's multinational corporate community. It is no overstatement to attribute our material standard of living to the enormous success of corporations and the very fact that in the aggregate they have indeed been able to wield their power and influence to create so much of value. Yet, at the same time we marvel at the material wealth that has resulted from their endeavors, we need to appreciate the full scope of their influence to understand just why they are such a threat.

For example, only about a dozen nations on earth have a larger Gross Domestic Product (GDP) than General Motors' annual sales, which roughly matches or exceeds the GDPs of countries like Switzerland, South Korea, Mexico, and Saudi Arabia, and the combined GDPs of Singapore, Portugal, Luxembourg, Peru, and Thailand.[5] In a sense then, the chief executive officer of General Motors has the kind of power comparable only to that of heads of state and, in some cases, it has become the envy of heads of state. Though they are not yet capable of declaring war, corporations can readily influence those who can. They often hold countries hostage to their needs for cheap labor, cash crops, and favorable tax and trade conditions in return for capital investment and the transfer of management expertise.

But, unlike heads of state, corporate leaders are at best only accountable to a relative handful of people that rarely if ever includes employees or the public.

Few people even know the name of the chief executive officer of the largest and most powerful corporations today, with the possible exception of those organizations with highly visible, charismatic chiefs who appear in the companies' advertising and public relations programs. Few people question their right to hire and fire, make job assignments, require personality assessments, conduct job evaluations, establish someone's job-worth, set retirement conditions and medical benefits, and allow or disallow employee access to employment files. Nor do many question its right to influence an employee's ability to file and carry through grievances or protest company policies, or "blow the whistle" on improper corporate behavior.

It is the corporation that assumes the hands-on governance of people at work. It is called management but no matter what one calls it, the new relationship is establishing a new power over individuals' lives. If one accepts a job, it is assumed he or she will abide by the employer's terms of service. As can be readily deduced (and verified through a massive literature on work and the conditions of labor), the corporation and its managers have an influence over each individual worker similar to that of the dictators, monarchs, and governments from which mankind struggled for millennia to wrest its fundamental liberties in the first place. The rise of the giant corporation with proprietary privileges extending to the purchase and management of people as if they are like any other resource, surely seems to place mankind back into a dependent position in which livelihood once again is determined by a fundamentally totalitarian social structure, this time emanating from giant corporate bureaucracies. Until very recently, the corporation was immune from adherence to basic constitutional requirements such as allowing its employees free speech, due process, and the right to organize. The relationship between employer and employee has been based on the principle of "employment at will" which enabled organizations to do just that: hire and fire people for any reason. Even now, though this principle has been somewhat constrained by new laws and court decisions, the expression of individual rights, as they are known in the larger community, is not secure within the majority of organizational environments.

The business press has reported many cases of employees who were dismissed for notifying their supervisors about questionable activities, health or safety risks, and other matters they felt, in good faith, the organization needed to deal with. "When MIT scientist Margot O'Toole exposed fudged research data for a scientific article signed by Nobel laureate David Baltimore, she lost her job. It was only in April—five years later—that she was vindicated when Baltimore admitted that the research was flawed. . . . Anne Livengood, a 51-year-old medical office worker . . . alleges she was fired from a physical therapy clinic in Fremont, Calif., after she notified management that its accounting system billed insurance companies for undelivered services. . . . Eric Schiffer, CEO of the clinic, says he will countersue for alleged theft of documents and libel."[6] In both cases, dismissal resulted from an individual's attempt to inform management of events they needed to know about and were handled with an apparent disregard for due process.

The relationship between the individual and societal institutions has been on an inexorable journey from autocracy to democracy. Though there have been dark ages and various regressions, there has been a fairly consistent move toward granting rights and entitlements to individuals which were once denied them. The struggle for individual freedom to create the kind of life one so desires first freed people from the authority of bandits and feudal lords, then the authority of established churches and assorted tyrants, and more recently from the domination of secular dictators and bureaucrats through the legal protection of a growing body of human and civil rights. Undoubtedly the future will witness the extension of democratic principles into our workplaces.

As the state declines in its visible day-to-day influence over our lives, the political struggle inevitably shifts to the corporation. Owners and managers of modern organizations are just the latest in a long line of ruling forces which have assumed powers over individuals in their neo-feudal realms.

While government has actually become an advocate, in many cases, for individual liberty such as protection of one's civil rights and equal employment opportunity, though there are still some glaring exceptions, corporations by comparison have usually disregarded the issue of liberty as irrelevant to organizational life until constrained by law or the courts. Because of this, the struggle continues for the inclusion of the democratic ideal within workplaces and for a resolution of the individual/organizational conflict.

As Harvard Professor Daniel Bell long ago pointed out, "In an industrial society, work is a game against fabricated nature, in which men become dwarfed by machines as they turn out goods and things. But in a postindustrial world, work is primarily a game between bureaucrat and client, doctor and patient, teacher and student, or within research groups, office groups, and service groups. Thus, in the experience of work and the daily routine, nature is excluded, and persons have to learn how to live with one another. In the history of human society, this is a completely new and unparalleled state of affairs."[7] It is a state of affairs which inevitably draws our attention to the creation of intentional democratic communities in our workplaces just as we have democratized other societal institutions.

Throughout their growth and coincident with the industrial era itself, private corporations have simply concentrated on their primary purpose of increasing their stockholders return on investment. In order to do this one major concern of owners and managers has been the reduction of costs. For most large corporations a major cost is labor. We can see over the course of corporate history the attempt by owners and managers to reduce that cost to its absolute minimum. In fact, over the last ten years, employment in the Fortune and Forbes 500 has declined while their economic power has increased and much of their operations have been moved off shore.

Peter Drucker, one of the world's foremost management consultants, reminded us, "indeed every manager, if he had sense, would be happy to get the job done without people. They are a nuisance. He does not want to be a 'government.' It only gets in the way of doing his job. For the Duke or the Baron of yesterday, people were 'subjects' and represented strength and wealth. For the hospital, the government agency or the business of today, people are 'employees' and represent 'cost'."[8]

This perception of labor as merely a cost of doing business has given rise to a sometimes violent, often belligerent and usually distrustful relationship between management and labor. As long as labor was simply a collection of hired hands, and employers had no legal responsibility to provide for even minimal employee welfare; and as long as government protected the rights of employers and denied rights to labor, what amounted to a system of industrial feudalism prevailed—and an enormously profitable one at that.

So, mankind has gone from being an asset on the farm to being a cost, a liability, in the factory and office. But the societal costs of the alienation, anomie, disenchantment, and moral decay proved too great and led to labor unrest. Concurrently, the natural tendency for organizations to rationalize their efforts and to husband their resources, coupled with vast societal and technological changes, led to thinking about the quality of work life itself. Is humankind simply another resource, such as steel, rubber, glass, and plastic, to be managed?

Through human resource management, productivity can be improved, obedience assured, and people reduced again to a state of dependency. But this dependency is one that individuals are led to believe they want; one that functions for their benefit.

Yet, there are many people who, despite the massive efforts at "human resource management" find that they simply aren't convinced. Their desultory performance, lack of motivation, underlying unease, and unexplained, unidentified malaise results in a decline in productivity, weakening loyalty, and eventually, when the hypocrisy of the human resource management programs are identified and understood, to total alienation. When this unconscious reaction is brought out into the open and dealt with in the newly politicized arena of large corporations the essential nature of the quality of work life issue can then be confronted. Then progress can be made toward transforming modern organizations into communities that work because of the conscious consent of everyone that works in them. When organizations stop dividing employees into owner/managers versus employees and unify them into a community structure, a healing of this fissure can take place and the organization can return to sustainable effectiveness. And that is precisely what leading edge companies are now doing.

Fortunately, the evolutionary process of technological and societal change shows that while dramatic short-term change seems unlikely the future looms large with hope.

National Steel Corporation has a policy of management-labor cooperation. There is a no-layoff policy and the company shares financial information with employees, "salaried and hourly employ-ees serve as cochairs of monthly meetings that provide workers with earnings figures, targets, and market conditions; hourly workers can be found acting as foremen and . . . the company-owned executive club has invited hourly workers to become members."[9]

Even U.S. Steel, once the scene of some of the most devastating labor/management disputes in the history of the labor movement is now recognizing the importance of labor management unity. Thomas J. Usher, president of U.S. Steel said that "There is a growing realiza-tion that we are not going to make it without the union and the union is not going to make it without us."[10] Managers and union workers now regularly consult and even visit customers together to get feed-back about the products they use.

These examples, however, demonstrate an individual decision to open up the decision making process. But just as it is opened up by an individual, so too can it be closed down at any time.

Since we are relatively free to choose among the corporations in terms of occupations which interest us and where we would like to work, we are led to believe that the system is working in our best interests. This cannot be the case until one is free not to work. But that is an eventuality we will not observe in our lifetime. So as long as people must work to earn a living, the struggle between the indi-vidual and the corporation will continue until a manner of equity is reached in the distribution of power and organizational rewards. Let me emphasize at this point that equity is fairness, not necessarily equality. So, each person may have an equal say regarding internal managerial issues and policy while compensation or the role one plays in an organization will be a matter of assessing the individual according to proven skills and the full complexion of one's experience.

While great pains were taken to cautiously assign powers to our political leaders, with many checks and balances and separations of responsibilities to guard against what was believed to be the inevitable corruption of those in office, we have neglected to address the full scope and use of executive power as it is applied to people in the workplace. Charters or constitutions will be necessary to specify institutional structures that will guarantee employee participation in decision making and a proceedure for amending the process, if neces-sary, through a consentual mechanism.

Economic participation is another matter. In this realm everyone is in agreement: money invested must appreciate in value—the quicker the better. There is no risk that participation in this realm will lead to discord. Stockholders' exclusive voting rights today (with the exclusion of employees) is the equivalent of property ownership as the sole basis for voting as was the case before the era of universal suffrage.

Can a democratic society that traces its foundation to a war over the right to self-determination force people to work without a policy and decision-making role? John Stuart Mill wrote: "The principle of freedom cannot require that mankind should be free not to be free. It is not freedom to be allowed to alienate his (or her) freedom."[11] Yet, when it comes to life in organizations we all too often do exactly that. Leading edge companies are forging a future that promises to correct this unfortunate state of being and, by building a shared community of interest among managers and employees, find they are better able to reach their economic objectives.

Most often, when companies focus on satisfying customers, shareholders, and employees, their economic results demonstrate superior performance compared to companies that focus solely on managerial benefits. There have been some dramatic differences. "Over the 11-year period, Messrs. Kotter and Heskett found that the 12 firms in the first group (satisfying customers, shareholders, and employees) increased their revenues, on average, by four times as much as the 20 companies in the second group (satisfying management only); their work forces expanded by eight times as much; and their share prices increased by 12 times as much (by 901 percent, against 74 percent for the second group). Perhaps most impressively, however, the net profits of firms in the first group soared by an average or 756 percent during the period, compared with an average increase of just 1 percent for companies in the second group."[12]

Thus there are benefits for eveyone when organizations begin to resolve the management versus labor dichotomy. In resolving this split, the first step is to establish a new relationship between employees and the organization. This in itself goes a long way to transform the entity into a unified whole, from the bifurcated situation, since a democratic, inclusive system of governance, by definition, leaves no one out. All are bound to the same system. It would be the corporate equivalent of universal suffrage.

INEQUITIES/INDIGNITIES OF WORK RELATIONSHIPS

As long as the manager/employee dichotomy exists, a double standard will persist. The personal anguish of being treated as an object, while at the same time treating others as objects, is an irony that rarely gets the attention it deserves. The *Harvard Business Review* ran an account of a top executive in "a global oil corporation" who was faced with a layoff of tragic proportions—his own. The account was a description of how, at age 54, he survived the ordeal. Of course the company gave him several months of salary, support, and expenses to relocate, counseling, and access to office resources including outplacement counseling.[13] But he never once mentioned the catastrophe that so frequently befell middle- and lower-level people at his hands who were given nothing except two weeks pay and a pink slip.

At a deeper level consider the occurrence of a boss telling his secretary that two people are to be laid off; one will be made uncomfortable so that, hopefully, she will resign and avoid the severance issue. The other, whom he hired, has become a personal friend but has been deemed the "odd man out" in his department. Thus he has to go— even at a time when the company was advertising a product that he developed single-handedly. Besides the lack of integrity on the manager's part in his handling of the situation, he continued his "friendship" with the knowledge that business is business; nothing personal. Consider the position in which he put his secretary. Knowing these two people and valuing them as decent human beings worthy of better treatment, she was bound to remain silent. The manager's remarks were confidential; the "organization" was acting and required her "loyalty." Here the manager has essentially asked his secretary to take part in the charade and to dehumanize herself in this game of treating her colleagues as moveable pieces in a corporate chess game. The boss's lack of integrity, and the audacity of making that kind of decision unilaterally and capriciously, typifies the imperiousness crippling business relationships today.

Here the secretary is made an accomplice in this hypocritical double talk claiming his act was an "organizational" one. Loyalty to the organization was implicitly invoked to assure her cooperation in remaining silent about the offhanded way people's lives were being treated. The decision was a personal act, though ostensibly on behalf of the group. The fundamental problem here is in the definition of the situation requiring managerial action and the process used to solve it. Apparently the problem was defined as a need to reduce the budget; not how to better utilize resources and increase revenue. Also, the process involved was a unilateral one. The manager in question simply acted as an individual in the name of the organization and the benefit of a full participative analysis of the situation was denied. In community, by contrast, individuals handle a problem like this as a group or through representatives. Conceptualizing each person as a respected member of the group entitles each to a meaningful role in decisions affecting him or her. Employees are entitled to maintain their dignity and humanity at work despite the fact that they receive a paycheck for being there. A manager has no right to be thoughtless and capricious; employees are still individuals—members of the community.

IGNORING HUMAN RESOURCES AS ASSETS

Like an Olympic marathon competitor wearing only one shoe, organizations cripple their ability to do as well as they can because while they focus on their financial resources, their human resources are neglected. An organization unconcerned with the management of its human resources is handicapped from the outset and is likely to become crippled during the competition. In a well-managed work-place, employees find work a satisfying experience with opportunities to reach their full potential as people and as contributors to the success of the organization. Isn't it time that we ask why processes for the proper handling of "human resources," employees as members of the workplace community, have been so contemptuously ignored while financial and accounting controls have been so totally and laboriously implemented? Clearly the controls for money have resulted in the most rigid of bureaucratic environments that stifle the full application of creative, imaginative, human endeavors. Possibly it is also because of the egocentric nature of the organization that conceptualizes all resources as an extension of the CEO's will and grants promotions to those most proficient at using power to enhance the CEO's perceived performance.

But our malaise in the workplace is also about dignity and freedom and self-determination. Why haven't we taken to liberating ourselves from the tyranny of an imperial management as we have from other forms of abuse of power. How is it that our democratic impulses have stopped at the organization's door? How can we assert our independence and liberate ourselves from racists, sexists, ageists, and bigots of every stripe, fight government excesses and defend our rights in courts throughout the land, while worshipping the CEO, accepting his right to rule, and subjecting ourselves to the virtually unchecked and frequently arbitrary whims of his minions in our largest enterprises?

THE SILENT SCREAM

America may be ripe for the first revolution in the history of mankind effectuated by inaction—by withdrawing either physically or psychologically from the system. And it might be successful beyond anyone's imagination in illustrating the fundamental bankruptcy of the current organizational world.

Turnover, absenteeism, inhibited initiative on the job, poor productivity or attention to one's role and contribution is a signal to the organization that people are feeling a disconnection—a lack of efficacy in the workplace.

Organizational upheaval is inevitable if upper managers are unable to resist the seductiveness of power. Yet the entire hierarchical nature of organizational life and its reward structure require pleasing those above as a political necessity. The system is deliberately designed to reward those most adept at achieving power. But whether they use it constructively and graciously, or wield it as if they were merely indulging in the use of a fringe benefit, determines if the workplace is problem/people centered, and decent, or a psychological torture chamber. Unfortunately, the mood in organizational America today is steeped in the latter. "Steadily growing legions of supervisory types, their livelihood endangered by cost cutting and recession, are angry, distrustful, stressed out and scared. . . . And because of their perception that the upper echelon has turned on the underlings, the white collar blues won't go away anytime soon, economic recovery or no."[14]

THE QUALITY OF WORK LIFE (QWL) ISSUE: HEADING TOWARD COMMUNITY

During the early years of the nineteenth century, Luddism appeared in England. The Luddites destroyed machines that threatened their way of life and have become a symbol of the forces of mindless anti-industrialism and anti-progress.

From the Luddites to the hippies of the 1960s, mankind struggled with the difficulty of first defining then creating the kind of quality of life and quality of work life that best serves its interests, reflects its values, and sustains a peaceful, profitable, and comfortable way of life.

That challenge continues today, of course. And though it might appear that even the most unfavorable working conditions are quite tolerable, particularly when compared to the atrocious conditions of yesteryear, each generation will want (and must take) the next step toward an even better way of life. When QWL issues are dealt with by all organizational members for everyone's mutual benefit then constructive, imaginative, and profitable change can take place.

Simply put, the QWL is a subjective assessment of the relationship between management and labor, and the overall work environment—

particularly as that condition fosters or retards human development and satisfaction with life in general. It implies a concerted attempt to negotiate the gulf between owner or manager and worker. In looking at this issue, however, everyone seems to have assumed a bifurcation of the organization into management and labor. Today it is becoming more and more apparent, as is argued here, that this adversarial distinction is no longer valid.

Leading edge companies have proven this for years. "The Gaines pet food plant in Topeka, Kansas, just celebrated 20 years of self-management. For two decades under three owners. . . . Topeka has always placed first when its labor productivity was compared with that of other pet food plants within its company."[15]

The move to bridge the gap between managers and workers is well underway. Soon the organization will be seen as a single entity serving a single vision for the benefit of all stakeholders encouraging the best from each contributor. "'The winners in the next few decades will be the companies with the most empowered work forces,' says Michael Dell, CEO and president of Dell Computer Corp. . . . To keep up in the race, managers must break with paternalistic business philosophies. . . . Rather than viewing themselves as practitioners of strategies and protectors of their people, they must look to their underlings for guidance—and spend their time creating an environment in which the expertise is shared and implemented. 'It isn't enough to just be a good employer anymore,' says Joanne McCree, personnel manager at IBM-Rochester. You have to find ways to help people make as much of themselves as possible."[16]

It is true that the ideal state of the workplace community is only limited by one's personal imagination and, no doubt, each person and company approaches the issue of the QWL and building community from a unique point of view. Nevertheless, there are some common areas of concern to all organizations that involve all individuals within each organization.

The QWL is defined as a "way of thinking about people, work, and organizations. . . . The focus of QWL efforts is not only on how people can do work better, but on how work may cause people to be better."[17] The QWL issue is broadening to deal with the fundamental assumptions and behaviors which influence cooperative human effort as well as the conditions of work itself. It is also an effort to study the organization to discover ways of making the treatment of all members reflective of the philosophy that people are ends in themselves and not simply means to organizational ends. So, QWL has everything to do with improving peoples' relationship to their work and to their fellow workers. Ultimately, the transformation of organizations into communities will facilitate this process, particularly since the workplace is becoming an ever more important focus of one's life experience.

The conventional wisdom regarding the operationalization of a QWL program as influenced by corporate management and designed and executed by personnel departments, typically suggests that there are eight major areas to consider:[18]

1. Adequate and fair compensation.
2. Safe and healthy working conditions.
3. Creating the immediate opportunity to use and develop human capacities.
4. Continued personal growth and security.
5. Social integration in the work organization.
6. Implementing constitutionalism.
7. Assessing the relationship of one's work to one's total life space.
8. Developing or enhancing the social relevance of one's work life.

When an organization is bifurcated, some managers deal with these matters as if they are something done to, or for, non-exempt or hourly employees. In community, as we shall see in the next chapter, the entire organization grapples with these issues through a participative governance process. These issues then become matters for the entire membership that accepts them as issues "we" deal with together.

THE QWL ISSUE TODAY

Work, as we know it, is changing dramatically. Our preparation for work and our expectations of work life have changed in such a way that we are coming to believe that work and career are as natural as play and should be challenging—even fun.[19]

Yet we find ourselves in the unfortunate position of depending on the benevolence of a CEO-dominated board of directors to achieve a humane quality of work life. Thus, nothing remains secure, even with the most well-intentioned individuals at the helm. Today, as corporations talk about reducing health care benefits they once again put their employees at risk. Companies once counted on to maintain a generous level of employee benefits, such as Ralston Purina, Boise Cascade, and Safeway, have shown that the pressures of increasing costs make one's good intentions another ephemeral aspect of contemporary organizational life. These companies and others are reconfiguring their benefits packages and employees will be taking more financial responsibility for the benefits they receive.[20] Before

Safeway was LBO'd (Leveraged Buy Out) it was considered a virtual lifetime employer. After the buy-out it laid off over 75,000 people, (though many were rehired) and undermined the morale and long-standing goodwill of its employees. "Their SOS motto, 'Safeway Offers Security' became a grim reminder of how drastically the company changed in just a few short months [after the buyout] . . . there were plenty of horror stories: One man was fired a month after his wife was diagnosed with cancer. Twenty-year veterans were told, with no warning, to clear out their desks and to be gone by noon . . . . When asked about the unceremonious disposal of one-third of his former work force, CEO Peter Magowan said only, 'There was a strong urgency to put the whole unpleasant matter behind us as soon as possible.'"[21]

In 1980, Louis Davis, then the chairman of the Center for the Quality of Working Life at UCLA reported that "what were once seen as privileges to be earned are now seen as entitlements which are slowly becoming rights. Young people are beginning to claim the right to have an interesting, self-fulfilling, self-developing, individually-centered job. We see this expressed through the extraordinarily high value being placed on people as individuals rather than as members of organizations."[22]

This creates pressures on organizations to justify their actions and to treat new employees in a manner they have come to expect. The QWL issue and efforts to transform organizations into communities is becoming for the corporation what the quality of life issue and the struggle of the individual for personal liberty was for government. This new focus of attention by the corporation is a recognition of three developments. First, its significance in our lives is becoming one of the most salient issue of the times. Second, we have for the most part, arrived at an equilibrium with government—that the exercise of freedom and the power struggles of various interest groups take place within a democratic framework. Third, focusing attention on the QWL issue recognizes that our organizational structures and underlying assumptions are out of tune with a changed work force and a changing technological environment, requiring a realignment.

There is growing evidence that corporate leaders are beginning to see the QWL issue in its broader sense and are willing to accept a role which recognizes business's responsibility to employees as well as its duty to shareholders. However, only a mere handful of companies are taking the necessary steps to institutionalize processes that demonstrate their growing awareness and many more companies that "talk the talk" but only "walk the walk" in good economic times. In both cases improvements in the QWL are still dealt with as benefits that are given by management to employees and not matters for the entire membership to decide and implement for themselves because it is their right to do so as legitimate stakeholders.

Developing community within a high quality of worklife environment makes sense not only because it is the right thing to do but because it is the profitable thing to do. In an era where organizations are shifting from manual to mental labor, activating worker motivation shifts from economic incentives to relationship and experience based incentives. Thus, the environment of the workplace itself becomes capable of motivating the individual when it is conducive to thinking, expression and cooperation—all essential in knowledge work.

The push for QWL improvements is coming from both blue collar and white collar workers. With blue collar workers, particularly unionized workers, QWL issues are often based upon contractual agreements which set out specific negotiable issues focusing on physical working conditions, compensation and fringe benefits.

Some corporations, particularly in the high-tech industries of computers, electronics, and biotechnology, once offered a paternalistic package of comforts unimagined not too long ago. When times are good, aspects of the QWL agenda were generously handled and extraordinarily comfortable. "Hewlett-Packard has 500 acres in the Santa Cruz mountains for company picnics and camping trips. Apple Computer has its own hot air balloon available for employee use, Tandem provides an Olympic-size swimming pool and Friday afternoon 'beer busts'. Advanced Micro Devices, on the other hand, is famous for its contests. Ten employees who wrote the most persuasive essay on the theme, "Why My Job Is Important," each won 50 shares of common stock. And last year, one AMD employee was selected at random to receive $1,000 each month for the next twenty years in a company raffle christened the 'American Dream'. . . . The phenomenally successful and innovative electronics industry holds out the promise not only of America's economic salvation but of a new way of working. What's more, high tech paternalism offers workers not just a job but a whole new style of life. It is a California dream of a holistic workplace where work is just one facet of the integrated human being and where, on the tennis court as well as the production line, the major product is the self. As Alvin Toffler says, workers enjoy the 'freedom . . . to be individuals.'"[23]

Perhaps for Tandem Computer that will soon become a reality. They ". . . may serve as the prototype for a twenty-first-century version of the nineteenth-century company town . . . . (Their) new campus . . . will have child-care facilities, a retail center, public and private parks and possibly a hotel. The property will be served by some form of company-sponsored transit. But most importantly, it will include up to 500 residential units for Tandem employees. 'We wanted to look at the whole picture,' explained Frank Robinson, Tandem's director of corporate real estate and site services. 'A lot of the community's issues in the '90s are also our issues, and we wanted to create something that's good for Tandem and good for everyone else.'"[24]

Unfortunately, in good times or bad, "For the production workers who make up half of the electronics industry work force, Silicon Valley means low-wage, dead-end jobs, unskilled tedious work, and exposure to some of the most dangerous occupational health hazards in all of American industry."[25] The situation hasn't changed much over the 10 years since this assessment was first made. "Low-paid assembly line workers, often ethnic minorities and occasionally undocumented aliens, cloistered in 'clean rooms,' elbow-deep in toxic solvents, have always been Silicon Valley's dirty family secret."[26] This dichotomy is not just a testament to the power of having a highly valued skill and being able to demand a comfortable work environment versus not having that skill and being ignored, it is also an indication that the underlying issues of the QWL question have not been faced: fundamental conflicts over the expressed values of the organization, the nature of interpersonal relationships in the workplace, the perception of who is included in the organization, and how the act of management is defined.

Now that the bloom is off the silicon valley miracle, middle management and the "techies" that made it all possible have racked up grievances similar to those of the blue collar workers, but theirs are of a psychological sort. "Some psychotherapists estimate that 60 percent of the valley's electronics workers are in therapy. . . . 'Corporations do not want to appear to encourage people to work themselves over the brink into having a nervous breakdown,' says Dennis Hayes, author of *Behind the Silicon Curtain: The Seductions of Work in a Lonely Era*, an incisive critique of Silicon Valley's dehumanizing work obsession. 'Yet the project assignments and deadlines compress the work into such small spaces that they, in effect, do invite nervous breakdowns, a slavish dedication to work that leaves little time for anything else—certainly for relationships and family.'"[27]

A QWL program can only be genuine, and not just another paternalistic gesture that can just as easily be taken away as it can be given, if it first addresses the question of how each person can become part of the process of determining what the QWL will be: How they can each help determine what their lives will be like at work. "Doing" it for someone robs them of their dignity and insults their intelligence.

Speaking of the QWL efforts at General Motors, a vice president of the United Automobile Workers Union emphasized the point. Management must accept the fact, "that workers are adults in the workplace as they are in society at large; that the democratic values we cherish as free citizens in our homes and communities are in good measure transferable to the place of work; that these democratic values entail direct individual and collective worker participation in the decision-making processes. . . . Not every worker will be amenable to participate in a quality of work life program. Some prefer the autocracy of the workplace as we know it today. Equally, not every job is subject to a democratizing shift in work life. But the genius of the human mind, once set on the course of 'humanizing' work and of bringing democratic values into the workplace, will perform wonders in satisfying the desires of workers to be part of the decision-making process at the workplace."[28]

QWL AND MANAGERS

Most treatments of QWL issues have intentionally or otherwise focused on the blue collar worker. Because working conditions, remuneration, career prospects and the work itself, for most white collar employees are so noticeably better than for blue collar employees, it is assumed that the QWL for them is high. It is also the result of a persistent bifurcation of the kinds of treatment each receives in the organization and the way responsibilities have been divided. This is the corporate equivalent of the split of military personnel into officers and enlisted ranks.

Programs involving white collar, professional and technical people are often termed organization development (OD) programs. Though the individual often meaningfully participates in the OD process, personal outcomes are usually secondary.

For example, increasing competence, skill, career choices, promotional chances, intrinsic job satisfaction, or reducing job stress, are usually secondary to increasing efficiency, reducing costs or resolving intergroup conflicts that slow the work flow. While this may be perfectly understandable, the emphasis of QWL programs must be on the mutual fit between individual and workplace; the impact of the organization on the individual is as important to consider as the individual's impact on the organization. Modern corporations have yet to fully demonstrate their understanding of this principle in their QWL programs or OD strategies. There are some notable exceptions, however, which have been frequently cited for their ground breaking efforts. Pitney Bowes, Tektronix, ROLM, Tandem Computers and others are often cited as examples of enlightened quality of work life environments. But even among them, the underlying assumption is that the system is inviolate, meaning that almost all employee programs are centered on making the status quo palatable rather than making the organization a true reflection of the specific needs and desires of its individual members. It is the growing legitimacy of this call for a fundamental reorientation of the conventional wisdom that is so irritating to many CEOs. Unfortunately, by conceptualizing organizations as extensions of their person, it is impossible for them to think of organizations as being inclusive of, and responsive to, the "hired hands." As Harold Geneen, former CEO of ITT, reputedly once said, "If I had enough arms and legs I'd do it all myself."

The effect of this mindset is that at a personal level, white-collar employees experience a much more insidious maltreatment than poor working conditions. The exercise of domination and control by an endless variety of bosses, and even an ever-present but elusive, unidentified "them" is the first source of discomfort and a sign of a low QWL. This is virtually unavoidable in a hierarchical environment that rewards the acquisition and use of power, often for its own sake. Shorris has written one of the most cogent indictments of this kind of tyranny. "Nothing can deter it, neither morality, nor reason, nor even self-preservation. The urge to dominate comes to dominate all those within the organization; men are but the means to movement, and movement is the only possible end."[29]

This urge to dominate is endemic to managers who make all important decisions. The consequence of this control is that persons with lower status are most subject to personal domination as well as organizational domination. One corporate memorandum made famous in a syndicated column by Mike Royko illustrates the point. "Any employee who does not want to adhere to the items mentioned above can quit. . . . I don't need a job—you people are the ones who need to get with it."[30]

The blue-collar worker in many large corporations at least has a union intermediary and this has, over the years, reduced some of the arbitrariness, capriciousness, and worker defenselessness, through a protective grievance procedure that gains a modicum of countervailing power. Among white-collar workers without the benefit of a union, perhaps the most important cause of mental disturbance is job stress induced by the seemingly irreducible urge to dominate by one's "superiors" and others in the typical organization.

Without unions, without the ability to pin down specific forces, even specific actions, without even being allowed blue-collar freedom, through alienation, white-collar employees often become struck by the stress and depression of being caught in an invisible, intimidating web of personalities, power, and pressures. These forces are usually successful in trapping them into misperceptions of what the so-called real world of corporate life is all about. Reinforced with the rough and tumble jargon of the "fast-paced," "upwardly mobile," "hardball playing," "wheeling and dealing" world of exciting projects, power bases, and promotions, it is easy for millions of people to willingly become caught up in the promise that they can "succeed" if only they play the game well. When disillusionment sets in, a new cadre has already been recruited and one must either accept personal "failure" or recognize the fact that indeed their perception of "success" has itself been the biggest trap of all.

The QWL issue for white-collar workers often becomes a matter of gaining more autonomy from these forces and individuals. There are other retardants to developing a high QWL for white-collar workers. Along with domination and control is, of course, intimidation and the suggestion that undesirable outcomes will result from not doing what one is expected to do. While this may be included under the broad issue of domination and control it is often a manifestation of one's adherence to or rejection of group norms such as hours of work, dress, amount of travel, willingness to relocate, agreement with the group on the kind and quality of one's contribution to it, informal status assignments and the distribution of variable perquisites.

What has become characterized as the "rat race" neatly sums up the kinds of pressures and circumstances that influence one's behavior through intimidation and peer pressure. One can become slightly paranoid due to second guessing the group and real and imagined "powers that be" by wondering what actions will gain their approval or their wrath. The degree of paranoia naturally is subject to one's degree of intuitive understanding of, and identification with, the group.

The way white-collar workers are kept on the treadmill is through personal evaluation exercises and the humiliation that often accompanies them. While there is an air of objectivity about the process, and rating scales, checklists, and a variety of forms to record the evaluation encounter, ultimately one's relationship with the evaluator and the performance pressures on the evaluator from his superiors

are the major determinants of one's review. Since actual personal performance and one's "real value" are virtually impossible to establish
apart from the larger context of the work group, the evaluation
process is often one which is more suited to dominating, controlling
and regularly intimidating subordinates, than an exercise in constructive feedback, personal growth and empowerment which is its osten-
sible purpose.

Perhaps blue-collar unionized employees understood this when
years ago they won the right for seniority to outweigh merit. White-
collar employees in conventional organizations, however, are still
subject to the annual review process and approach it with trepida-
tion, not just because of the uncertainty and arbitrariness of the
encounter, but because it "removes the privacy from men's lives,
reduces men to objects, converts the human complexity of them to
pale generalizations, and stores away this arbitrary reduction of a
human being to be used against him later."[31] The development of a
personal file on each employee is a lifelong transferable shackle. As
an instrument of control and intimidation, it so far surpasses its usefulness as a true evaluation and development tool as to make any
claims of objectivity at the evaluation encounter simply ludicrous.

The white-collar aspects of the QWL issue have far reaching implications since they raise questions about the most fundamental workings of the large corporations and the assumptions we make regarding
their rights and obligations as instruments of society at large.

It goes without saying that we need and depend upon our large
organizations to sustain and improve our existing way of life. And, it
doesn't matter what political ideology prevails, organizations
develop their own systems and influences that have so far been
resistant to democratic ideals and, in the vast majority of cases, have
even adopted totalitarian methods to achieve their objectives.

To most people that judgment is too harsh, too radical. After all,
business is different from life; "business is business" suggests that a
separate and equally legitimate set of rules exists for business conduct in addition to civil conduct. If those rules don't include the luxury of
democratic processes which the society has struggled for so long to
attain, well, it has to be that way. The irony is that, "In business, men
do not arrive at totalitarian methods because they are evil, but
because they wish to do the good in what seems to them the most
efficient way, or because they wish merely to survive, or with no
more evil intent than the desire to prosper."[32]

Hence, like blue collar QWL issues, but in a somewhat different
way, white-collar QWL issues strike at the heart of our relationships
with one another and our organizations, and our responsibilities to

the larger society. These questions may have appeared only vaguely implied in the white-collar QWL issue of employee loyalty. Being part of an organization places an individual in a confidential relationship of trust with others. He or she is expected to keep the group's interests at heart. But how should one act when he or she is fully aware of corporate misdeeds, deliberate legal or moral transgressions, or cover-ups of errors with unfortunate public consequences? Here the pressures to remain silent or face the wrath of the corporation if one speaks, can be overwhelming. The individual has no protection against these pressures and must usually leave the company, and then, incurring its wrath, often suffers long afterward.

BALANCING ORGANIZATIONAL POWER WITH INDIVIDUAL RIGHTS

To be employed is to be beholden. As a "subordinate," experiencing all that that term implies, one is made dependent on individuals who wield, literally, the power of economic life and death. The political maneuvering that surrounds the conduct of one's work efforts in order to secure favorable treatment by the organization is remarkable in its commentary about the demeaning, servile, experience of working in America. We seem to have veered way off course from reaching the state of interpersonal equality that democratic philosophers and the founding fathers had in mind. Though we have freed ourselves from governmental tyrants, we willingly succumb to the petty tyrants in the workplace and believe it is the natural order of things.

For the ambitious, the politicking is intense and every nuance of one's interpersonal relationships, particularly with "superiors," or others in a position to facilitate one's career, is fraught with multiple levels of meaning and a great deal of anxiety. For the less ambitious, and those simply interested in an honest days wage for an honest days work, a concern for their economic well being and job security may still create a measure of anxiety—particularly in an age of mergers and recession. Underlying both positions, however, is the implicit understanding that one's connection to the organization is tenuous indeed. Individuals are simply not guaranteed employment and possess few rights in the workplace. While this may have been acceptable in the early days of capitalism when few people were touched by the factory system and had an extended family to fall back on in hard times, it is increasingly being challenged today.

Individual rights are not fully or uniformly safeguarded from corporate intrusion, though Federal laws and court decisions are making some inroads in extending rights into the workplace. Workplace safety, equal employment opportunity, and some measure of due process is now being regulated into business practice. Court decisions have also moved in the direction of extending personal rights into the work-place but the corporate world has become the most conspicuous hold out of authoritarianism since the democratization of nation states and public institutions.

Though infrequently examined in the context of an organizational experience individuals' are also beginning to demand considerations that only a few years ago would have been unthinkable. Robert Smith outlined 14 freedoms of concern to all workers. They serve as the basis for an extension of constitutional safeguards into the workplace and are not proffered as the end point of concern about democratiz-ing organizations.[33] In addition, Robert Levering has added several, though more esoteric "rights" that are morally justified.[34] All, it could be argued, will become rights in tomorrow's organizations if they aren't already respected by organizations today. Together they are:

Freedom in the Hiring Process

The kinds of tests individuals can be made to take; inquiries into their personal lives; and, discrimination based on age, gender, race, religion, and in some states, sexual preference, handicap, or preg-nancy are now being proscribed by law.

Freedom of Trust

The use of a polygraph (lie detector) and some other methods of determining one's honesty or behavior such as drug testing or hiring a detective agency or credit bureau to investigate an employee is now regulated in some states. Involuntary use of the polygraph has been banned by federal law but some employers still seek voluntary use as a confirmation device when suspicions arise. The applied standard tests the organization's need to know and the employees right to pri-vacy and security in one's reputation. At one time the Coors brewing company used a polygraph test to ask job applicants how often they changed underwear and whether they had ever done anything with their spouses that could be considered immoral.[35]

Freedom of Speech

One of the most incredible reversals of logic regularly occurs when a company fires one of its employees for "blowing the whistle." Accused of being disloyal, an employee is dismissed for having revealed an illegal or unsafe or questionable corporate act. What many believe should be seen as a positive act to help the organization stem misbehavior early and face its responsibilities squarely, often results in the humiliation of the informant as a corporate pariah. Employees at Lockheed Corporation working to eliminate racism and sexism in their Northern California facilities ". . . are only now adopting more militant tactics because of their deep frustration after years of working for change without success." One of the leaders of an employee coalition raising discrimination issues with management, Gil Jaramillo ". . . saw his once promising management career stall after he became active in the coalition, an independent auditor found."[36]

Many sympathize with organizations and see whistle-blowers as somehow traitorous, despicable, snitches. In virtually every case where cost overruns, tax evasions, unsafe work practices, bribery, price-fixing, systematic discrimination, or knowingly deceptive advertising have been shown to be accurately reported by the whistle blowers, it is also demonstrated that they first, and persistently, went to their superiors with the information. In each case, they believed that the company should, and would, correct the matter. In too many cases the individual either lost his or her job or suffered the ridicule of fellow workers—frequently both.

Even in a milder attempt to exercise free speech, such as expressing oneself honestly at a meeting where the boss is present, most individuals are under severe pressure to self-censor their comments lest they result in disapproval. It is not a matter of competence but of point of view. Intimidation buttresses the pressure to conform to the conventional wisdom and to the wishes of the powers that be.

A more insidious infringement of an individual's freedom of speech is being fired or censured for what one says on his or her own time, off the job. "Daniel C. Winn made nearly $9 an hour setting up machinery at Best Lock Corp., Indianapolis. He was fired after he testified in a relative's legal hearing that he drank socially from time to time: Best Lock forbids alcohol consumption by employees, even after work. Best also contested his right to receive unemployment benefits, claiming he was fired for cause. A state court ruled Winn eligible, but Best notes that the court didn't hold its 'no drinking' rule invalid."[37]

Freedom of Expression in All Forms

Employee communications among one another must be protected, not just their right to unionize. This might be manifested through an uncensored newspaper, or through meetings on company premises during company or personal time. Along with this is the implication that one has the right to be listened to, the right to be wrong, the right to make a mistake and the right to practice one's fundamental convictions and to be excused from doing work contrary to one's convictions without being penalized.

As companies are transformed into communities, this and the other rights mentioned herein will become viewed as "natural" aspects of workplace life contributing to the participative development of a high quality of work life.

Freedom from Intrusions

When an employee is suspected of wrong doing, organizations often assume they can search the individual, their offices or their belongings at will. Court cases are finding in favor of employees who have been improperly accused and searched but the federal constitutional guarantees against unreasonable searches doesn't apply to employer-employee situations. "At least five states—Connecticut, Georgia, Ohio, Virginia, and Wisconsin—have laws that specifically restrict searches and surveillance of employees, and some of them are quite powerful. In Connecticut, for example, an employer who repeatedly uses electronic devices such as video cameras or audio tape recorders to monitor employees in restrooms, locker rooms, or lounges can be charged criminally and sentenced to jail for 30 days...."[38]

Tapping phone lines, monitoring mail, work-site surveillance, and automatic computer supervision of workstation productivity and usage are all devices used to check on individuals' performance and whereabouts. They are also powerful tools to convey a general suspicion of the work force to each employee.

Item: "In Wabash, Indiana, Janice Bone lost her job as an assistant payroll clerk at the Ford Meter Box Co. The reason? The firm which will not let its employees smoke either on the job or at home, insisted that she take a urine test, which proved positive for nicotine."[39]

This form of personal intrusion is a particularly repulsive and invidious act on the part of the employer because it so totally disregards the dignity of individuals and forces their submission to what might be deemed an illegal procedure to determine if an individual is partaking in a lawful though undesirable act.

Freedom of Safety and Health

What may surprise some people is the fact that 1990 was the worst year for on-the-job injuries and illnesses since the record has been kept from 1972. The total topped 6.8 million cases, with factory injuries and illnesses accounting for about a third of the total. It may come as a surprise since there is virtually no widespread discussion of workplace conditions and because so many people enjoy rather comfortable office surroundings.[40] "While many industrialized countries have succeeded in making their workplaces safer, the United States—with the highest occupational fatality rate of any industrialized country—is not among them. A 1989 study by the National Safe Workplace Institute in Chicago revealed that during a single year about 11,000 American workers are killed on the job, nine million are injured (70,000 of them permanently disabled), and one out of six of all workers eventually dies of an occupationally related disease."[41]

There are obviously dangerous jobs and then there are jobs that are hazardous but invisibly so. Only recently has a concern been raised that windowless, centrally air conditioned offices containing synthetic materials in carpeting and furniture may be leading to a form of illness peculiar to the artificial office environment. This may not be as dramatic as the on-the-job risks to a fire fighter or toxic waste handler but have become a concern nevertheless. The obligations of the employer to ensure a safe and healthy work environment are now being codified by state as well as federal regulatory bodies such as OSHA (Occupational Safety and Health Administration). For example, by designating many workplaces as smoke free, they have thus helped clear the air.

Freedom from Stress

As long ago as 1972, work-related stress was identified as debilitating. Robert Ellis Smith quoted a government report asserting that "Dull and demeaning work, work over which the worker has little or no control, as well as other poor features of work also contribute to an assortment of mental health problems. . . . From the point of view of public policy, workers and society are bearing medical costs that have their genesis in the workplace, and which could be avoided through preventive measures."[42]

Freedom from Assignment/Reassignment without Consultation

Full participation among colleagues and the reconceptualization of the organization into community demands that each person play a meaningful role in determining the full breadth of their job responsibilities including collaborating with others about what they will do and where they will do it. Leading edge companies empower employees to determine work assignments in a fully participative fashion. At an NCR plant in Atlanta "the core work force of production workers (called 'manufacturing associates') have complete responsibility and accountability in the areas of production, quality, work style, and work environment. They are cross-trained in multiple jobs, set their own hours, determine their job tasks, conduct peer performance reviews, play a major role in developing compensation packages, and screen applicants, conduct interviews, and make hiring decisions. Part-time ('on call') workers have the same status as management associates."[43]

Personnel Journal reports that a survey of Fortune 1,000 companies shows that corporate reliance on teams is increasing dramatically and the payoffs have a tremendous positive impact on the bottom line. "Northern Telecom's Morrisville facility, for example, has experienced major increases in revenue (63 percent), sales (26 percent), earnings (46 percent), productivity per employee (60 percent), and quality (50 percent)."[44]

Freedom in Off Hours

For white collar workers, the work day is elongating. With modems for computer access via the home, work, for a growing number, is ever present and in some professions putting in 14, 16, even 18 hours a day has perversely become a badge of honor! Where "work life" ends and "real life" begins is blurred for an increasing number of people who find it impossible to escape their work. Total customer service and total quality products demand responsiveness from individuals around the clock—whenever and wherever the need arises.

Carving out "quality time" the yuppie catch phrase of the 1980s is becoming ever more difficult. Kids are placed in day care almost as soon as they arrive home from the hospital. Though that may be necessary because of the increasing need for both parents to work, many parents choose it as a way of partially relieving them of their child rearing chores. Business trips, of course, frequently consume days on end and usually don't earn compensatory time off at some future date; for many companies that would be a laughable if not disloyal request.

Weekends are increasingly used as an opportunity not to get quiet time at home but at work when the phones stop ringing (until people learn you're there on weekends) and colleagues aren't around (until they realize they'll lose the competitive edge by ignoring weekend work). Though this 1980s stereotype of the corporate go-getter may not be receiving the same respect in the 1990s, the workweek has indeed dramatically increased. According to Harvard Economist Juliet B. Schor, ". . . the average employed American works the equivalent of one month more each year than he or she did 20 years ago."[45]

These issues involve work seeping into personal time off the job but companies have also been famous for meddling in other personal areas such as one's social life, for example, when it becomes known that an employee is friendly with people working for competitors or get involved with political or environmental causes not of the employers' liking. The typical intrusion today is around the so-called lifestyle issues. "Turner Broadcasting System Inc.," for example, "won't hire smokers at all. We think we have the right to employ the kind of person we want to have—and that's a non-smoker," says William M. Shaw, vice president for administration."[46] In the name of lowering health care costs for the employees, as a group, many companies have shown a keen interest in not only one's smoking habits but drinking, exercise, and weight control. The city government of Athens, Georgia, once eliminated job applicants if they had a cholesterol level in the top 20 percent. Other companies such as Multi-Developers Inc., according to *Business Week*, ". . . won't employee workers who engage in 'hazardous activities and pursuits [including] such things as skydiving, riding motorcycles, piloting private aircraft, mountain climbing, motor vehicle racing, etc.'"[47]

Freedom from Sexual Harassment

The confirmation hearings for Supreme Court nominee, now Justice Clarence Thomas, exposed yet another of our dirty little secrets to a national audience and placed the issue of sexual harassment squarely on the corporate agenda. It isn't a new issue, of course, but it is now getting the attention it deserves. Twenty years ago the issue was seen as frivolous. As recently as fifteen years ago in a U.S. district court a judge declared in Bundy v. Jackson, (24 F.E.P.) that "sexual intimidation was a 'normal condition of employment.'"[48] Ten years ago that decision was reversed on appeal, [Cases 1155 (D.C. Cir. 1981)], and today women's mistreatment in the workplace encompasses many specific issues including unequal pay for equal work, discrimination in promotion, lower pay for jobs women dominate in contrast to comparable jobs dominated by men, and discrimination in benefits. Furthermore, they suffer disadvantages created by their need for maternity leave, day care facilities for their children, and flextime to attend to family concerns. All of these are unlikely to have a similar impact on men but they are gaining attention.

Many larger companies are facing these issues squarely. Providing day care facilities (or subsidies for day care) are increasingly becoming a natural part of employers recruitment lures as well as other aspects of the benefits package offered to employees. Paternity leave and time off for males to be with their newborn is also gaining respectability.

Freedom from Organizational Harassment

Perhaps the single most important contribution of the Anita Hill revelations about sexual harassment will be the attention given to all forms of intimidation in the workplace. While sexual harassment is seen as mostly a women's issue, men and women have been intimidated in a number of ways to comply with the dictates of their boss or to conform to the prevailing norms of acceptable behavior defined by their organization or work group. The threat of plateauing in one's career or being reassigned to an undesirable locale for failure to meet a sales goal is also an affront to an individual's dignity. Forcing the relocation of an entire family to a corporate Siberia is also a form of intimidation we need not allow in the workplace.

Freedom of Information

Limits to the disclosure of information affects employees in at least three ways. According to Smith, "They are denied information about the organization they work for and thus are less able to participate in guiding its destiny, or even in working effectively for its success. They are denied crucial information about their specific jobs within the organization, including information necessary to protect their own safety, health, and rights as citizens. Lastly, employees are left in the dark about information that is kept on them as individuals, in the personnel files of the front office, as well as about how that information is collected, maintained and disclosed to others."[49]

Dependency is assured when access to information is limited. Until the computer revolution, organizations could deny access to individuals on the grounds that it was too time consuming or costly. Today through computer networks all employees can access needed information to make well informed personal and professional decisions regarding their work, their performance and their future needs. Whether or not organizations will allow access through computer terminals is another issue. To deny individuals the information they want and need will become increasingly indefensible since computers are already being distributed throughout the organization as an essential work tool and the cost of access is virtually non-existent because the information is already on-line. The issue will clearly be divided along political interests according to the stakes perceived by current centers of power.

Marion Labs, a prescription drug manufacturer employing about 2,000 'associates' may be setting an enlightened lead in this area. They have a policy that employees can access any information except others' personnel records, financial matters that are prohibited by law from early distribution and specific plans that could be used by competitors.[50]

Andy Grove of Intel, a high tech computer chip manufacturer that one might naturally think requires secrecy in its highly volatile and competitive market environment, notes that "people formulate strategy with their fingertips. Day in and day out they respond to things, by virtue of the products they promote, the price concessions they make, the distribution channels they choose."[51] Charles Garfield adds, "Old story strategic planning is inappropriate in this fast-changing environment; what is required is strategic thinking on the part of every employee."[52]

Freedom from Propaganda

Whether a company pressures employees to vote for certain political candidates that represent its interests, or to contribute to charitable organizations it deems worthy, or "trains" employees to become motivated through the selective disclosure of information or organizational rewards, the individual in each case, is being unfairly manipulated and subject to sometimes not so subtle intimidation to serve the organizations political objectives. If Harry stands in the way of a unit's 100 percent participation in a United Way drive or Martha's refusal to contribute $10 prevents her "team" from winning a trip to Las Vegas, they risk suffering the wrath of their peers. The organization that encourages these activities may feel civic minded and have the highest motives, but unless individual choice to participate is respected, the effort is simply another form of workplace intimidation for organizational ends. This is especially so when the decision to engage in this activity as an organization is itself beyond the purview of full employee participation.

Freedom to Participate

Workplace democracy is around the corner. The democracy movement in Eastern Europe, China, and the Soviet Union, regardless of the degree of success or the specific reforms already achieved, can't help but spill over into other aspects of life in those countries or in our own. The issues we face are taking a personal toll. They are no longer academic abstractions. The environment is deteriorating and in serious danger. Communities are falling apart. Personal relationships of every kind are under enormous stress. And the workplace is becoming increasingly demanding of us, while remaining unresponsive to our needs. It is a natural venue for agitating for change. Besides the social reasons, technology is making workplace democracy not only a good idea, but necessary. Computers facilitate communication and the flow of ideas. As the hierarchy flattens, workers become colleagues and their role becomes more participative, for example, when they are formed into teams to solve problems.

The arrogance of unilateral decision making is becoming less and less palatable to a weary work force increasingly fed up with the shortsightedness and self-centeredness of following the myth of managerialism. Access to information contributes to the general awareness of the abuses which so characterized management's lopsided behavior in its own (not the organization's) interest. For example, according to *Business Week*, "Twenty-five top executives of General Dynamics Corp., the nation's No. 2 defense contractor, have booked $18 million in incentive bonuses in just the past six months (1991). Not bad for a company that's even now dismissing thousands of workers in order to better position itself in what Chief Executive William A. Anders admits is a 'nongrowth market'."[53]

Freedom in Fringe Benefits

Perhaps the most important fringe benefits Americans have are health care and retirement packages. Today, more and more companies are beginning to reduce their health care coverage and/or require employee contributions—both actions that dilute this vital benefit at a time when health care costs are astronomical. We have also seen that the conditions which an employee must meet to be vested in a retirement plan, as well as the control of that plan, have been subject to the cost cutting interests of management resulting in lost benefits for millions of workers.

There are many other types of benefits from employee discounts on company products and services to full reimbursement for educational expenses to stock ownership subsidies. But with record levels of mobility in this country, there is an effort to at least create uniform health care and retirement plans so individuals need not sacrifice earned assets and personal security when changing jobs—either voluntarily or involuntarily. The need is for fringe benefits that travel with the employee and this makes particularly good sense with retirement and health benefits.

Freedom of Due Process

In matters of dismissal, denial of promotion, or interpersonal conflict with one's superiors, few organizations provide a process through which an individual may get a fair hearing. "There's no process for challenging—or changing—bad decisions made by the authorities. There is no mechanism to vote for people to represent you in decision making bodies. There's no Freedom of Information Act to help you discover what is going on behind closed doors. There is no presumption of innocence or trial by peers."[54]

Federal Express is an exception. It has a policy of guaranteed fair treatment which it terms GFT. It begins with a hearing with one's supervisor and if necessary that person's supervisor. Then, if a further review is necessary the divisional senior vice president will make a decision or create a board of review. The board consists of five members, a majority being selected by the employee filing the grievance. At that point the decision is final and binding on all parties.[55]

The issue of due process is more poignant in organizations with the greatest imbalance of power, usually in the most hierarchical, the most traditional. It is a fundamental consideration in establishing fairness in the workplace that some measure of due process be assured. It is necessary for the resolution of differences that inevitably arise at work. Without it, few rights can be established or kept secure.

Freedom from Abusive Firing

Abusive firing occurs when an employee is laid off for reasons other than inadequate performance or organizational economic distress. Often this reason is disguised under a veil of false acceptability. For example a personality clash results in one party finding fault with another or exaggerating performance weaknesses in order to present a case for a "safe" dismissal. At one point in the not too distant past airline stewardesses would be dismissed upon turning 35 years old or getting married or gaining weight; and female newscasters would be assigned or released because of their appearance. These reasons were rarely acknowledged formally, however. Even in situations where an employee is performing inadequately, an organization has a responsibility to attempt remediation and allow the employee to improve his or her performance. Nevertheless personality clashes and strategic changes often result in employees being dismissed without consideration and this is increasingly being defined as abusive. The obligation incurred by an employer upon hiring individuals is being challenged to include some measure of enduring responsibility as long as the employee performs assigned duties competently and in good faith. The employers traditional right to hire and fire at will is under assault.

Additional Concerns

To the above compendium of freedoms must be added the concern for ethical behavior in dealings with all community stakeholders. This is implied in many of the freedoms but covers a broader range of activities. It would also be inclusive of non-employees such as dependents of employees, suppliers, customers or clients, and members of the neighborhood in which the organization is situated.

The idea of corporate social responsibility is itself an umbrella concept for a host of concerns that range from producing safe products, disposing of waste in a form that offers no hazards to others and aspiring to behave, as an organization, in a fashion that exemplifies the best practice and best thinking of our culture as a whole. This would include doing no harm to people or the environment in any way.

TOMORROW'S WORKPLACE

As with all human endeavors, the past is prologue; the vistas and prospects for change are indeed vast. We have seen that the QWL originally defined in terms of working conditions and benefits has changed enormously over the past few decades and now includes fundamental issues of interpersonal behavior, democratic processes and even the legitimacy of the conventional organization system itself. As basic survival and security needs are met through legislation, union protection, court interpretations, professional influences on standards, and rising expectations about how one should be treated on the job, questions regarding quality of work life issues have been elevated to a new plateau.

In addition, as issues of pay, benefits and working conditions become more or less settled, serious attention is drawn to the "traditional law of the master-servant relationship, which in the main holds that management can fire an employee for cause, for no cause, or for cause morally wrong."[56] Since the early 1970's this tradition has come under fire and is now on the verge of revocation. Today, "In more than half a dozen states, including Michigan and New Jersey, legislators have written statutory exceptions into the so-called law of master and servant. In many more state legislatures, bills have been introduced to protect certain kinds of employees from dismissal."[57]

Employee rights to privacy; due process in matters of grievance handling and firings; free speech, particularly for so-called whistleblowers who attempt to alert corporate officers and the public to wrong-doing or questionable practices; access to one's personnel file, especially to know about evaluations, recommendations by others, and, whether non job-related or inaccurate materials are present; and, the right to equal treatment including the right not to be harassed for political or sexual favors, are all maturing.

As these issues unfold, enlightened personnel practices, government regulations and union-management agreements influence the extent to which companies today define and protect employee rights. There are, however, tremendous inconsistencies and the burden of proof still seems to be on the victim who is, from the start of any complaint (or dismissal due to filing a complaint), at a tremendous disadvantage vis-a-vis the corporation.

The first effort by corporate reformers, then, has been to stress the adoption of an employee "Bill of Rights".[58] It is fundamentally a way of extending to the corporation the same considerations one is entitled to in his or her socio-political environment. With the adoption of a bill of rights, "rights then become not what one can give a worker, but what no one can take away."[59] The second area of concern moves away from merely protecting oneself from corporate abuses or the infringement of personal rights. Rather, the QWL issue will move into the larger arena of corporate governance itself. It is not difficult to see how employees would consider full participation in the decision-making process a logical extension of their "rights" since their livelihood for the most part depends on decisions by people far removed from them in the organization.

The self-management or industrial democracy movement has been gaining much attention lately because it asserts that employee rights must include a measure of control over one's work by the individual. Its goals are to secure, in addition to rights, equality of treatment and opportunity, respect, and a proprietary feeling about one's work. As Einer Thorsrud, an advocate of self-management said as far back as 1974, "We have to make people think there is hope for them. If we are not successful in giving meaning to their lives, then we may see the terrible turmoil of the end of technological society. . . . If you don't make changes in the way people work, an increasing number of companies . . . will find that there are simply no more people to do the work for them, even when these people are going hungry."[60]

To implement a self-management program is to literally transform organizations into communities; to articulate new relationships among people and to enable each worker to make decisions about his life. It fully abolishes the dichotomy between manager and worker; and, in the final analysis a self-management program enhances the growth and development of individual, company, and society alike.

The self-management model in its many varieties strives to replicate many aspects of community. Michael Parenti catalogued the breadth of community concerns in which everyone shares an interest. "In modern Western societies the social desiderata are usually thought to include such things as material comfort; financial security; adequate and safe diet; clean natural environment; good health and good medical care; sanitary living conditions; opportunities for recreation, learning, self-development, and self-esteem; autonomy of choice in personal affairs; opportunities for participation in social affairs; gratifying personal relationships; meaningful and useful work, freedom from exploitative and degrading labor, and other such tangible and intangible life values."[61] To succeed in achieving this transformation both a new managerial and a new worker's consciousness is required. All organizational members belong to, and benefit from, the company. "Labor is an asset to be enriched rather than a production input to be consumed and discarded once no longer needed."[62] Each person needs to be imbued with the notion of taking personal responsibility for the success of the organization and, in some ways, developing a sense of responsibility to society at large. Unfortunately conventional management co-opts the agenda and summarily dismisses employees' desire and abilities to contribute in a meaningful way.

Clearly, developing a sense of community and transforming the organization into a self-managed system result in the QWL issues becoming as vital as the productivity and economic issues facing organizations. Forces are amassing which are pushing the organization in this direction. When the transformation occurs the old organizational paradigm is replaced. Instead of organizational success being attributed to a distant and impersonal leadership and organizational failure attributed to hapless subordinates, success and failure becomes the product of a combined effort, a mutual sense of responsibility and a self-managed process inclusive of all organizational participants.

The methods of self-management as well as the concept itself often appear radical to contemporary owners and managers because of the tremendous burden which results from what seems like a very laborious consultative process and the consequent decline in managerial power and prerogatives. The methods may not need to be so radical if basic principles of work are established such as:

1. An understanding that jobs need to comprise some variety and be reasonably demanding for those that want them.
2. Opportunities for learning on the job.
3. An area of a person's job that allows for individual decision making.
4. The existence of social support and recognition at work.
5. The establishment of a clear link between what a person does or produces and his social life.
6. The existence of the feeling that one's work can lead to some sort of desirable future.[63]

What self-management and community building offer people is a way to develop a meaningful relationship to their workplace and a sense of purpose with real responsibility for their lives. Not everyone wants this or is capable of working well within such systems but the current momentum for change is clearly headed in the direction of a lot more, not less, employee involvement. Building community enables employees to become members in a shared enterprise and helps each to become a contributor. It unleashes potential that can not be anticipated because the attention one gives to a workplace community leads to frequent serendipitous contributions and combinations of ideas among people who begin to express themselves freely and wish to work together.

This tendency, as we have seen earlier, is simply an extension of the forces that have been struggling for individual autonomy, dignity, and freedom of choice throughout Western history. The full adoption of the principle of participation, not just in structural terms or the rearrangement of formal relationships, but emotional terms as well requires the acceptance of, and commitment to, a set of values, attitudes, norms and interpersonal processes compatible with the active involvement of an ever increasing number of employees within the organization.

Community building concepts are a reflection of this. The point is not the form that participation takes, however, but the fact that organizational systems are now in a transformational process with the aim of increasing participativeness and developing community in organizations. The aim is also to be thoroughly consistent with the quality of life found in the society at large and reflective of the best interests of the organization as an economic entity as well as the individual interests of those within the organization.

In the early stages of the participation revolution it seemed to many managers that the impetus was solely among those who promoted it as a matter of faith. It was democratizing. It was humanizing. It was the right thing to do. But it wouldn't work. It wasn't economically sound. Supposedly it was blue sky, false hopes and utopian to the point of ruin. Time has now shown beyond a doubt that the interests of both individuals and the organization are achievable through participative systems. It is not an exaggeration to say that such systems are now necessary for the economic survival of most organizations and the satisfaction of people in them. One need only read the business press and the daily newspaper for evidence of this truth.

"Full worker participation in running companies . . . has already won converts at the likes of Ford, Goodyear and General Electric. . . . Chairman James Hagen [of Conrail] authorized workers to assemble problem-solving teams on their own initiative. One such group met with an irate steel shipper last spring to reduce the error rate on the customer's bills to a manageable 3 percent from an exasperating 14 percent." and, reports Stanley Gault, Chairman of Goodyear, "The teams at Goodyear are now telling the boss how to run things. And I must say, I'm not doing a half-bad job because of it."[64] In the complexities of competitive business, two heads are indeed better than one.

To understand why this is so, we must appreciate the changes that have taken place throughout the industrial world. First, technology has changed. The way we work, the tools we have, the information we need, all require that teams of people and networks of teams must function cooperatively and accurately. Not only is our organizational world more complex than ever, errors are more costly and extra-organizational concerns such as with competitors, customers, regulators and suppliers force us to be consultative and participative. No one person or group has the intellectual ability to know all there is to know or to have the oversight capability to manage without the participation of a wide variety of other necessary sources each important in their own right and each, perhaps, in an interdependent relationship with one another. Hence, participation is simply a requirement of organizational survival.

Second, people have changed dramatically. Because publicly supported education extends to at least 12 years for most of the industrial nations and because the mass media provides a constant barrage of information to all households, we find our social awareness and our expectations of a uniformly middle class quality of life very strong. Given the material comforts provided in the typical household since the end of World War II, it is no surprise that values have now changed to reflect more of the individual's spiritual and emotional needs than more basic and security needs.

Underlying these changes is a fundamental questioning of social and organizational hierarchies. The legitimacy of old categories, the prerogatives of the rich and powerful and the arbitrary separation of people into management and labor is no longer in a corporation's best interest; it serves no useful purpose. Participation is now being viewed by enlightened CEOs, as well as workers, as a legitimate right to influence one's own destiny in the workplace, a right which can be exercised while simultaneously improving the organization's performance. It is indeed an elegant solution to the management-worker conflicts of the past.

BEGIN AT THE BEGINNING

Before creating new policies, seek out participants to examine the conditions suggesting a new policy is required. Identify people who have a stake in the issues. Get them to represent the broadest possible constituency and empower the group to create the new policy if it determines the need is there. Empower it also to look into existing conditions and to suggest remedies to dysfunctional behavior or inappropriate systems that may obviate the need for new policy at all. Start by encouraging a voluntary team to lay the groundwork by studying the issues and making recommendations. Later, perhaps a permanent ombudsperson could be appointed to begin settling disputes and creating avenues for phasing in and expanding opportunities for participation in a wide variety of circumstances of immediate relevance to the quality of work life issue generally and individuals' jobs or work relationships, in particular.

Let the group also create a scenario reflective of the members' conception of what the work life environment could become. This is the first step in establishing a future direction and visualizing the necessary steps to fulfilling the vision.

CONCLUSION

The corporation will, in all likelihood, serve as the venue for many of the struggles to fulfill the promise of the paradigm shift now underway. The corporate world appears to be the next political frontier. The implications this has for all of us, not only in our workplaces but in all aspects of our lives, are exciting. In a sense the new paradigm gives birth to limitless human potentialities which can be and probably will be nurtured in our workplaces. And as the next four chapters will show, the challenge now appears to be to build workplace communities, develop an appropriate new structure for their governance and new skills for managers to succeed in facilitating the success of organizational communities in reaching their objectives.

NOTES

[1] N. Machiavelli, *The Prince* (New York: Mentor, 1952), p. 49.

[2] *Annals of America: Great Issues in American Life, A Conspectus* V. II (Chicago: Encyclopaedia Britannica, 1988), p. 182.

[3] M. Parenti, *Power and the Powerless* (New York: St. Martins Press, 1978), pp. 179–180.

[4] Ibid., pp. 179–80.

[5] J. W. Wright, *The Universal Almanac* (Kansas City, KN: Andrews and McMeel, 1990), pp. 389–503.

[6] "Blowing the Whistle Without Paying the Piper," *Business Week*, June 3, 1991, pp. 138, 139.

[7] D. Bell, *The Coming of Postindustrial Society* (New York: Basic Books, 1976), pp. XVI-XVII.

[8] P. F. Drucker, *Management, Tasks, Responsibilities, Practices* (New York: Harper and Row, 1974).

[9] M. Milbank, "National Steel Claims Strength in its Labor-Management Alloy," *Wall Street Journal*, April 20, 1992, pp. B1, 4.

[10] J. P. Hicks, "The Steel Man With Kid Gloves," *The New York Times*, April 3, 1992, pp. 1, 3.

[11] G. Himmelfarb, (Ed.), *J. S. Mill, On Liberty* (Harmondsworth, Middlesex, England: Penguin, 1987), p. 173.

[12] "The Caring Company," *The Economist*, June 6, 1992, p. 75. In a review of J. Kotter and J. Haskett, *Corporate Culture and Performance* (New York: Free Press, 1992).

[13] G. C. Parkhouse, "Inside Outplacement—My Search for a Job," *Harvard Business Review*, January-February 1988, pp. 67–73.

[14] A. B. Fisher, "Morale Crisis," *Fortune*, November 18, 1991, p. 70.

[15] "The Search for the Organization of Tomorrow," *Fortune*, May 18, 1992, p. 94.

[16] P. Burrows, "Power to the Workers," *Electronic Business*, October 7, 1991, p. 98.

[17] D. E. Nadler and E. E. Lawler, "Quality of Work Life: Perspectives and Directions," *Organization Dynamics*, Winter 1983, p. 26.

[18] R. E. Walton, "Quality of Working Life: What Is It?," *Sloan Management Review*, Fall 1973, pp. 11–21.

[19] Digital Equipment Corporation could be the first major corporation to legitimize fun as a corporate objective. The 125,000 employee electronics firm includes "fun" on its list of organizational values at its Enfield, CT, plant.

[20] J. Main, "The Battle Over Benefits," *Fortune*, December 16, 1991, pp. 91–96.

[21] M. Moskowitz, R. Levering and M. Katz, *Everybody's Business* (New York: Doubleday, 1990), pp. 81, 82.

[22] L. Davis, "Individuals and the Organization," *California Management Review*, Spring 1980, p. 9

[23] R. Howard, "Second Class in Silicon Valley," *Working Papers*, September–October 1981, p. 22.

[24] J. McCloud, "Tandem Plans a 'Town' In Silicon Valley," *New York Times*, September 22, 1991, Real Estate Section p. 29.

[25] R. Howard, "Second Class in Silicon Valley," p. 22.

[26] J. Whalen, "Fried," *Metro*, May 29–June 5, 1991, p. 15.

[27] Ibid., pp.13-17.

[28] I. Bluestone, "Implementing Quality of Worklife Programs," *Management Review*, July 1977, p. 46.

[29] E. Shorris, *Scenes From Corporate Life* (New York: Penguin, 1984), p. 198.

[30] M. Royko, "The Birth of a Living Corporate Legend," *San Jose Mercury*, January 1978.

[31] E. Shorris, *Scenes From Corporate Life*, p. 315.

[32] Ibid., p. 16.

[33] R. E. Smith, *Workrights* (New York: E.P. Dutton, 1983).

[34] R. Levering, *A Great Place to Work* (New York: Avon, 1988).

[35] R. E. Smith, *Workrights*, p. 67.

[36] M. Levander, "A Battleground of Discrimination: Critics Allege a Long History of Bias," *San Jose Mercury News*, March 15, 1992, pp. 1A,18A.

[37] "If You Light Up On Sunday, Don't Come In On Monday," *Business Week*, August 26, 1991, p. 68.

[38] D. Lacy, *Your Rights In The Workplace* (Berkeley, CA: Nolo Press, 1991), p. 12/5.

[39] J. Elson, "Busybodies: New Puritans" *Time*, August 12, 1991, p. 20.

[40] Associated Press, "On the Job Injuries at Highest Level Ever," *San Francisco Chronicle*, November 20, 1991, p. A3.

[41] S. Murray, "The Silent Epidemic," *Utne Reader*, July/August 1992, p. 21.

[42] *Work in America:* Report of A Special Task Force to the Secretary of Health, Education and Welfare (Cambridge, MA: M.I.T. Press, 1973), quoted in Smith, p. 115.

[43] T. Catchpole, "Empowering Part-time Workers," *Industry Week*, March 16, 1992, pp. 18–24 reported in *AT Work: Stories of Tomorrow's Workplace*, July/August 1992, p. 5.

[44] Schilder, "Work Teams Boost Productivity," Personnel Journal, February, 1992, pp. 67–71, reported in *At Work: Stories of Tomorrow's Workplace*, July/August 1992, p. 5.

[45] T. Gower, "The Overworked American," *Metro*, October 17–23, 1991, p.14. From an interview with Juliet B. Schor, author of *The Overworked American* (New York: Basic Books, 1991).

[46] "If You Light Up On Sunday, Don't Come In On Monday," p. 69.

[47] "Ibid., p. 69.

[48] R. E. Smith, *Workrights*, p. 142.

[49] Ibid., p. 154.

[50] R. Levering, *A Great Place to Work* (New York: Avon, 1988), p. 214.

[51] C. Garfield, *Second To None* (Homewood, IL: Business One Irwin, 1992), p. 145.

[52] Ibid. p. 145.

[53] J. E. Ellis, "Layoffs on the Line, Bonuses in the Executive Suite," *Business Week*, October 21, 1991, p. 34.

[54] R. Levering, *A Great Place to Work*, p. 63.

[55] Ibid., p. 64.

[56] D. W. Ewing, "A Bill of Rights for Employees," *Across the Board*, March 1981, p. 42.

[57] D. W. Ewing, *Justice on the Job* (Cambridge, MA; Harvard Business School Press, 1989), p. 32.

[58] D. W. Ewing, *Freedom Inside the Organization* (New York: McGraw-Hill Book Company, 1977), pp. 146–49.

[59] Ramsey Clark quoted in D. W. Ewing, "A Bill of Rights for Employees," *Across the Board*, March 1981, p. 44.

[60] T. Wicker, "A Plant Built for Workers," *New York Times*, July 1974.

[61] M. Parenti, *Power and the Powerless* (New York: St. Martin's Press, 1978), p. 64.

[62] I. Adizes and E. M. Borgese, *Self-Management: New Dimensions to Democracy* (Santa Barbara, CA: ABC-Clio, 1975), p. 35.

[63] Ibid., p. 108.

[64] J. Greenwald, "Is Mr. Nice Guy Back?," *Time*, January 27, 1992, pp. 41–42.

Chapter Five

Beyond Teams: Creating Workplace Communities

"We live in a culture of brokenness and fragmentation. Images of individualism and autonomy are far more compelling to us than visions of unity and the fabric of relatedness seems dangerously threadbare and frayed. . . . We have all but lost the vision of the public (as understood as) our oneness, our unity, our interdependence upon one another."

—*Parker Palmer*[1]

During the enlightenment, at the dawn of the industrial revolution, people asked questions about their role in the political system and the legitimacy of the long-standing principle of the divine right to rule. For centuries, that principle effectively convinced the masses in Europe of the inevitability of the various royal houses.

Today, as we have seen, the industrial paradigm is shifting toward a new consciousness of personal empowerment. This is happening at a time when corporations are supplanting governments as the foci of the polis. Once again people are asking crucial questions about the structures that dominate their lives. Now, many people are asking about the legitimacy of the exclusivity of investors interests over those of employees in organizations and over the interests of the public at large. This is as dramatic a turn of events as when the American colonists demanded representation in determining their own laws and taxes.

The call for community now arises to align empowered individuals with their organizational environments. It is as heretical as demanding independence from the United Kingdom and disavowing divine right. The emergence of the corporation as the next political frontier is testimony to the fact that this process is well under way.

This chapter takes a look at how to establish community in the workplace and how it might be operationalized. Some examples of community building and a method to approach its development in your organization are presented. Undoubtedly many variations are possible but the fundamental principle remains the same: to institutionalize personal empowerment in a way that cannot be revoked and that enhances organizational effectiveness.

When consciousness changes, everything is seen anew. The transition from an old way of being to a new one is often accompanied by a long period of debate, skepticism and adjustment. Change cannot occur until individuals perceive the need to change. Yet change occurs quite rapidly as one's way of seeing the world is altered. Thus the wisdom of a popular saying, "Believing is seeing." Today, it seems, a multitude of people are believing in and searching for community.

WE'VE DONE IT BEFORE

Community in America is based on a long history of voluntary association. Consider the Mayflower Compact. It was the first written record of a conscious attempt by a self-selected group of strangers to create a community—". . . a civil body politic, for our better ordering and preservation . . . and by virtue hereof do enact, constitute and frame, such just and equal laws, ordinances, acts . . . (that) shall be thought most . . . convenient for the general good of the Colony. . . ."[2]

Thus began the colonization of New England in those moments at dawn off Plymouth Rock, Massachusetts. All families aboard the Mayflower signed the compact and "promise(d) all due submission and obedience" in the beginning of a quite remarkable democratic experiment.

The Fundamental Orders of Connecticut, the U.S. Constitution and even condominium by-laws represent continued attempts by strangers to create the rules under which they will live and are a conscious effort to create the kinds of environments that promote their mutual well-being while still remaining true to their own pursuit of happiness.

TOWARD COMMUNITY RENEWAL

Today there has been a breakdown of community in society due in part to a diminishing sense of connection with others. Life in urban America, where the vast majority of us live, is characterized by the lack of a shared sense of purpose; a dwindling concern for each other, and an unwillingness to reciprocate care.

The ever-presence of crime and violence leads to a generalized fear of strangers and tends to reduce our personal participation in the larger cultural experience.

Rising illiteracy amidst the technological revolution is another indication of the ineffectiveness of societal institutions to socialize new members and reinforce positive, shared values. The family is fragmented, the schools are in disarray, the church is no longer a unifying force, the police cannot guarantee public order or even handle most emergencies, and the legal system can't resolve disputes in a timely or equitable manner. Few supporting mechanisms exist to ensure the implementation of any code of conduct aside from the law in terms of what once may have been considered a community influence.

The immersion in a hyper-stimulated society wherein television as a purveyor of instant gratification increases the level of routine excitement necessary to sustain social life and further aggravates our inability to connect with others in a meaningful way. Instead it isolates us from one another. In fact, TV, through its advertising, has become the communicator of mass personal inadequacy and the creator of superfluous, but very intense material want. Through its programming, TV conveys the expectation that in our personal lives problems can be immediately, though superficially, solved and the rather ironic notion that violence is a painless remedy of last resort to getting interpersonal satisfaction without negotiation, compromise, or effort.

Though the pursuit of freedom and individual choice has long been our national mandate, it seems that the realization of diverse lifestyles has led to a shift away from a generalized sense of community toward compartmentalization, separation and isolation. Thus, only shallow bonding takes place, if at all, with those near at hand, through work, or in one's neighborhood, but most likely bonding is limited to one's immediate family and acquaintances.

Material gain is the most consistently recognized community goal. It has replaced a host of intangible values as the single most shared cultural understanding. It is easy to define, measure and display and is a yardstick that all can agree upon. In a material culture, acquisition and consumption is the only way of life that counts. It is virtually a patriotic act to spend money. "Shop till you drop!" or, whoa, a recession will befall us!

There is little belief in the several virtues and less motivation to abide by moral or cultural rules when it seems that only the rich get richer and everyone else doesn't. There is no pay off for conforming to a set of generalized principles traditionally reinforced through home, school or church. Situationalism and personal advantage seem to dominate individual decision making.

This rather unfortunate cultural state of being seeps into the organization and makes the experience of work a process of inauthentic or somehow incomplete relationships. It results in mixed feeling about how much to contribute, how much to invest of oneself in the process of work. This is particularly so when the future is uncertain and one is led to expect casual, dismissive, treatment by the organization.

When the state of the interpersonally-shared cultural experience that we do have is so bad, why bother making it better? The ultimate antimotivational stance against an employer, and one becoming more and more common, is psychological withdrawal. This is most dramatically felt by those conventional companies that haven't realized that the most pressing problem today is creating meaning and rewarding achievement in the workplace among all employees and not just the managers.

In order for employees to become motivated and committed to their work, their experience must justify their effort. They must either find intrinsic pleasure in their work, enjoy a monetary benefit for doing it well, or have a sense that their participation in the organization is meaningful—that they are part of a community that needs them.

The call for community renewal ultimately arises, of course, among those who have lost it. Community is absent from the mobile middle class who have been uprooted since first going off to college and following careers coast to coast in the hope of climbing the corporate ladder. Being rootless and disconnected seems to be a useful investment in one's future when it is a temporary state of being that one hopes will result in a greater sense of accomplishment. When this sacrifice persists and midlife arrives without the sense of connection or accomplishment one hoped for, there is an inescapable feeling of having lost something of value and a growing disenchantment with society. This is especially so when one's neighbors are not only strangers but hostile as well. If there is no sense of community either at work or in one's neighborhood the loss is that much more poignant.

Louis Harris' "alienation index" went from 29 percent in 1966 to 62 percent in 1983. The belief that "the rich get richer and the poor get poorer" grew from 45 percent to 79 percent and those who believed "What I think doesn't count very much" went from 37 percent to 62 percent.[3] By 1991 the situation hadn't improved. "Americans today have little or no sense of belonging to a community that is important to their lives. The thousands of people we interviewed averaged out their level of community involvement below three on a scale of one to ten. . . . Not surprisingly, more than two-thirds of us cannot name our local representative in Congress . . . [and] we don't know our neighbors, either. The great majority of Americans (72 percent) openly admit that they don't know the people next door."[4]

There is a tendency to blame ourselves and take it as a personal failure that we experience so many tragedies of isolation, disconnection, and alienation. We rarely see our personal predicament as the result of societal forces, rooted in consumerism, competition and fear. Consequently we hesitate to look at the system—the structures of our society—for explanations. Yet, it is precisely those structures that need to be altered to accommodate the new social reality. One of those structures is the work organization. Built as a method to expedite the control of resources for one or a few people, they contribute to the very separation, alienation and isolation people feel and wish to overcome.

The sense of disconnection is also evident among the younger generation because they, too, have not experienced much stability in their lives. They respond to the idea of community because it suggests both a connection with a meaningful group of people and an engagement in something worthwhile.

Frequently coming from single-parent households, effected by the transient nature of a plethora of rapidly changing fads and fancies, they have yearned for direction in their lives. School and career in the late sixties meant much more to their parents. It was a liberation, a ticket to a cornucopia of material goods and experiences never imagined by previous generations. Leaving home was a chance to become independent and exercise a new set of values that would have otherwise been stifled. Today's youth are in a different situation enjoying the fruits of a liberated society with an acceptance of diversity as a natural order of things. Yet, they respond to the ideas of community for the same reasons their elders do, to create meaning in their lives.

For many organizations and their employees, the current path is pointing in the wrong direction—toward greed, self-centeredness, exploitation, alienation, separation, and isolation. To many people a new path is needed: toward a shared sense of meaning, cooperation, community and the hope that one may derive personal growth, life-long learning and enjoy the challenge of a creative, useful life by being part of an organization moving along that new path. Community building seems the most sensible next step.

DEVELOPING WORKPLACE COMMUNITIES: ORGANIZATIONS OF CHOICE

Community is a form of organization. It is enabling. It obviously isn't something that everyone wishes to participate in routinely but as a structure of relationships, a process of working with one another and as a mechanism for establishing personal and group expectations, it allows fruitful participation when it is necessary and when individuals have the inclination to get involved. It is not a mandate. It is a matter of choice.

Workplace communities encompass a set of values and a way of being that is only now developing in the business world. There are models in civil government at the local level, such as New England Town Meetings and in community-based organizations and volunteer groups. They can easily be adapted to organizational life in the business world especially since business organizations have both the right to choose members who will hold the same values and behavioral agreements, and the right to dismiss individuals for not living up to their expectations. The nature of organizational life is becoming more and more team based; meetings, conferences and corporate events are now routine. Using current opportunities to enlarge or replace parts of the existing agenda with time for discussions of community issues could be arranged quite easily. And it works.

"Many decisions at Tandem Computers are made by consensus. Most departments meet frequently, and often an entire department interviews job candidates to see if they get along well with the team. 'Town meetings' are held regularly for employees to discuss new developments. . . . Tandem nurtures the spirit of community and communication among employees in many ways from consensus meetings to 'weekly popcorn parties.'"[5]

Modern economic entities have been successful when conceived as a mutual endeavor—one of the intentions of building a workplace community. The best examples of this are found on the roster of large employee-owned companies which lengthens every year. A few of the most visible employee owned companies are Avis (14,000 employees), Publix Supermarkets (65,000 employees), Arthur D. Little (a global business consultancy; 2,600 employees), The Milwaukee Journal (6,200 employees), Republic Steel (4,900 Employees), and W. L. Gore Associates (makers of Gortex fabric; 5,000 employees). The distinguishing feature of many of these organizations is that all employees are participants in the re-creation of their organizations into entities that serve all members. And they succeed.

The challenge of organizational society is to realize a collective vision—to effectuate a way of life, a state of being, that enhances the choices made by the members of the community. Organizations of choice select members from among a group of willing applicants or are formed by like minded individuals who have freely chosen to associate. Unlike society at large there is a built in advantage. The association is a conscious effort to work toward a mutual objective. The groups we form are, in a sense, an extension of our selves, our lifestyle choices and other interests. Though we already have the ability to create business organizations that facilitate our material as well as spiritual fulfillment, rarely do we conceive of them this way. Rather we see organizations as being owned exclusively by a few people for their own benefit; not for all who become a part of them or for the larger group of stakeholders that have a natural interest in their survival.

ORGANIZATIONAL COMMUNITIES FOR THE 21st CENTURY

Given our current diversity of lifestyles and interests it is likely that several types of organizations will evolve. There is, however, a very strong indication that one form of organization will represent a vital and compelling model for large organizations to adopt. That is the community model proposed here. Perhaps the most important reason for building a community is that its features meet the needs of a society in transformation. Teamwork, learning, flexibility, caring, a sense of belonging, and gainsharing for example are qualities to be found in community and they perfectly complement the managerial requirements of the new paradigm.

Unlike its predecessors, the community model is a dynamic system of people at work. It is not a static, regimented bureaucracy. It's main task is knowledge based: the sensing, gathering, interpretation, processing and reevaluation of information, concepts and ideas. The operative environment that is established is inclusive, responsive, created and recreated by its members for the purpose of doing their work effectively but also in order to develop a high quality of "work life" for its own sake. In this way workplace community becomes a living organization.

Given the inadequacies of bureaucracy, mentioned earlier, and the loss of connectedness, people are developing a hunger for community and the application of democratic principles in the governance of their work lives. When the social cohesion of neighborhoods and other institutions diminishes, the individual must develop his or her own connections and guiding lights or accept those of an interest group or that of his or her work organization. Something will fill the void. The rise of many evangelical and fundamentalist religions is attributed to people simply filling the void in their lives. Since work consumes more than half the waking hours of so many people, it seems appropriate for business organizations to become workplace communities and help their members meet this need.

This form of organization can be a vehicle for tremendous personal as well as economic growth. The rate of growth and personal goals are set by the participants as their careers and their work group's job expectations of them unfold. Ultimately, community is a process that is inclusive and allows much room for individual benefits to accrue because it respects individuals and their ability to make intelligent personal decisions as well as participate constructively in organizational activities.

One's behavior is ultimately derived from one's values and environment. The self-fulfilling prophesy is an example of how a person's expectations materialize simply because they are what is expected. If, for example, one believes that people can't be trusted or will take unfair advantage of unsupervised opportunities at the earliest possible moment, their managerial behavior will be to supervise closely, minutely define expectations of subordinates, institute detailed and rigorous control systems, etc. On the other hand, if one believes people are basically well-intentioned and want to do a good job then their supervisory style will be more empowering. They will delegate and give a large discretionary area of freedom to subordinates to act as they see fit.[6]

Because of this process and the hierarchical, rigid, control-oriented nature of conventional work bureaucracies, we hold "superiors" responsible for their "subordinates" and thus put in motion an often counterproductive and over regulated system. The system eventually stifles everyone since each person is being subjected to an inordinate fear of making mistakes and this fear cascades down the hierarchy from the CEOs office door. Community relieves the fear in part through respect for the individual, the establishment of work groups, and a process of problem-centeredness that is guided by the explicit goals of the group and organization. When actions are aligned to those goals and people are empowered to act on their competence, fear is not an issue. The way this happens is through the process of maintaining community which serves as a gyroscope for the organization. No one needs to take the burden of always being right and knowing everything that must happen in order to direct others. The process, being inclusive, becomes the source of constant course correction and the education of each member. The process thus expands the realm of awareness of what's happening and what needs to be done by including all members of the organization in an appropriate decision making context.

In return of course, each person's view of the organization is enlarged. The organization becomes an entity of personal importance and each person is expected to accept responsibility for its performance in the marketplace through accepting responsibility for his or her work. This reciprocal involvement with the organization, as a social system, can be compared with one's place in the ecological system. In the latter case we are raising our consciousness about the responsibilities we have for the welfare of the planet and are beginning to take personal actions that reflect this new awareness. Similarly, people are eager to connect with one another in pursuit of a common vision of organizational success.

The new paradigm recognizes that the old ideas about how to manage are no longer working; there are simply too many exceptions, mini-crises and breakdowns. By reaching a higher level of consciousness about our connections with one another and our work we cut through the need for bureaucratic controls and compartments and move into the realm of coordination and process. A change of consciousness is the most powerful force we know.

If organizations are transformed into communities, they have the potential of helping us establish the kinds of connections with one another, the work, the goals of the group that can fundamentally alter our motivations. Changing a way of thinking changes reality. To use a marketing example: H. J. Heinz was able to put a perceived disadvantage to advantage. Because its ketchup was a lot slower than others it had a problem: it was harder to pour because it was a lot thicker. Therefore, it was thought that the ketchup must taste a lot better. By advertising this point of view it turned a potential disadvantage into an advantage and market share rose from 19 percent to 50 percent.[7]

COMMUNITY EMERGING

Many organizations are evolving into communities. They have begun to take on the same responsibilities for their constituents of employees as the larger political state has done for its constituents of citizens. A visit to any of the larger corporations or government bureaucracies will confirm this. Our right to access the premises and establish that we belong to an organization is granted with an employee ID which serves as our "birth certificate" or "passport" and authenticates our membership in the corporate "family" with access to certain privileges. Membership is subject to socialization, training, and an on-the-job induction into the corporate community with its exposure to the peculiar culture inclusive of rites, heroes, myths, celebrations, norms, rewards and punishments. Membership requires service to the community and, in return, members are paid and also provided with a plethora of benefits even citizens of the political state envy.

Consider universal health care. Once thought of as a socialistic evil and anathema to the deregulated capitalist state, it is provided to each employee-citizen of most of our larger organizations. Furthermore, educational and training programs, that would rival the best public and most private educational programs, are subsidized at a per-capita rate for employees. Large corporations support the arts, provide recreational and social activities, and, through extensive employee assistance programs, provide social welfare services which today surpass that of most governments on the face of this planet. And that is just the beginning of the impact the larger organizations are having on employee-constituents.

Examples abound of corporate efforts to address the larger quality of life and quality of work life issues. A benefits handbook from any major company will be a catalog of a social welfare program unrivaled by any municipality. In the largest corporations such as IBM, Exxon, General Motors, Kodak, and Westinghouse, a review of some of their benefits programs includes everything from profit sharing, reimbursement for educational programs, paternity leave, retirement and financial planning services, use of corporate retreats for vacations, counseling services for a variety of ailments, to paid sabbaticals and matching grants to community fund-raising endeavors. They have made a difference. The combined effect is tremendous. The corporation has turned to these matters as a way of attracting talent to a desirable community as well as to build a high quality of work life.

Organizations have only recently become surrogate communities for a growing number of people. Some who seek community in their workplace have become rootless, estranged by their mobility, and on a demanding career track that allows little time for non-job-related activity. For middle managers and executives, leisure time has actually declined since the late sixties. "[T]he total hours worked by Americans of both genders, has increased since 1969 by 163 hours per year to nearly 2,000, on average—and that's not counting another 900 hours of work done in the home."[8] Though many are seemingly on a Japanese corporate schedule with an established norm of 12-hour work days, many middle and upper managers are finding themselves putting in long hours which also includes time at the in-house gymnasium and spending time in corporate sponsored social activities. Many singles committed to the organization are finding after-hours time an important opportunity to mingle and catch up on reading while still at the workplace. For some workaholics long days allow the pleasure of missing time at home with their families. The corporation is increasingly providing around-the-clock access to facilities and after-hours amenities for those who stay on. Combustion Engineering hosts MBA classes in its conference rooms at its world headquarters in Stamford, Connecticut, in part as a public convenience for busy executives, and in part for the convenience of their own staff enrolled in the program. It saves the two hour commute to the university's campus.

EXAMPLES OF COMMUNITY BUILDING

Johnsonville Foods

Tom Peters described a work team at the Johnsonville Sausage Company in Wisconsin that is building community through its actions though it may not call itself a community just yet. "A typical Johnsonville work team, (a) does its own recruiting, hiring, personnel evaluation, and firing; (b) regularly acquires new skills and then conducts training for everyone; (c) formulates and tracks its own budgets; (d) makes capital investment proposals as needed (with all necessary staff work); (e) is responsible for all quality control, inspection, and subsequent trouble-shooting; (f) suggests and then develops prototypes of possible new products, processes, and even business; (g) works on the improvement of everything, all the time; and, (h) develops its own detailed standards for productivity, quality and improvement and makes them tough standards."[9]

Levi Strauss

Levi Strauss & Co. has developed an "Aspirations Statement" that spells out its intention of creating a company where employees get involved and where together they attempt to "affirm the best of our company's traditions" and close "gaps that may exist between principles and practices." The essence of the statement is to help employees focus on building a company "that our people are proud of and committed to, where all employees have an opportunity to contribute, learn, grow, and advance based on merit, not politics or background. We want our people to feel respected, treated fairly, listened to, and involved. Above all we want satisfaction from accomplishments and friendships, balanced personal and professional lives, and to have fun in our endeavors."[10] Levi-Strauss is building community, though they haven't specified it by name.

Gordon Forward, CEO of Chaparral Steel, is also at the leading edge of building community. "To help them use their noggins, Chaparral makes sure at least 85 percent of its 950 employees are enrolled in courses, cross training in such varied disciplines as electronics, metallurgy and credit history. How does all this lower costs? In scores of ways."[11]

Work teams differ from community as a caterpillar from a butterfly but they are similarly on an inexorable path toward gaining their wings. Fully becoming community results in the following characteristics being operationalized:

A shared purpose is established; community assumes a balance between the individual and the group. Once a person is selected there is an obligation to sustain that person's relationship in the organization so long as he or she lives up to designated responsibilities. Community conveys a felt concern for the success of the organization and the individual members in it and that concern is felt at a fundamental personal level.

Community is and must be inclusive. The group must justify exclusion—of saying no—rather than justify inclusion; commitment, the willingness to coexist is crucial. There is a sense of personal efficacy in the role one plays by participating in the creation of the ends toward which the community strives. Each person determines how she or he will serve the community and the means through which each achieves his or her personal responsibilities. All roles are necessary and there is no hierarchy of importance even though some jobs are more pressing or are more fun or more visible or more central to the fulfillment of the organization's goals than others at different times.

Community requires continuous learning. Pay and privileges vary but are determined by the community. There is a fair and equitable package of financial and other benefits reflecting each person's contribution, knowledge, and skill.

Community, by encouraging individuality as it does, can never be totalitarian; it strives to move beyond democracy to consensus yet it focuses on realism; accommodating multiple perspectives and dealing with dissent. There is total decentralization of all authority. Community strives to become a group of leaders; managers or facilitators of projects may serve for the duration of the project or for a designated period of time after which the position rotates or the group reappoints them.

There are no sides, cliques; a group can disagree gracefully without creating a win/lose situation. However, a grievance system with trained mediators presides over interpersonal and organizational/personal disputes and is independent.

Community develops a structure that provides avenues for the expression and resolution of conflict and protects the existence of diversity of thought. Power is task centered not person centered. Unilateral veto powers, if they exist at all, are assigned by the workplace constitution as are other rights and responsibilities while the separation of powers, and checks and balances, are built into the process.

Each member can be as involved in additional responsibilities as he or she chooses through being allowed to serve on administrative, policy and maintenance committees. A community forum exists for decision making in these areas. Each person is directly or indirectly involved through the election of representatives. Operating rules and processes are determined by work groups and the community process.

Community allows the full, authentic expression of one's whole personality and encourages completely honest communication; and also encourages humility, self examination and vulnerability—the ability to truly be oneself; (this violates the norm of pretended invulnerability where one must always be 'covered' and correct in the eyes of fellow workers).

The community allows spirit to emerge from within the group as a natural outgrowth of the community building process.[12]

BUILDING COMMUNITY AT WORK

For an organization to become a community certain conditions must prevail. Each person who is selected by and freely joins the organization is expected to be involved in decisions affecting day-to-day work and the governance and maintenance of the organization. The form may be direct or representative involvement.

Community means more, of course. It means mutual aid, cooperation, respect, friendliness, individual efficacy, responsibility and good treatment of strangers—those we don't work directly with but who are part of the organization. Quad/Graphics corporation tries to create this kind of environment through its belief that management, like marriage ". . . is a close personal relationship that is worked at daily."[13]

It means no layoffs or personnel policy changes without consent. Representative bodies of employees—of everyone through the CEO's office deal with these and other issues in an effort to keep everyone in the governance process and informed. The work group or representative body would also decide issues of hiring, socialization of new members, performance expectations, assignments, scheduling, benefits, rewards and punishments, and dismissal. It would also arrange for the mediation of disputes between individuals and would handle grievances rooted in the organizational policy, rules, or structure. These ideas are being instituted quite successfully by companies embracing self-managing teams. Often situations that were believed to require laying off people have been turned around through imaginative pain sharing programs. "When the computer chip manufacturer Intel was forced to reduce personnel costs, it chose progressive salary cuts according to employees' individual paychecks. Pay cuts ran from none to 10 percent, with the lowest-paid workers losing nothing from their pay checks."[14]

Many more imaginative ways involving shortened work weeks, voluntary leaves-without-pay, early retirements, and others, help ease the blunt edge of the cuts. But when these measures are insufficient to meet the economic needs of the moment, and redeployment of talent to potential growth areas or other parts of the organization isn't possible, it shows enormous respect for those involved to ask if they would be part of the solution instead of simply treating them as part of the problem. Inviting employees to be involved in the process of cutting back empowers them with an opportunity to save the company as well as their jobs. If even after that possibility is exhausted, executing the layoffs based on a predetermined formula would certainly demonstrate fairness and at least show respect for all of those affected.

Community means inclusion, acceptance, efficacy, freedom of expression and having social as well as organizational goals legitimated. It also means being able to communicate openly and freely and to observe all constitutional rights in the organizational context.

The individual's acceptance by, and usefulness to, the organization is assumed. Personality and relationships issues are dealt with separately from competence and task-related issues. This requires agreement on fundamental values at the time of recruitment. It also requires the individual's willingness to recognize and to commit to the legitimacy of the fundamental values and associated requirements of the employment agreement. Each person accepts responsibility to make the agreement work and accepts a given process for changing the agreement to meet his or her needs as they evolve. The United States Constitution has an amendment procedure and companies such as Perot Systems and Digital Equipment Company (DEC) offer corporate policy statements that suggest that they are moving in this direction. Motorola, S.C. Johnson, Lincoln Electric, and New United Motor are among a dwindling number of companies in the United States that have a no layoff policy.[15] Their regard for the employee places them on many lists of best places to work in the United States and they are committed to employee participation in creating a suitable work environment.

In short, the acceptance of individuals is dependent on their living up to their role, responsibilities, and group function. In return, the individual takes part in determining the organization's objectives and in pursuing his or her own career objectives within the work community. The community stimulates its own growth and group development by creating a learning environment and providing opportunities for individuals to develop fully.

Involvement is Essential

Because organizations are conceptualized as an extension of the personal resources and prerogatives of the owner or manager, talking about involvement at work is often a subversive act.

There seems to be a struggle between those who have used the corporate system to acquire and hoard power, and those who rightfully wish to become full partners in the organization. The irony in the struggle, however, is that it is in part financed by the companies themselves as they continuously train their middle managers in new management techniques and organizational development strategies, virtually all of which advocate personal empowerment, team building and open communications. Self-managing work teams are themselves becoming the launch vehicles for a final push toward workplace community.

Involvement isn't about voting on every decision. It is about being a legitimate participant in a process of determining the nature of one's work life. It is having the opportunity to express oneself and to be recognized as an equal member of the community on the same footing as everyone else. It is not a matter of equal pay or equal responsibilities any more than it would be a matter of having the same job as everyone else.

It's a matter of accountability. The impact of the biggest corporations is obviously commanding in our contemporary society and will get larger. The need to activate a democratic consciousness within them is pressing as never before, particularly since the locus of societal influence has shifted to the Board Room from the Capitol. This is evident as the corporation, indeed all workplaces, looms as the next political frontier in the struggle for the attainment for human rights and economic security. The fact that employers still exercise the right to fire virtually at will is itself a powerful force. Though regulatory bodies and court decisions made some inroads, they have only touched the surface of the issue. Individuals within large organizations may be better situated to influence the scope and direction of corporate power and its effects on the larger society through internal activities to democratize and win accountability to the stakeholders.

Some organizations will recognize that a necessary transformation to participative community is essential to compete in the global economy, and they will apply democratic principles to release enormous personal energies in service to the company. An organization must be participatory to encourage the natural flow of people, information and resources to solve problems, coordinate activities, serve customers, improve processes; and, to give and receive accurate feedback about its impact. Community and its attendant attitude of commitment stimulates synergies and serendipity. These kinds of outcomes are inhibited, if not destroyed altogether, unless individual initiative is released. Only democratic processes and overcoming individual fear, can accomplish this. Thus a participatory system is not only useful to solve complex problems and to coordinate various aspects of the work flow, it is a necessary motivational mechanism to encourage individuals to enter into the process. As the new paradigm sweeps the land, managers will discover that people at work will need to be treated much differently. The real distinctions between manager and employee will quickly dissolve as the roles change to colleague reflecting the fact that they are equally trained, socialized, and able to do what needs to be done.

Organizations of choice will actively represent themselves as organizations intent on building community and will select those applicants inclined to get meaningfully involved in a working community. The act of management will become a matter of creating an environment conducive to thinking and expressing oneself freely. Community does this.

Remember: Participation is not permissiveness and self-actualization is not license. Resisting the implementation of democratic principles by upper management is usually symptomatic of the fear of loss of control at a personal level which gets projected onto the organization as the conviction that the principles won't work. In light of current realities that defense is no longer sensible.

Group Decisions

Decisions, formerly removed from those directly involved, are devolving to the relevant work groups which are, in turn, becoming

self-managing teams: issues regarding hiring, performance expectations, benefits, rewards and punishments are increasingly made at
the work-group level within uniform guidelines. Social issues and the
fallout from group decision making are also being handled by the
group so that individuals feeling unproductive competitiveness, or
stress overload, for example, can turn to the group for help.

Recruitment and Training

Recruitment by the group helps select individuals who will fit in with
their group-centered, self-management responsibilities. Continuous
on-the-job processing of issues regarding interpersonal relationships
and individual performance serves as socialization into the organizational community as well as a vehicle to renegotiate job expectations
as work demands change.

Leadership

Process observation, leadership, and facilitation skills are taught to
everyone. Mediation and arbitration skills are also taught. Full-time
leaders are not needed when the leadership functions are shared
though some individuals may be chosen as facilitators at different
work sites to take on a coordinating role or initiate the leadership
function when necessary. In effective teams, "We're all leaders
because we all want something to be good."[16] At more and more
companies such as General Mills, Chaparral Steel, and Federal
Express, self-managed work teams are becoming routine forms of
organizing and group centered leadership is developing.

According to Harvard Professor Chris Argyris, "Group-centered
leadership is maximized when the members (1) are free from dependence on a formal leader, (2) are permitted to determine their own
goals and the skills they intend to use to achieve these goals, (3) are
permitted to define and initiate for themselves any changes within
their group, (4) are not led by any one individual all the time, and (5)
are free to depose their leader (physically or psychologically) whenever they desire."[17]

Applicable Models

In addition to the evolutionary forces at work transforming organizations into community, there are many models available to businesses
to help them accelerate the transformation to community. Some popular models, such as Deming's method,[18] promulgating total quality,
ultimately lead to community building when they are utilized to their

logical extreme. Starting from the bottom up, they advocate "whole jobs" for individuals and everyone's continuous education in order to understand the entire work flow process and the rationale for actions. It also enables each person to rotate jobs or help out in other areas as needed. The impact of this is to make each person conscious of all that has to be done and stimulates the creation of a team awareness and willingness to help others.

Other useful conditions for the establishment of community include: giving everyone some personal decision making responsibilities, social support and personal recognition in the workplace, a feeling that there is a relationship between what the individual does and what he or she produces and that there is a link between the job and some desirable future.

A Basic Blueprint for Building Community

In moving toward community the following steps, derived from standard organization development practices, would be useful:[19]

1. Establish a membership planning committee with representatives of all groups. Guarantee employment during the community-building process in order to insure active participation and support. This group first develops the personal skills required to create community, (these will be discussed in detail in Chapter Seven), and develops an appropriate process to spread the learning throughout the organization.
2. Assess the organization's ability and willingness to proceed with an extended change program given present conditions.[20]
3. Determine the appropriate depth of the community concept to be implemented; the degree of personal participation; the areas for involvement in organization policy making; the structure of the community; feedback processes, goal setting procedures; and a time frame for accomplishing implementation by phases.
4. Determine personal and work group needs assessment to sustain the change effort; institute a continuous training, education and feedback program.
5. Establish action committees throughout the organization to take over specific implementation from the original membership committee. Each action committee is taught the skills required to guide the change process in their specific areas.
6. Choose a subgroup to begin a pilot program.
7. Create a catalog of baseline measures; measure all key variations in performance both in terms of job output and interpersonal

issues (climate, culture, morale); look at communications processes particularly the difference between espoused and actual patterns; assess satisfaction/dissatisfaction of all members of the organization as ground work is laid and implementation of the change program begins; wage and salary reviews should reflect changes as well; perhaps a reformulation of compensation should include a plan for gain/pain sharing at this point.

8. A program for change is drafted by and for the experimental group which includes: cross-training employees to handle different work roles in partly or fully autonomous groups. Instruction and reinforcement of group-centered leadership techniques would be useful.

9. Institutionalization of change and feedback of continued learning through community-wide diffusion of results.[21]

Thus, the broad steps are: Sensing the need to create an intentional community, total involvement in planning, building commitment, developing action plans, implementing change and seeking out and incorporating feedback into the change process. See any of the Total Quality Management/Quality Control Circles or Action Research models[22] as an aid in developing a continuous process of goal setting, building commitment, finding divergence, resolving conflicts, solving problems and honing the person/task fit.

There are certain positive qualities that facilitate the transformation to community and it would be good to help prepare the organization for the change process by focusing first on developing them. For example:

1. A willingness to think and act in terms of the good of the whole, not just in terms of personal needs and opinions. This is a willingness to grow toward unselfishness.

2. Tolerance for differences and open-mindedness towards different points of view.

3. A willingness to work out conflicts; having a realistic belief in the possibility of resolving differences to mutual satisfaction.[23]

These qualities may not be widely distributed in any specific company but while entering the change process they can be developed and supported.

At this point it should be obvious that community requires that gain/pain sharing be incorporated into the process to make the exercise a genuine one for each person. Remember, there is no motivation to put oneself out and to make the extraordinary effort to become a community if it is simply another "program, panacea or quick fix" in order to enrich investors or streamline the system. This transformation can have a profound effect on the organization and its profitability and each member must be a beneficiary of the effort—success or failure. Each must feel the impact of community on profits, losses. Consider this: Charles Garfield reported a study by the Public Agenda Foundation which found that "Some 75 percent of the respondents reported that because of their exclusion from rewards, they deliberately withheld extra effort on the job."[24]

IMPLICATIONS OF CORPORATE COMMUNITY

Creating New Rules

Community builds into the organization checks and balances so that no one person or office abuses the powers bestowed in trust by the organization as a whole. There is a system for the redress of grievances, based on the principle of due process. Each person with duties that influence the work group is also accountable to the organization. Obviously we will continue to depend on many people exercising power within the organization. An organization development or education department plans the continuous improvement of community-building skills and personal assessment techniques and creates opportunities that help meet individual job-related, as well as community-building, needs.

Remember when playing or watching pick-up baseball how teams agreed to change the rules when it was necessary? Sometimes no more than two foul balls were allowed or no one could hit to right field while playing seven on a side or perhaps only two outs were allowed. The players created a mutually agreed-upon alternative to accommodate either short manned teams or a pressing time factor. Corporations can do the same thing. They can create whatever rules are important to them to facilitate achieving their goals and satisfying their members. If eight-hour days are what people want then eight-hour days is what they get. If four-day weeks is what they want then they can create four-day weeks. If they want to decide how to measure the accomplishments of one of their team members or any other myriad managerial task then they can decide how to do so in a way that is appropriate for them. In each case the group uses a single overriding criteria against which to measure the appropriateness of its decisions: "Does what we are deciding to do help us reach our organization's objective while meeting our needs?"

Creating rules and policies through a members forum or council could easily be accommodated as part of the process of organizational citizenship. When rules remain dormant for a period of one year, they automatically terminate like sunset laws. If they turn out to be inappropriate they should be revised immediately. The formal rules themselves should be kept to an absolute minimum. The point here is that when organizations conceive of themselves as deliberate, intentional communities, members take control of their lives and can arrange the dimensions of work life within the organization in any manner they choose. Frequent assessments of the workings of any organizational system would be a useful exercise and would be appropriate for members' forums.

Employees as Members

Jack Welch at General Electric is trying to create a boundaryless organization. According to James Baughman, GE's head of management development, "We wrote the book on bureaucracy. Now there aren't any books, just real people talking about real problems face-to-face, sweating it out and grunting through. It's a revolution, nothing less, from control to let'er rip."[25]

In a corporate community that, in part, exemplifies a boundaryless organization, new avenues to group success and personal recognition need to be created. Multiple career paths and innovative ways to recognize quality performance and important contributions are required. An organizational community begins to put an end to the era of hero worship and dependence upon a father figure to show the way, solve all problems, decide all issues.

Some of the options for new methods of utilizing talent other than to promote people up a chain of command might include:

- doing internal consulting as recognition of one's talent and competence in a particular area
- becoming a mentor to younger staff
- taking internal sabbaticals to work on personal interests as they relate to the organization
- developing a professional or operational career path with significant gradations that recognize one's developing expertise and experience without removing that person from applying that expertise, and
- allowing innovators to spin off ideas into entrepreneurial joint ventures.

Professor Edgar Schein of MIT, one of the most articulate students of organizational culture has described the importance of establishing a conscious understanding of the entity's mission, philosophy, work group goals, and acceptable means to achieve the goals.[26] Without ownership of the process, however, few members of the organization will buy into the culture as formulated by only a few managers. It wouldn't be a natural outgrowth of the group's experience and would thus be presented as an artificial and irrelevant public relations construct.

According to Robert Blake,[27] one of the foremost management consultants over the past 30 years, there have been many efforts made to manage change through decrees from the top. They have included an impressive roster of techniques developed for use by middle managers to increase the performance of their work groups. All of them are techniques that come and go with the interests of the individual manager and depend on the willingness of top management to sustain the effort. It is a very transient affair because organizations lose interest, managers are often ill suited to the implementation process, and the individual workers quickly grow cynical as they feel "done to" rather than "worked with." Do you remember: QCC's, skunkworks, suggestion boxes, brainstorming, MBWA, New Age Management, Wilderness Training, TQC, Empowerment, MBO, Ombudsman, Role Modeling, Assessment Centers, Integrity Circles, Productivity Improvement Groups, T Groups, Theory Z, Participative Management, Excellence?

Why have so many of these potentially powerful tools come and gone? Because innovators are reluctant to take the next step— empowering everyone; recognizing the organization IS everyone. Instead, ideas are imposed on, and not worked out with, those ultimately required to implement them.

This has been the case since the first proposed management reforms over 150 years ago. We have developed quite a panoply of very sophisticated social technologies, but they seem transient. In recent years, for example, we have considered quality circles, Japanese management, and even "reinventing the corporation"—a popular but short-lived concept again suggesting a humanistic attitude about running organizations, but not the hard changes necessary to nurture that concept into reality. Currently, the "learning organization" has grabbed our imagination.

Each technique is really quite good and promises to move organizations toward a higher degree of effectiveness and a higher sense of personal fulfillment, at least for the professionals instituting the innovations. Each technique fine tunes an aspect of our relationships at work and truly helps us improve. However, they often fail and become passé because they are inappropriately grafted on to a system that rejects them. At their worst, the new technologies become irrelevant, something like developing a nuclear fuel tank for a horse and buggy. At their best, they are like providing a narcotic to a terminally ill cancer patient. In either case they have missed the point.

What is necessary is an alignment of technique with the condition of the system. In creating community the intention is to reconstruct the organization so that the system itself fosters acceptance of development as a way of life not subject to the idiosyncrasies of a CEO or the whims of any one manager. Rather, it institutes a way of life that, because it is based on systemic change, with all the checks and balances we enjoy in our political world, builds in the process of continuous consideration of individual and group needs. The community concept thus provides a mechanism for the expression and satisfaction of needs as they arise.

Once we understand the significance of interrelatedness between our behavior and the constraints of the system within which we are embedded, we can look at both ourselves and the environment to determine where necessary changes are required. Rarely have we looked at the conventional organizational system, however. Somehow, the organizational environment has escaped serious attention and meaningful reform efforts. In fact, it seems to have grown a protective shield of invulnerability. It is truly a wonder in its ability to survive waves of scandals, debacles, horrendous incidents of immorality, exposure as an exploitative device, and virtually total agreement in the business press that the way we manage our organizations is seriously amiss. Clearly, the system needs a restructuring to align with the new realities as Peter Drucker calls them.[28] Then we will begin to see the futility of panaceas which address the most severe of the symptoms of organizational dysfunction but not the causes. What I am calling for here is first the partnering of employee forums with boards of directors and eventually a single board of stakeholders to guide the community. I am also calling for the creation of corporate constitutions and a members' bill of rights and responsibilities to become the framework for life within organizational communities. More will be said about this later.

New Responsibilities of Managers and Members

The effects of blind obedience to authority. The single most powerful barrier between people at work, particularly at different levels in the hierarchy, is the perceived authority of one over the other.

In one particular study almost twenty years ago, "The workers accepted production as a goal but refused to tolerate demands for obedience for its own sake, arbitrary assertions of authority, close supervision, invidious status distinctions, demands for deference, etc.; if these were insisted upon, the workers reacted with hostility toward their supervisors and with apathy towards their work."[29] A study in 1991 found that disenchanted workers are more actively resisting. "Almost half of us admit to chronic malingering, calling in sick when we are not sick, and doing it regularly. . . . Only one in four give work their best effort. . . . After all, half of us genuinely believe that you get ahead not through hard work but through politics and cheating."[30] The use of managerial or supervisory power for its own sake without checks and balances frequently results in conflicts and damaging relationships that diminish the productive capacity of the organization.

This perception inhibits free and open communication which is an essential aspect of community. Until we deal with this issue all efforts to change the organization will remain handicapped.

The insidious effects of the implied powers of one person over another or of "the organization" over the individual are extraordinary. According to psychologist Stanley Milgram[31] ". . . it is not so much the kind of person a man is, as the kind of situation in which he is placed, that determines his actions. . . . With numbing regularity good people were seen to knuckle under the demands of authority and perform actions that were callous and severe. Men who are in everyday life responsible and decent were seduced by the trappings of authority, by the control of their perceptions, and by the uncritical acceptance of the experimenter's definition of the situation, into performing harsh acts."

In his experiments he was able to demonstrate that "subordinates" almost unthinkingly responded to a "superior's" request to administer a painful electric shock to an uncooperative learner simply because they were "following orders." They assumed the orders were "valid" or legitimate.

Isn't it typical to obey, to act as if the authority is allowed (indeed, expected) to make demands of us as "subordinates"? Don't we find most requests not a matter of giving orders but simply a part of the boss's prerogatives which we obey because they fall within our zone of indifference? Where there is some discrepancy between what is demanded and what we feel is legitimate aren't we caught in a difficult position to decide if this issue is the one to risk taking a stand on or, to save the fight for a more worthy cause? Each attempt to resist will have an associated cost that will be to the subordinate's disadvantage.

Do we need to be told its OK to disobey? Is loyalty more important than integrity? In conventional organizations, yes. In work communities, no. Once again, the group needs to separate position power from person power. (Loyalty may be a positive force when applied to institution, goals, values, and purpose but harmful when applied to person, position, clique.)

We know all too well that compliance is expected and rewarded while failures and the refusal to obey are punished.

According to Milgram[32] obedience is based on: (1) believing oneself an instrument for carrying out another's wishes; (2) politeness, as if a guest in someone's house; (3) a desire to live up to the expectations of others. Thus, one becomes responsible to the authority.

There are other reasons we are all too familiar with: one focuses on his or her own task and doesn't see (or care about) the larger picture; there is a counter-anthropomorphism—one denies human power over the system, i.e., the rules of the company as if they exist in their own right.

One insidious explanation for blind obedience is apparently the systematic devaluation of the impact of one's action on victims. For example, to fire someone is an impersonal, professional, business decision due to a poor individual-to-job fit. The action, of course, is required for the good of the company. That's business. Attachment to the personal ramifications of such a decision would be too painful for anyone to deal with emotionally. In describing the "new thinking on firing" a *Working Woman* article discussed the advantages of acting quickly. "One of the advantages of the quick method is that it's so fast there's not enough time for an employee to break down, or for a manager to let his own emotions get the best of him. Still, a number of executives don't take any chances. They schedule other appointments in order to cut the encounter short. 'Personally, I like 11:45,' says [Emily] Koltnow (author of *Congratulations You've Been Fired*). 'Once I've explained the situation, I use a lunch appointment as a polite excuse for having to leave.'"[33] Business is business, no offense.

Another explanation is that those in authority become larger than life, become the institution they control. CEO's like Iacocca, Sculley, Gates, Perot, and others have reached this level in the public's eye, not to mention in the eyes of their employees. How can you challenge such people when they seem to represent so much?

Who wants to be personally vulnerable and responsible for what happens after a challenge to authority? Open conflict over reasoning and motives, is incompatible with polite social exchange. Simply refusing to obey is a challenge enough to the most mild of authorities.

Obedience is so much a part of the organizational milieu that standing up to authority is an embarrassment that many are unable or unwilling to face. Individuals are perceived to have the authority (right) to make decisions relevant to their jobs which others are expected to acknowledge.

Finally, one has the expectation that an individual will be in charge and that the dissenter is burdened with his action not the obedient one.

This is an impressive catalog of the very subtle forces that, in a conventional organization, are arrayed against freely communicating to superiors. In an organizational community one has the obligation to think carefully about one's responsibility and the impact of one's actions on the work flow. In that respect, communication is an obligation to serve the larger good and of reaching organizational objectives.

Thus in the new social contract in workplace communities, obedience to authority for its own sake and the resultant dependence that is required are transformed into a sense of commitment to the overall tasks/vision/mission of the organization and one makes an independent decision to become part of the community.

Brainpower v. Manpower

The fundamental issue facing all organizations is "How can we apply our intelligence and use our resources to meet the needs of our market?" The next logical question might be, "How can we organize and work together to stimulate each member of our community to give of their best?"

These kinds of questions turn the conventional wisdom upside down. Instead of seeing employees as a necessary evil, a cost, they are viewed as a resource that adds value to the processes that constitute the organization's mission. It is the only resource whose utility expands or contracts as environmental circumstances change. People do not produce at a constant rate nor do they reach their potential merely because they are expected to. Rather they must be nurtured in a way that supports their motivation to contribute. As long as the act of managing remains an egocentric privilege at the highest levels of the organization, the management of human resources will remain a helter-skelter haphazard affair with uneven effect on the individual members in the community.

Now managers and employees are becoming indistinguishable in background, education, and commitment to the goals of the organization. They are changing, blending. The separation between managerial and labor functions is blurring. More value-adding activities are moving lower in the organization. When this happens a sense of a shared community emerges as middle management is reduced or merged with, or replaces supervisory personnel. The hierarchy is vanishing as we have seen earlier. Paradigm Two organizations look more like a fried egg where the strategic core activities are imbedded in the performance arena and integral to the rapidly changing environment influencing the entire entity.

As problems become jointly owned and as both are rewarded in gainsharing the mental model of work changes and the organization is conceptualized as a joint experience; as a community a common vehicle for the well being of each member.

Making Communication Work

As part of community building everyone is involved in meaningful meeting opportunities which guarantees the members' right to communicate freely and openly. This process can include discussions about one's job, informational meetings about job related future demands and prospects for the company, consultations on team training needs and assessment, company related social matters, issues involving the individual's supervision, customer relations matters, intergroup relations issues, grievances/fairness issues, governance matters or any member-initiated concerns at open forums. The meeting opportunities are held frequently as the group and individuals continually seek alignment between actions and goals. They are always meaningful in clarifying expectations and reviewing conditions or developing new ideas, skills or assessments.

The evolving social contract is made explicit and ambiguities or misunderstandings are continuously explored through the multitude of opportunities to discuss differences or relevant issues in general. Completely open, authentic and constructive communications is of prime importance. Without this all other aspects of work will be handicapped.

Implications for Management

The changing role of managers leads to, or complements, the changing functions of management, especially in light of the computer revolution and the decimation of middle management; computer terminals and self-managing teams replacing them. Managers will become facilitators helping to add value to the product of their work teams rather than controllers of subordinate individuals.

In the near future, managers will need to develop a new way of behaving not only because community will replace bureaucracy but because the societal and technological conditions have also changed so that the managerial role will be completely different. They will need to develop competence in team building, learning facilitation, responsiveness and be accessible, resourceful, and flexible

EXHIBIT 5–1
Some Differences Between an Organization and a Community

	Organizational Type:	
Variable	*Organization*	*Community*
Goals:	Exclusively & mainly economic (for industrial organizations)	Comprehensive social, economic, political goals (for all organizations)
Social goals:	Means to economic goals	Goals in their own right
Authority to determine goals:	Legal owners, probably outsiders to the organization, represented by management	The total membership of the community
Organization is legally a vehicle for:	The investor (owners)	The total community
Decision-making centers:	Primarily a state of centralization	Primarily a state of decentralization
Legal flow of authority:	Top down delegation	Bottom up and top down (circular)
Distribution of managerial prerogatives:	Policy and administrative decisions made by professional management (The dominant coalition.)	Policy decisions made by total membership; administered by professional management in consultation with members forum of individual employees
Contribution to society:	Direct, mainly economic	Direct, economic and socio-political
Assumed environment:	Atomistic (competitive)	Holistic; integral part of societal system
Conflict resolution between inputs (capital and labor):	Via bargaining with management	Via consensus of the total community
Board of Directors representation:	Exclusively representatives of the owners or government, and mostly consisting of "outsiders"	Representation or participation of entire community of stakeholders.

Source, with significant adaptations: I. Adizes and E. M. Borese, *Self Management: New Dimensions to Democracy* (Santa Barbara, CA: ABC-CLIO, 1975) p. 19.

CONDITIONS FAVORING THE DEVELOPMENT OF WORKPLACE COMMUNITIES

Organizations select their members, can assign them to training and development programs, can give or withhold promotions, benefits, and assignments on the basis of the degree of individual compliance with the training objectives and can dismiss them if there isn't a fit between the community's needs and individual's performance.

In addition, organizations can depend on a well-educated group of professional talent that has already been partially socialized to expect communitarian treatment and to behave in a like manner befitting professional standards acquired in collegiate and post graduate education as well as in corporate training programs. The community ethic is widely accepted as legitimate.

Organizations are also finding that community-like behavior is an attractive recruiting tool for those who believe in their professional competence and who seek out organizational environments accommodating their need for independence, empowerment, and efficacy on the job.

These powers coupled with the individual's right to quit and to participate in the internal change process attempt to balance the needs and inclinations of the individual with the needs of the group.

Why We Hesitate to Do The Inevitable: Fear

Humankind, not the machine, is the essential core of organizational processes in the postindustrial age. How people apply their resourcefulness and imagination determines the success of the enterprise. As one wag put it, "People are capital on legs. If they aren't properly tended to, your business will simply walk away."

Two particular cultural artifacts remain from our nineteenth century social history that placed the burden of performance on the individual, not the group: the glorification of rugged individualism (self-sufficiency) and the acceptance of Social Darwinism (the spoils to the victors, usually the "fittest" person, race or class) as a way of life. These ideas have also been intimately related to the Protestant work ethic and Puritanism: delay gratification, work hard to earn your place in heaven, and if it feels good, *don't* do it.

As these ideas have evolved and been internalized over the years we have reached the point in our culture where: (1) if we haven't succeeded in the competition for worldly possessions we consider ourselves losers in this society; (2) people need to be tough and fight hard for what they get; not to do so, or to be assisted by others, is a sign of unacceptable personal weakness, and; (3) if it feels good *do* it, but feel a little guilty about it.

These notions set up a powerful framework for the denial of societal or organizational responsibility for our malaise. They also retard progress in the establishment of organizational communities because of the contradictory assumptions implicit in community. To think of group performance as part of the facilitative responsibility of managers and for individuals to cooperate with others and to be allowed to enjoy one's work, is somehow incongruous. The most vehement ridicule comes of course from those who believe in competition and personal responsibility as the only measure of merit and the only method for getting the best performance from people within the organization as well as from the company in the marketplace. This is the power of myth five: there's only one way to manage.

At some point this may have been adaptive behavior, especially in a threatening physical environment. In today's organizations the challenge is almost entirely intellectual and the nature of motivation has shifted from getting the body to show up at work to engaging the brain in a creative act. This is all very new and, to many people, a scary turn of events. It requires a new social technology for the workplace—one we have not been familiar with or very comfortable in creating elsewhere in society. Creating community has that Sunday-afternoon aura about it and not the tough, rough-and-tumble rush of a macho marketplace where the strongest survive and the winner rises above the rest as "king of the mountain." But building community is precisely what is necessary to stimulate the eager, innovative and creative mind to flow with ideas that will determine the success of the organization in a postindustrial world. It is also necessary because the jobs to be done are bigger than any one person can handle alone. It is that simple. Necessity, in this case, may indeed be the mother of invention since a postindustrial world offers so little choice other than to build working communities for the achievement and coordination of complex creative acts.

Why have writers on organizations, social alienation, and management been so reluctant to:

- take the next logical (though certainly radical appearing) step in proposing fundamental systemic change?
- show that organizational accountability to the entire group must be a property of every person's role, not just to those "above" or a board of directors?
- show that gainsharing is essential to give each contributor an incentive and a reward?

- show that stakeholders have a legitimate right to access the organization's decision making process?
- show that social responsibility, no less than personal law abiding behavior, is a requirement for doing business and not a luxury?
- demonstrate that the era of virtually unrestrained managerial personal prerogatives must come to an end and that a sense of commitment to develop communities is necessary to engage the hearts and minds of the employees in the organizational world?

These hard questions still go unanswered. Indeed, they hold the key to dramatic productive increases but, because of their implications, remain ignored as if they are simply too painful for the organizational world to face.

Yet, we've all been there. When Congress began debating whether or not to impeach President Nixon it was the beginning of the realization that we must take responsibility for our society and work together. It was a demonstration that our fear of the superhuman image of the presidency was mistaken; that behind that facade was a frail powerless mortal just as when Toto pulled the curtain on the Wizard of Oz. It was the end of dependence. Though we fear responsibility and often hope for a wizard or boss to take care of us, or for us to blame for our failures, the fullness of the experience for us and the results we achieve help us conquer the existential temptation to surrender to purposelessness in return for order in our lives. It is the American historical legacy that we can transcend apparently insurmountable difficulties and find strength within ourselves to build a better environment in which the rewards for personal involvement, effort and responsibility enrich our entire community as well as our personal lives.

The Watergate hearings and the eventual resignation of the president without catastrophe confirmed the workability of the political system that built in this check on the abuse of power. It was the beginning of the end for myth two: dependence on a messiah instead of ourselves. Many feared a collapse of the system into anarchy but precisely the opposite happened. The nation grew stronger. Congress "pulled the curtain" and the nation realized the fallacy of placing too much faith in the ability of others, even of the highest positions, to know more about conducting our affairs than we, ourselves.

Fear is our only block to community. It is the fear of letting go of some of our cultural mythology. If we alter the system we are most familiar with, if we turn bureaucracy into community we rid ourselves of the notion that our future can only be a function of our past. There is the fear that somehow we'll lose something of value or the new system won't work. This in spite of the enormous evidence that the present system itself isn't working anymore.

The fear is evident because we play intellectual charades trying to find ever newer panaceas or quick fixes to help individuals change or for middle managers to champion motivational programs in the workplace, but we refuse to acknowledge that it is the form of the workplace itself and our acceptance of it that must first change. The time to create a new way of organizing is now. That new type is community and the new structure is "solacracy" which will be defined and discussed in detail in the next chapter.

CONSEQUENCES OF THE SHIFT TO COMMUNITY

When community is built, bureaucracy is replaced. Power shifts to a negotiated relationship and to teams and networks. Communications are open and authentic. Evaluations of work and assessment of personnel are based on contributions and the process of working with one another as individuals and groups. Feedback is continuous, assessments are frequent, occurring during the normal course of doing one's work and when relevant to achieving group goals.

In addition, the individual is accepted as a whole human being. Work is recognized as a personal experience. The individual is also more than a resume but a person in the process of "becoming."

Due to challenges made available on various work teams' and/or members' representative bodies, one has an opportunity to show his or her capabilities in a variety of ways to community members and the process of growth in the organization is not so much a climb up a ladder for control as it is assignment to increasingly challenging work teams and community service bodies.

Initially, until the system stabilizes, the leaders and community activists will need new skills. The organization as a whole will need to undergo an intensive training exercise to acquaint all members with the concepts of community and how one can meaningfully participate. Part of the training will focus on how to deal with the unexpected and the anxiety that sometimes accompanies ambiguous situations.

Individual motivation to build community will result from being an integral part of the organization and being directly effected by increases or decreases in its effectiveness. Higher levels of satisfaction or well-being will be reflected at a personal level. The organization will probably experience greater commitment to the success of the group while each person will experience a greater ability to contribute. This will be especially so if the community becomes the nexus of one's interpersonal life.

In addition, workplace communities can help individuals develop a connectedness to others at a level previously experienced only through the extended family and neighborhoods. It may even be a more meaningful experience since it is by choice and each person, as a partner, can fully participate in the development of the social contract and take responsibility for their future. In so doing the workplace community helps reduce fear and skepticism of strangers and enables the individual to participate in the larger world in a meaningful way. For some, it may also reawaken an optimism about the future and the ability to tap into the culture's potential. Workplace community does indeed offer the possibility of unleashing some powerful creative impulses waiting to be realized.

CAUTION: WHAT WORKS AGAINST COMMUNITY?

Our educational system and culture of competition where "winning is everything" and there is no "second best" may be an enormous obstacle to building community. Our exposure to constant hyperstimulation to encourage our seeking immediate gratification for every need and conceivable want; our incessant focus on short term rewards or returns on our investments (even $500 CDs get careful attention by comparison shoppers); anti-intellectualism and the impulse to act first, think later—all these have been integral parts of our culture of competition, in which there is always time for Monday morning quarterbacking when our ill-conceived action fails on Sunday afternoon.

The idea of transforming organizations into communities is unacceptable to many people who believe that involvement beyond the exchange of time for wages is inefficient, costly and not a matter for business to be concerned with in the first place.

The strongest case for caution may be that proposed by one of the founders of humanistic management himself. Abraham Maslow has written that "Freedom and trust given to authoritarians . . . will simply bring out bad behavior in these people. Freedom and permissiveness and responsibility will make really dependent and passive people collapse in anxiety and fear."[34] Rather than abandon experiments in community, however, there will simply be a safeguard holding power users accountable to the group where their abuse can be held in check or punished. Fortunately the great number of Americans today are not only capable of dealing with the system appropriately but are demanding greater influence and participation in every area of their lives.

The greatest concern to owners and managers is of course the risk of diluting one's vision and jeopardizing one's position due to the involvement of other people in decision making and the establishment of interpersonal processes that take time and encumber the boss as well as everyone else. In that sense, one's concern is with the burden of bureaucracy being transformed into yet another burden but this time one of process. In addition, the motives of others' involvement may not be as pure as the motives of management and owners; that their interest will be diluted to more personal or social concerns than the financial concerns of the enterprise which, after all are central to the establishment of the organization in the first place. Finally, there is the concern that evil doers and the pathological or even the mildly neurotic will come to drive the group because of their obsession with continuing personal agendas brought up in the workplace—the community, the only forum for the expression of these concerns open to some individuals. Thus, managers want to know, "How can we control for the pathological and create boundaries to keep out the evil doers while not sacrificing the openness and participation of each person in the organization?"

One must distinguish between the pathological individual and the individual reacting to ills in the environment. On the one hand the individual may truly bring inappropriate or damaging behavior to the community. On the other, the organization could be stifling or provoking the individual to respond in a way that may be inappropriate; not because of a personality flaw but because the milieu has itself become an irritant or is violating the social contract. Thus, ". . . to some extent the goodness or badness of an individual depends upon the social institutions and arrangements in which he finds himself."[35] Intentional organizations such as the workplace communities described in this book encourage the group to come to grips with what it will take to build the good organization and an environment which facilitates positive work-centered behavior.

There is also the fear of the people who hold an incompatible world view: doomsayers, cynics, pessimists, fatalists, or martyrs to narrow causes. But as in any democratic or participative gathering they are welcomed to contribute their ideas which are then accepted or rejected on their merits. The organizational advantage, however, unlike in the outside community, is its ability to select its membership so that pathologies are minimized.

Is it possible to select thousands of people for large complex economic organizations who will have a commitment to support one another and become personally responsible for building a communicative and effective workplace? Can the intention to allow another person "to develop," "to be authentic," work in such large organizations? As earlier examples testified, it may take time, but working toward community aspirations suggests that it is possible.

There is more to life than work life. Might there be a danger in work life substituting for other forms of life? Like personal social life? Family life? But isn't it a fact that the time at work does exceed that spent in neighborhoods or with families? And isn't it a sad commentary that there is often more quality or purposeful time at work than at home? One study by the Institute for the Future[36] suggests that building teams at work may actually improve activities in other areas of one's life such as at home and in other organizations. Isn't attention to these issues legitimate for a society to raise? Isn't the issue of building an appropriate environment one that deserves the attention of all companies? Isn't it the responsibility of people in a democracy to democratize all institutions and to work toward building a better society?

The worst case for business, however, will be to defend the status quo long after the societal consciousness grows to demand a higher quality of work life. Might not state and local governments begin to mandate certain organizational behaviors as the federal government has? Might plant closing laws and the concern for employee rights, for example, be expanded to include liability for denying employees the expression of their civil rights? In fact, might not civil rights be extended to the workplace through state or local law? Might not the state or locality in which a business is situated levy extra taxes or fines for negative effects to the local community in more imaginative ways such as imposing a heavy plant closing tax?

Can we afford not to raise these questions?

A FAIRY TALE?

Describing community in these terms must sound peculiar to those in organizations rife with political intrigue, back stabbing, mistrust, game playing, posturing, self-protective behavior, inauthenticity, and tyrants at the helm. There are an overwhelming number of examples of such places and I am sure every reader of this book has experienced at least one.

In examining those times, however, when you were caught in that kind of a destructive environment, ask yourself if there were any avenues for grievance handling, due process, questioning superiors, objecting to dictates from above or any opportunity to give meaningful feedback with any hope that change would be possible. It is not an outlandish hypothesis to suggest that the miserable autocratic, pathological conditions you experienced were the result of unchecked power and the inability to resist abuse emanating from the highest levels. In most of these cases the entire organization is permeated by the influence of the CEO and there is little natural barrier protecting those below from being buried under the demands of a sadistic boss.

Yes, community will sound like a fairy tale if your experience has been with a pathological organization or an abusive boss. The point you have probably already surmised, however, is that it doesn't have to be that way. People who choose to form and work in an organization can exercise choice; organizations can select and reward those who promote the highest standards and values that represent the will of the entire organization. It is the right of the corporation to select and choose individuals and it is also their right to require training and adherence to an explicit code of behavior that creates the best environment.

If you have ten, twenty or thirty more years left before you retire, you can make a valuable contribution toward aligning your organization with the new paradigm. You help build the future you imagine.

The possibility is very much a real one if we choose to create it—to exercise our right to freedom of assembly and expression. It is also the right of each employee to seek a job in an organization that reflects his or her values and aspirations and it is each one's right to quit when conditions become intolerable. It is also every employees' right, even obligation, to establish a dialogue with others at work for the purpose of raising the consciousness of those in the workplace in order to create change. It is their right to challenge the rules and to construct a mutually satisfying workplace and not tolerate the pathologies emanating from the dominant coalition of top executives who misuse their authority. As in any political system, forces for change can assert themselves and demand a revision of undesirable conditions.

When the conditions are right (or made right) the process of building community can take place with a very good chance of success.

Community can be created from within when existing management is enlightened and understands it is the best way to become competitive in the new postindustrial environment. Otherwise, organizations will be involved in political struggles for control and, ultimately, change will be forced upon them or they will collapse. Some of the structural changes are being imposed through the mobilization of external forces such as regulatory bodies and the courts.

Really, what is the alternative to participative, humanistic management and to the establishment of corporate communities? Lives of alienation and abuse? Consumerism as a palliative? Drugs and virtual realities as substitutes for the natural experience of life? Who will work toward the resurgence of our economic power if they are not to benefit through finding meaning in their work, gainsharing and personal satisfaction? Shall we all forsake the fullness of life for the balance of trade and still be laid off at will? Be forced to strike for wage increases? Work the night shift? Be accountable to an incompetent manager? Do work that is mind numbing and soul crushing? Or treated with less than full human dignity while we work?

Easy? No. And building community is not a panacea. It is one way of re-conceptualizing conventional organizations and some of their fundamental characteristics that block their ability to change in order to successfully meet the demands of the new paradigm as it unfolds.

In any case, however, failure to change with society is a death knell for organizations that will, through their self-destructive behavior and ignorance of their environment, simply consume their capital and disintegrate.

Is community really unrealistic? Only if *you* say so.

NOTES

[1] Quoted in H. C. Boyte, *Community is Possible* (New York: Harper & Row, 1984), p. 10.

[2] H. S. Commager, *Living Ideas in America* (New York: Harper & Brothers, 1951), p. 111.

[3] H. C. Boyte, *Community is Possible* (New York: Harper & Row, 1984), p. 25.

[4] J. Patterson and P. Kim, *The Day America Told the Truth* (Englewood Cliffs, NJ: Prentice Hall, 1991), pp. 171, 172, 239.

[5] D. Dreher, *The Tao of Inner Peace* (New York: Harper Perennial, 1991), pp. 186–87.

[6] Douglas Mc Gregor first postulated this dichotomy as a contrasting set of beliefs; one being a "Theory X" and one being a "Theory Y." They were archetypes representing extremes from totally authoritarian and controlling to totally open, participative and responsive. See: D. MacGregor, *The Human Side of Enterprise* (New York: McGraw-Hill, 1960).

[7] J. Sculley, *Odyssey* (London: Fontana, 1987), p. 45.

[8] G. Schwartz, "Making the Case For Taking A Break," *Fortune*, March 9, 1992, p. 155.

[9] T. Peters, *Thriving on Chaos* (New York: Alfred A. Knopf, 1987), pp. 30, 287, 300, 327.

[10] Levi Strauss' Aspiration Statement as reprinted in: Howard, R., "Values Make the Company: An Interview with Robert Haas," *Harvard Business Review*, September/October 1990, pp. 133–44.

¹¹ B. Dumaine, "Unleash Workers and Cut Costs," *Fortune,* May 18, 1992, p. 88.

¹² These characteristics were adapted from M. S. Peck, *The Different Drum* (New York: Touchstone, 1987), Chapters V and VI; R. Levering *A Great Place to Work* (New York: Avon Books, 1988), and the common body of literature on organization development.

¹³ R. Levering, *A Great Place to Work* (New York: Avon Books, 1988), p. 23.

¹⁴ R. H. Rosen, *The Healthy Company* (Los Angeles: Jeremy Tarcher, 1991), p. 119.

¹⁵ Cited in M. Moskowitz, R. Levering. and M. Katz, *Everybody's Business* (New York: Doubleday Currency, 1990), p. 593.

¹⁶ Sculley , p 515.

¹⁷ C. Argyris, *Personality and Organization* (New York: Harper & Row, 1957), p. 196.

¹⁸ See for example, R. Aguayo, *Dr. Deming* (New York: Fireside, 1991).

¹⁹ For an overview of the discipline of organization development see: W. L. French, and C. H. Bell, Jr., *Organization Development,* 4th ed. (Englewood Cliffs, NJ: Prentice Hall, 1990).

²⁰ For an assessment instrument, see, for example: T. V. Rao and E. Abraham, "The HRD Climate Survey," *The 1990 Annual: Developing Human Resources* (San Diego, CA: University Associates, 1991), pp. 143–51.

²¹ For a detailed, practical guide for developing self-managing teams as a prelude to community, see for example, J. B. Orsburn, L. Moran, E. Musselwhite and J. H. Zenger, *Self-Directed Work Teams: The New American Challenge* (Homewood, IL: Business One Irwin, 1990).

²² For TQM see W. E. Deming, *Out of The Crisis* (Cambridge, MA: Institute of Technology Center for Advanced Engineering Study, 1986). For QCC see, O. L. Crocker, S. Charney and J. S. L. Chiu, *Quality Circles* (New York: New American Library, 1984). For an Action Research model see: W. L. French and C. H. Bell, Jr., *Organization Development,* 4th ed. (Englewood Cliffs, NJ: Prentice Hall, 1990).

²³ C. McLaughlin and G. Davidson, "A Checklist for Those Wanting to Join Communities," in L. S. Baltrusch, *The New Age Community Guidebook* (Middletown, CA: Harbin Springs Publishing), pp. 8–9.

²⁴ C. Garfield, *Second to None* (Homewood, IL: Business One Irwin, 1992), p. 248.

²⁵ "A New Age for Business," *Fortune,* Oct 8, 1990, p. 162.

²⁶ See for example, E. Schein, *Organizational Culture and Leadership* (San Francisco, CA: Jossey-Bass, 1985).

²⁷ A presentation to the *International Organization Development Association's World Congress,* Caracas, Venezuela, November 25, 1990.

²⁸ P. Drucker, *The New Realities* (New York: Harper & Row, 1989).

²⁹ P. Blumberg, *Industrial Democracy* (New York: Schocken Books, 1973), p. 101.

³⁰ J. Patterson and P. Kim, *The Day America Told the Truth* (New York: Prentice Hall Press, 1991), p. 155.

[31] S. Milgram, *Obedience to Authority* (New York: Harper Colophon, 1975).

[32] S. Milgram, *Obedience to Authority* (New York: Harper Colophon, 1975), Chapter 11.

[33] A. Siegel, "The New Thinking on Firing: Do It Quickly," *Working Woman*, August 1991, p. 12.

[34] A. Maslow, *The Farther Reaches of Human Nature* (New York: Viking, 1971). p. 245.

[35] Ibid., p. 20.

[36] Groupware Users' Project, *Business Team Participation: Impacts on Family Life* (Menlo Park, CA: Institute for the Future, 1991).

Chapter Six

New Organization, New Structure: Introducing Solacracy

"Every force evolves a form."

—*Shaker Proverb*

As the societal transformation continues, and the new paradigm spreads, it will become harder for organizations to adjust course without a correspondingly more painful reformation, if they don't make an immediate effort to adapt to the changes, as they occur.

Bureaucratic rules codified in an operations and policy manual can't begin to account for all the conditions each work group will face. Nor can a rigid hierarchy even pretend to meet the increasingly shortened time span available for decision making. Bureaucracy simply doesn't work under the emergent conditions. In community, given normal budget and reporting constraints, the task group or work team decides matters regarding its output including sub-task assignments, implementation, evaluation and coordination. In order for this decentralized, group centered organization to succeed, it needs to have a simple and fast way to determine if its decisions are on course. One way to do that is through the creation of a mission statement and operating philosophy.

Jack Welch understood this when he took over General Electric in 1981. Almost immediately he tossed out 27 volumes of policy and replaced them with a one page mission statement. It is remarkable how rapidly change can occur when the mindset changes. It is also remarkable to see how bureaucracy and red tape can expand when clarity is missing from the mission statement. As reflected in Taoist advice to ancient Chinese Monarchs: "When the Way is lost, then come laws. . . ."[1]

The search for a structural replacement for bureaucracy and auto-cratic organizational systems is occurring among people who are creating the new political frontier within organizations. It is their attempt to achieve quality of work life goals consistent with the transformation. The drive for humanistic workplace communities is based on the desire for responsive, participative, institutions in all areas of life. It involves the search for whole jobs; basic rights such as due process, freedom of speech, tolerance of differences between people, and gain/pain sharing.

The purpose of this chapter is to develop an operating philosophy and organizational structure for establishing a workplace community. It will attempt to translate the principles of the transformation into a workable and robust organizational system that aligns it with societal, technological and market forces that are driving the changes we are experiencing. It will also try to respect the importance of the intangibles by de-emphasizing controls we use seemingly for their own sake.

NEW ATTITUDE, NEW NAME, NEW STRUCTURE

I have coined the term solacracy (so•LOCK•ra•see) to describe the dynamics of large postbureaucratic organizations. It is a conjunctive of the stem sol implying a solar entity such as the Sun as well as an individual person such as in sole with -cracy a suffix from Greek meaning a structure of governance. Solacracy is the result of transforming the bureaucratic chain of command. Instead of the cumulative power of each level in a supervisory pyramid rising to a pinnacle where a CEO retains ultimate control over the organization, in solacracy a network of multiple power centers exists, based on task relevance.

Solacracy is the successor to bureaucracy, a counterpoint to the conditional paternalism and authoritarian forces that dehumanize people by treating them as means to an end rather than ends in themselves. It is a structure that combines democratic governance including a division of powers, accountability, and personal responsibility. Solacratic organizations adhere to the same democratic principles of representation, shared decision making and universal accountability that have been built into national, state and local governments, professional associations, interest groups, and, volunteer organizations. Acknowledging that corporations will inevitably assume an even bigger role in our lives, solacracy is a structure designed to insure that organizations become responsive by accelerating the transformation of organizations into workplace communities. Concurrently, forming a solacracy is also a means for organizations to cope appropriately with the societal forces now at work that are causing the transformation.

Solacracy is a form that accommodates both the self-managed team and network concepts but two fundamental differences exist; first, team autonomy is much more extensive and second, the nature of the relationships therein are balanced and reciprocal.

It is my intention in choosing the term solacracy to convey a visual image of a system in constant motion much like the solar system. The associated symbolism of enlightenment, holism, empowerment, and movement are enveloped in the definition. At the core is the emanation of the central idea, the essential purpose of the organization.

In a more ethereal sense, physicist and philosopher of science, Fritjof Capra, described the physical processes underlying matter as ". . . engaged in endless motion and activity; in a continual cosmic dance of energy."[2] In our knowledge society, organizations, once thought of as relatively stable and predictable, like molecules, are found to be enormous bundles of energy persistently gathering, generating, breaking down, reforming, transmitting and receiving information as if they were the human equivalent of subatomic particles "engaged in endless motion and activity . . ." in a continual earthly dance of progress.

Solacracy also symbolizes the holistic, dynamic, interdependent relationship that exists between all individuals and groups at work regardless of function. People in solacracy are subject to interpersonal forces much like gravitation influences the relationship between celestial bodies. The strength and characteristics of the relationships between people and work groups in the community become the focus of a deliberate conscious effort to improve interpersonal dynamics.

With multiple pathways and connections, solacracy organizes people's intelligence and resourcefulness as if in perpetual motion to accelerate the creation of a new, more useful state of being represented by finished products or services from disparate inputs of data, materials and ideas. It is a configuration of relationships mediated by the ease of communicating with and meeting each others needs in the process of working together. It only exists when activated to achieve a mutual endeavor. Otherwise the network becomes dormant, then after falling into disuse, ultimately, dissolves if new uses are not created and if new products and services are not forthcoming.

Organizational settings are dynamic. Solacracy recognizes that all organizational variables are continually changing; a change in one influencing a change in the others in varying degrees over time. Life within solacracy changes with individuals' moods as well as with the normal vicissitudes of the work flow process in satisfying the many demands that ebb and flow through the workplace environment. Because change is continuous and omnidirectional, interactions are created that cannot always be controlled or anticipated. Conceptualizing organizations as a dynamic entity makes it necessary to break through the bureaucratic mindset which freezes people into rigid roles and stereotypes within the static structures and functions of conventional organizations.

Because change eddies around each individual and because each moment is a slice in a flow of energy, we need a new word that captures the process. Solacracy describes this rather bounded chaos—the system of surging energy—the energy of gathering and enhancing the information which constitutes the raw material of our work and the basis of our work relationships.

Viewed this way organizations begin to take on an everlasting plasticity where relationships, roles and the governing rules themselves are malleable, contracting and expanding as they respond to the ebb and flow of changing requirements. They hardly reflect the organization charts and job descriptions that bury so many of today's conventional organizations in red tape.

Steelcase has experimented with this form of organizing. "There are no separate departments for different functions anymore," according to former CEO Frank Merlotti. "We tried to remove anything that got in the way of people communicating, discussing ideas. We wanted to get rid of this top down thing."[3]

The network structure of interdependent relationships requires a fundamentally new management philosophy and style in order to make optimum use of the solacracy.

A WAY OF BEING

Solacracy represents an attitude as well as a structure. It is a positive representation of what is possible when people consciously choose to associate. Given the new social contract, people need not fear and resist change. Rather, they can face circumstances squarely and be proactive in appropriately shaping them to meet existing needs. People are prepared to become part of the process that flows with events rather than being cogs in a traditional organizational machine that is jammed by periodic and threatening change. The attitude of the possible frees the imagination and truly harnesses mankind's potential as it envisages a future worth striving for. It helps people set out on a process which is itself a source of a meaningful sense of purpose. And it is the process which helps people enjoy and share in the success of an effective workplace organization. This attitude will only develop, however, when members of the organization are secure in place and purpose. That is what a community mindset is all about.

Rigid hierarchical structures are beginning to dissolve into the precursors of solacracy in some of our biggest organizations. For example, once moribund AT&T, according to their in-house journal, reports that critical management skills include the ability to thrive on a high level of ambiguity while managing diverse teams. "Bosses" are being asked to become "champions."[4] This has profound implications. Primarily it means that the groups being "championed" need to develop the consciousness of independent, self-management and the skills to implement action on their own initiative. These groups thereby become like solacratic work teams (which will be described more fully later). Solacracy is thus characterized by a flatter, more fluid structure with open, more direct lines of communication between all members representing the necessary flow of information to achieve the tasks at hand.

Because of computer workstation technology, much of this will take place in a totally electronic environment where management as we know it becomes irrelevant. Rather, the interaction in the problem solving and work process is a matter of personal resourcefulness and negotiation skills in a work team or between individuals unrelated in a power hierarchy. In effect, the control aspects of management will be transferred to computer data bases or the workgroup responsible for its own output.

CREATING A PHILOSOPHY

Developing a community philosophy with an aligned culture may be the ultimate competitive advantage because it can't be copied. Though it certainly can be imitated, its strength lies in its uniqueness. A philosophy and an associated organizational culture develops into community practice much like personality in an individual. Like one's personality, the community philosophy and its manifestation in the organizational culture is a genuine reflection of the actual sentiments and behaviors of its members. When the organization manifests principles and practices which reflect its philosophy, it becomes interpersonally efficient in executing its goals because the context of communications and behavior are understood and lead to easy agreement and synchronicity between people working together. If the underlying philosophy stimulates the creation of an environment which nourishes individual growth and develops an expressive way of being, it generates ideas, innovations, creative serendipity, positive relationships and an ambiance that facilitates group success. No one can copy this nontransferable software. They can emulate it, but that is just pure flattery, not a threat.

Though almost all organizations have an espoused philosophy, and some demonstrate a clear philosophy without articulating it, where it is imposed by a CEO or simply the creation of top managers, it loses its power as an organizational guide to actual behavior. It is important to establish a community-based philosophy for three critical reasons. First, having a philosophy embodied in corporate practice establishes a benchmark for behavior. It conveys a message about what is important and what behavior will be rewarded or punished. Where daily work involves many unknowns and unpredictable circumstances, all participants benefit from a set of general principles which guide their behavior through ambiguous decision-making situations.

Second, it helps the individual know exactly what the real purposes of the organization are and minimizes arbitrariness and uncertainty about what is valued. Personal performance and personal integrity can readily be matched against the workplace community's values. Further, it helps ground individuals; it clearly guides the development of useful personal skills while discouraging the display of behavior that is inappropriate.

Third, it establishes a community wherein deliberate, enlightened interpersonal behavior is accepted and encouraged. Mutually determined norms and expectations are created and support of those norms is encouraged. Yet, it is important to establish a baseline that includes a healthy acceptance of personal differences so that members need not fear feeling stifled by the need to conform. There is a healthy pressure to personify the community norms that promote the organization's achievement of its various goals. Unhealthy pressure to conform for its own sake without a clear connection to the organization's purpose must obviously be discouraged.

Solacracy thus develops many of the same qualities as social communities, allowing for the natural development of relationships under a new social contract that creates a bond between its members which leads to a feeling of shared community. A sense of mutual loyalty is developed. The individual becomes committed to live up to the organizational philosophy and culture yet still retains his or her right to influence its change through a participative process. While each person plays a role in community building and is an integral part of the decision making process, the organization in return, fosters personal security for each participant.

In the development of a specific philosophy many companies such as Nordstrom's and Quaker Oats reach for the highest ideals. Statements regarding equal opportunity, individual integrity and democratic processes pepper their corporate philosophies and permeate the fabric of their policies and interpersonal behavior. In Nordstrom's case, service to customers is legendary and people in their primary market in western states frequently have a story of outrageously good service. To listen to the tales is to think you are listening to a fisherman describing the one he caught last summer. "Why, it was THIS big!" "New Nordstrom employees are handed a statement summing up the company's philosophy. It reads, 'Welcome to Nordstrom. We're glad to have you with our company. Our Number One goal is to provide outstanding service. Set both your personal and professional goals high. We have great confidence in your ability to achieve them. NORDSTROM RULES: Rule No. 1: Use your good judgment in all situations. There will be no additional rules.'"[5] For these and other companies, the philosophy brings out the best among their associates who strive to live up to the organization's ideals. Pitney Bowes Business Systems is another company that identified several key values for mention in what they termed a "Direction Statement". Continuous innovation; positive relationships; integrity, respect and fairness are all mentioned.[6]

Other companies, in examining their own culture, often fear a "loss of control" over their employees or that such ideals are impractical for business organizations. Some managers even think of these ideals as subversive of capitalism since, on the surface, they temper the assumed proprietary "rights" of owners and managers. Beneath the surface, however, such ideals simply recognize the historical imperative of American society which has been to move toward democratization. The organization is no longer considered management's or stockholders' to do with as they please. It is a societal instrument which must be responsive to all stakeholders and the operating system to employees in particular. Clearly, society is coming to believe it is the employee and not the investor that has most at risk. For the investor it is only money; for the employee it is his or her livelihood. One company that intends to divide its stock equally between the employees, customers, and owners is the Red Rose Catalog.[7] This novel approach recognizes the integrated nature of business employees and the community. Perhaps crafting a constitution and a set of principles would be useful as well. One might also choose to integrate a new social contract into the governing documentation of the organization.

THE NEW SOCIAL CONTRACT

The idea of a social contract in the Western experience dates from at least the fourth century B.C. when Plato first grappled with it. The emphasis in our time has been the development of an agreement between the individual and the society, the state. During the American enlightenment, Jeffersonians believed in a democratic society but also in the protection of the individual from being overrun by the majority no matter what the mandate. Americans were the first in modern history to attempt structural and legal safeguards to protect the individual from the power of the state. In fact it was America that first developed a government that actively advocated individual rights and safeguards to personal liberties, most recently demonstrated by the equal employment opportunity statutes and prosecution of corporations for unsafe work environments.

Here we are concerned with the relationship of the individual to the workplace and whether that relationship is synchronous with institutional—individual relationships in the larger culture. Though traditionally the relationship at work was a simple exchange of time and obedience for money with which to live our lives in the so-called "real world" away from work, increasingly the workplace is becoming the focus of our lives; it is becoming THE world. Working for someone else or a government bureaucracy is not an alternative to life on the family farm or in a small family business. It is a fact of life for everyone but the heirs to economic fortunes. At the time of the revolution the vast majority of freemen worked for themselves as farmers, tradesmen or small shopkeepers. The outrage in the colonies in the 1770s was the control exercised by the political state over people's daily affairs. Today as we have seen earlier that role is shifting from the state to the organization to which we are all tethered and the issues now arising in the workplace challenge the assumption that there is even equity in the notion of a fair days work for a fair days pay—especially so in light of the recent outcry over wildly excessive CEO compensation.[8] Being a wage slave for eight to ten hours a day is no longer acceptable. Employees want an equitable role to play in the governance of the organization and in establishing policy, rules and the parameters of their working relationships.

We need some role boundaries, however, to know what is proper to expect of each person and for people to know what is fair for the organization to expect of them. The current stress epidemic is both personally and organizationally rooted. Balancing personal and group demands is important for mental health as well as to establish an equitable relationship between the individual and the group. Within organizations there is a fierce replication of the earlier economic and political rivalries found in communities and among neighbors. Vying for status symbols, bosses favors, the perks of promotion or the gold watch while not as vital now as it once was in one's community life certainly seems so inside the workplace. The boss and one's peers can become the source of great personal stress in how the assignments and demands are made upon us. In short, the workplace has become the neighborhood today and they can vary psychologically and materially as much as Beverly Hills and the South Bronx.

The difference between an Exxon and a Herman Miller demonstrates this point. Exxon has become a depressed place to work where morale is low and facilities, as everywhere in the oil business, are often dangerous. "In the words of one Exxon employee, '"I don't know anyone who is happy, and I know a lot of people who are looking to leave.' A pipe fitter at Exxon's refinery at Billings, Montana, said after the Valdez spill: 'Morale is as low as I've seen it in my 14 years here.'"[9] It wasn't always that way of course but over the past several years one outrage after another has plagued employees' sense of well being. With short notice they are fired, reassigned or bullied. Lawrence Rawl, the CEO that transformed Exxon from a steady paternalism into an unpredictable dictatorship was known for his particularly insensitive attitudes to employees. Perhaps that's a necessary position to have when you cut the work force by 28 percent, over 50,000 people.[10] The organizational culture in such a workplace is typified by competitiveness, low morale, backbiting, envy of others, and fear.

At Herman Miller, by contrast community is represented by a sensitivity to all employees. Their Scanlon Plan, a profit-sharing tool, was designed by representatives of management and labor and voted on by all employees before adoption.[11] That kind of concern and involvement leads to high morale, cooperation and motivation to contribute one's best at work.

Building community at work is a function of a social contract between the individual and his or her work environment. The social contract establishes our relationship to the workplace regardless of whether it is explicit or implicit. It is an understanding between ourselves and our colleagues, between a supervisor and the organization itself through policies, rules, benefits and other group-based expectations.[12] The social contract is a strong influence on behavior because it underlies individual's expectations of work roles and responsibilities as actually performed and it also establishes a benchmark for what the individual considers fair treatment.

Under the economic model of man where the only motives seen were a drive for money to provide one's basic needs, organizations needn't worry about a social contract. Coercion and fear kept people at their jobs. As the consciousness of one's relationship to the workplace changes and as the federal government and the courts actively mitigate the employer/employee relationship, the social contract actually becomes more important to understand since it becomes a more important factor influencing the circumstances of work. Where safeguards to one's job expand and the employee is entitled to certain considerations and better treatment, nuances in workplace relationships become more meaningful.

With the new consciousness of organizations and the idea that a primary purpose of the workplace community is to foster individual growth, relationships become a central matter to be equitably determined by all parties involved. It is in effect a negotiable aspect of life within organizations to be determined by everyone. Eventually, with attention to the interpersonal processes at work, the social contract becomes a more explicit representation of mutual understandings regarding each individual's role in the group and the kinds of treatment one can expect from associating with a particular organization. Not everything will be immediately explicit but attending to interpersonal relationships and the process of working together eventually will enable all issues of concern to be openly discussed as legitimate matters for group attention.

In a sense this is bringing the concept of justice to the workplace where individuals begin to share their mutual destiny on the basis of shared interpersonal understandings. Rawls (no relation to Exxon's Rawl) explained that the foundation of justice rests, initially, on two principles: "First: each person is to have an equal right to the most extensive basic liberty compatible with a similar liberty to others. Second: social and economic inequalities are to be arranged so that they are both a) reasonably expected to be to everyone's advantage, and b) attached to positions and offices open to all."[13]

The current system has clearly not been to everyone's advantage and the numbers it benefits appear to get smaller and smaller each year. The professional middle class is now acutely aware of the inequities because it feels them personally each day. Overworked, stressed, and sacrificing a life for the system has not paid off. As people see how easily they are discarded after a merger or when new technology makes it feasible they feel a profound betrayal and the golden handcuffs that may have seemed so rewarding begin quickly to tarnish. Clearly they no longer believe that they will win a place in the executive dinning room. The pressure among the disillusioned yuppies of yesterday is building to an explosive level. If the executive class, which is fast becoming an imperial class, stays the course, it will trigger a massive upheaval amounting to a bloodless, psychological revolution.

Elements of a Social Contract

A social contract encompasses specific guidelines governing behavior. Sometimes the guidelines are established by external bodies such as the courts or legislatures. The most recent example of a new element to the American social contract is the prohibition against sexual harassment which has resulted in requirements for all businesses to implement in regard to intergender relations. In order to realize the full potential of any social contract it is a good idea to create a formal framework within which each person can be assured that the organization will not vary, retaliate, renege or reverse itself without violating established procedure. It is in effect writing a forerunner to a constitution and bill of rights for the organization which would spell out precisely how rules are made and enforced as well as the rights and responsibilities of each member of the community.

We know that "Every reciprocal relationship has a social contract, even if it's an unwritten one. The more explicit and clear the expectations and understandings of a social involvement are, the more likely the association is to succeed and to proceed gracefully along its course."[14] It behooves the organization to deal with these issues forthrightly.

Social involvement inevitably means confronting differences as well as similarities. In the workplace it isn't convenient, efficient or sensible to expect that unpleasantness can always be avoided or that it is always a completely negative experience. When work becomes heavily process centered, issues that were never addressed before surface quite frequently because the process itself requires working through interpersonal understandings. There are limitless aspects of personality: personal needs, wants and perceptual interpretations that can either be points of conflict or cooperation; agreement or disagreement. The new social contract needs to build in the expectation that attention to these areas is not only a valid concern in the workplace but necessary to reach optimal effectiveness and to fulfill the vision of the organization. That's why attention to process becomes so important.

Some of the many areas of interest to examine include: the basic tenets of the philosophy mentioned earlier, rules for interpersonal relationships and defining the broad parameters of one's role, rights and obligations of community participation, the structures for decision making and the distribution of power and economic rewards, how individual and group evaluation will be carried out, the dispute resolution process and the selection and dismissal of leaders and members. In community all of these matters are determined, directly or indirectly, by those affected by them.

Toward a Constitution and Bill of Rights for Organizations

In community, management is a public trust. Organizations as we have seen are emergent polities; they regulate our lives to a large extent. Our good fortunes are inescapably tied in with their behavior. The managerial role in any organization whether it be a work organization or a volunteer organization, a government body, or a school, still must be driven by community-based principles that guarantee the fair treatment, responsible behavior and organizational accountability of all members to all members. Accountability to the organizational community means the community has the right to remove an individual in gross, or persistent violation of community requirements (the social contract). And the individual can instigate actions to override policies or decisions perceived as against the individual's or community's good.

Stemming Abuse of Authority

The exercise of conscience and self-restraint is insufficient, alone, to prevent arbitrary and capricious behavior. We have seen the extent of greed and corruption that is possible on the part of many CEO's and others in the recent past. "At some 80 percent of the companies on *Business Week*'s list of America's 1,000 most highly valued corporations, one person rules the roost as chairman and chief executive. He controls the meetings of directors, who are theoretically monitoring his performance on behalf of shareholders. It's no wonder CEOs often confuse who works for whom. As John Nash, president of the National Association of Corporate Directors, put it recently: 'Their attitude is, 'It's my company and it's my board.' They don't get it that it's not'"[15] The fact is many boards are hardly able to serve as a watchdog committee. Thus a separation and a limitation of powers may be necessary to safeguard the rights of individuals and the participative structures in community. Each organization, in a fully participatory manner, must determine for itself the kind of community it wishes to establish and to create a constitution that effectively controls the use of authority and prescribes how it can be amended.

The Levi Strauss aspiration statement mentioned earlier approaches constitutional status. In part, it claims that "When we describe the kind of Levi Strauss & Co. we want in the future, what we are talking about is building on the foundation we have inherited: affirming the best of our company's traditions, closing the gap that may exist between principles and practices, and updating some of our values to reflect contemporary circumstances."[16]

A SAMPLE SOCIAL CONTRACT

A social contract must include a framework for establishing the relationship between the individual and the organization. It must spell out both obligations of the individual to the group and what rights the individual can expect to enjoy as a member of the community. It should also indicate how the organization is structured and the role one will play in the continuing development of the workplace community.

For community to be established and for it to be truly different from present day teams and self-managed work groups the following is designed as the basis for developing an operating contract.

Basis of Community

The vision, values and objectives, and operating philosophy, policies, and rules of the community will be articulated through a process inclusive of each member (or his or her representative) established by the governing stakeholder forum.

Rewards for membership shall be established to reflect one's contribution to the work as well as one's membership in the community. Salary and benefits will reflect the former—a bonus the latter.

Individual Obligations

Each member of the workplace community has the responsibility to perform at or above the requirements of his or her role as established at the time of membership. In addition, members are expected to participate in both individual and work group-based learning experiences to upgrade existing skills and to acquire new skills and competencies throughout their tenure with the community.

Each member of the community assumes the responsibility for and will cooperate in achieving the community's financial and social objectives. Individuals are expected to contribute to the maintenance and improvement of the community through personal participation in decision making opportunities at the work-group level and in other bodies that have a bearing on the quality of work life environment, the quality of our output and the economic performance of the community in the marketplace. In doing this individuals are expected to honestly share their personal points of view and to express themselves authentically in all of their relationships.

The manner in which one's obligations will be fulfilled shall be determined by each work group in accordance with general policy designed by the representative forum and in a relevant manner determined by the individual.

Individual Rights

Each member of the community is offered employment security as long as he or she perform their obligations in good faith. Any penalties, sanctions or alteration in one's status with the community shall be determined by the representative forum. Each member will enjoy due process in the administration of work rules and in any grievances arising from one's experience in the community.

Members shall have access to information and the right to express one's self.

Each person will have the right to establish the level of intimacy with the community and its members that is most comfortable to her or him.

Note.   Clearly this is to suggest thinking on the topic and is not suggested as a social contract that can stand alone. Each company must establish its particular contract in light of its unique circumstances and labor-management history.

RENEWAL/RE-CREATION

Building workplace community portends the renewal of individual liberty, the right of free expression and the legitimacy of striving for personal growth on the job. It will recognize the managerial function as a public trust much like other public office holders. A new dynamic should be established reducing the dichotomy between manager and worker; organization and individual. All members of the community should be responsible for the combined output of the organization. The role one plays will be in part determined by the kind of work one does as well as the requirements of the group one is a part. But the degree of involvement in the management of the organizational community will be determined by each individual according to their interests and needs much like one's role in the larger polity is so determined.

The business world itself is now beginning to sense the need for a transformational change that includes attention to process and continuous education. "A handful of visionary leaders—General Electric Chairman Jack Welch chief among them—are going beyond training seminars to a fundamental reordering of managerial priorities . . . (this movement recognizes) that reality is not absolute but a by product of human consciousness. . . . Even the primacy of the profit motive (is) being questioned by those who argue that the real goal of enterprise is the mental and spiritual enrichment of those who take part in it."[17] Jack Welch, once known as "Neutron Jack" for his mass firings, restructurings, and downsizing in the early days of his tenure as CEO has apparently gone through a personal transformation of his own. In the 1991 annual report to stockholders, Welch "declared that 'GE cannot afford management styles that suppress and intimidate' subordinates."[18]

Organizational renewal is the process of realigning the consciousness and efforts of all members to the community's vision, its sense of purpose, and each person's daily efforts in achieving operational goals.

As Welch has realized, change is needed to tap the full potential of all employees. In creating a more accepting, participative, cooperative environment even huge (290,000 employee) GE is taking a step closer to community. When you free people from the command and control constraints you not only tap into their resourcefulness and ideas but you are inviting them to become equal partners in the renewal of the organization. In so doing other systems in place from the earlier bureaucratic era will need to be changed to align with the new energy unleashed by the participative impulse. Compensation systems, methods of selecting supervisors, indeed their very role and function changes. It sets in motion very powerful reform processes which must be seen through to their logical conclusion to most efficiently harness the human energy suddenly being released from the bureaucratic pressure cooker.

Just as progress and belief in human potentialities can benefit us, belief can also retard us. Superstition still powers many cultural systems in the preindustrial world. Fanatical religions still chain their adherents to inaction in the name of fate and their doctrinal interpretation of scriptures or other divine messages. The reforms spoken of in these pages assume two primary values: one, a volitional person, willing and able to make choices to further the condition of the planet; and, two, the belief in endless creative possibilities. The marketplace now sets the challenge as competition ultimately spurs organizational creativity, learning, and the widespread ownership of the process. Soon that tide will be splashing upon the corporate sand castles that represent the bureaucratic past.

It is important to focus on the process of what we do because we live with it, not the product of what we do. The product or service is external, it is what we transfer to the consumer. It deteriorates and is lost as the process is refined to produce new and better things and new and better services. It is the process that makes it happen.

If we assume that people are good and that failure to nurture that goodness and growth may result in either the decay of the goodness, stifling the growth need, or the atrophy of the natural process of growth toward maturity, then organizations need to devote attention to the issue of fostering the right climate.

Components of a Philosophy of Community

In general a community philosophy could profitably be premised on the following tenets derived from the principles of humanistic management. The following were adapted from Abraham Maslow's[19] compendium which he created from studying the works of Barnard, Likert, Drucker, Herzberg, Argyris, and MacGregor[20] while studying a manufacturing facility in California.

1. Everyone is to be trusted. Under random or otherwise extraordinary conditions this may not be wise. However, modern organizations, unlike society at large, do have the privilege of selecting and training their members. With the expansion of the professional class and its socialization to a high level of integrity the selection of trustworthy individuals is likely. Once in an environment where trust is practiced as well as preached, the vast majority of emotionally healthy individuals endeavor to live up to, and maintain it. In addition, one's peers will, if necessary, apply pressure to conform to a high standard of trustworthiness. This is especially true when the truth, as pleasant or as unpleasant as it may be, is dealt with authentically, sincerely, and honestly. Trust in our society is so valued and sought that even among nonprofessionals, those most regarded with suspicion by managers, it can be assumed once the traditional barrier between the managerial/professional and non-managerial/non-professional classes can be overcome. In large part that barrier has been erected by bureaucratic managers who have during the industrial era threatened their employees capriciously and who, due to their own insecurity, have been unable to act trustworthily in control-based, blame-centered uncommunicative bureaucracies.

In solacracy that fear among participants is removed, and trust between all parties can be developed. In fact it must be developed since the nature of solacracies, as they are now emerging, focuses on concepts, knowledge and information which is so vast, and often amorphous, that to succeed everyone will depend upon the collaboration of others in performing their work. Furthermore, collaboration requires trust and open communication. W. L. Gore and Associates provides one of the best example of this. It was among the first companies to abandon traditional hierarchy and bureaucracy and replace it with what it calls a lattice organization. Some of the characteristics quoted in an early account of the firm are still in effect: "No fixed or assigned authority; sponsors, not bosses; natural leadership defined by followership; person-to-person communication; objectives set by those who must make them happen; (and), task and functions organized through commitment."[21] By 1990 employment at Gore reached 5,300. Today organizations using a variant of this approach are looking more like a solacracy; they are sometimes called networks.

In a fast-paced information world it is perhaps ironic that one needs to trust more strangers than ever before in providing the goods and services we desire. There is little room for not being trustworthy since one simply cannot do business any other way. Time for doubt and personal assessment of one's trustworthiness is diminishing. Professional socialization and a widespread understanding of the importance of acting trustworthily, however, have impressed this upon us. Failure to live up to a high standard of trust and honest behavior is one of the surest ways to violate the new social contract within the community and the surest way of losing customers and business in the marketplace.

There is always the danger that the selection process will nevertheless not guarantee trustworthy, emotionally healthy individuals and the conditions set forth for solacracy, including a trusting environment, may have, as Maslow has warned, a ". . . bad, even catastrophic, effect on a certain small proportion of the population" some of whom may pass through the screening process.[22] This fear of the small percentage of deviants has always poisoned the environment by the establishment of harsh controls for the vast majority of people capable of living up to and thriving under conditions of trust, empowerment and personal responsibility. Solacracy, however, cannot survive under such tight controls. Hence, rather than stifle the organization because of a small minority, counseling, training and support are generously given to help each participant successfully deal with the environment. Where that attention fails, individuals may need to be assigned to a low-interactive position so they do not destroy the environment for others, or be released by the organization. Establishing community means creating a new social contract as mentioned earlier. It means living up to expectations or learning how to do so. Failure to do so may require dismissal. Community and the solacratic model creates the reciprocal relationship of both rights and responsibilities.

One dramatic example of how trust leads to improved performance was reported by Paul Bernstein, Dean of Graduate Studies at the Rochester Institute of Technology. He found that creating a trust culture results in a variety of advantages to the individual as well as the organization. In one manufacturing facility "instead of 14 percent of the work force tied up in rework (1984), only 1.7 percent had that job by the end of 1986."[23] These results have been so widely replicated where a trust culture has been deliberately established, that it is now a truism that trust benefits the organization.

2. Everyone is to be fully informed. In community each person is entitled to know all about the organization, particularly if a trusting, collaborative environment is to be built. In the industrial era there was an aura of secrecy because of the exploitative nature of organizations and because secrecy was used to maintain the myth of managerial superiority. Since exploitation and managerial superiority do not exist in solacracy, because of the recourse individuals have to challenge and or remove the abusers, and because each individual is in agreement and must comply with the new social contract, secrecy is dysfunctional, and unnecessary.

Naturally, there are a handful of facts, which, if known by competitors, might damage an organization. Critics point to disloyal, disgruntled or opportunistic employees who would abuse their knowledge of organizational information. Further, with mobile employees who readily change jobs there is a potential threat to the company if they take important information with them, even when there is no malice intended. It may be necessary to keep formulas, blends, components and perhaps, a very few key strategies or future plans secret, but usually they are so few in number and obvious to everyone, that secrecy per se is not a problem. But what is often kept secret such as financial data, salaries, personnel and resource projections and allocations, the budget process and plans for organizational restructuring, only upset people's sense of fairness, involvement and trust and do not contribute to organizational effectiveness or security. In community there is reduced secrecy. Decisions are inclusive and require that members be well informed.

The ultimate purpose for keeping people fully informed is for them to become better able to do their job and to stabilize the social system. An informed participant knows the resources available to him, their limits, what to expect from the many interdependencies at work and the social milieu. There are few work related surprises; rumors can easily be dealt with.

Marion Labs has a policy that employees can have access to any information except others' personnel records, financial matters that are prohibited by law from early distribution and plans that could be used by competitors. "A policy of no secrets does much to build trust . . . (and) can stop rumors that erode people's confidence in each other."[24]

The late Sam Walton was the most successful contemporary American businessman, a legend as the wealthiest man in the country, who built an organization of 345,000 associates in an industry no more likely to attract honest employees than any other—retailing. According to him, "What sets us apart is that we train people to be merchants. We let them see all the numbers so they know exactly how they're doing within the store and within the company; they know their cost, their mark-up, their overhead, and their profit. It's a big responsibility and a big opportunity."[25]

One additional benefit to disclosure is keeping the political environment honest. If information is power, full disclosure devolves power to the members where it should ultimately reside.

One move to make the free flow of information a meaningful exercise would be supporting an employee daily newspaper. Not a publication of a communications office it would operate much like a campus newspaper and either pay for itself or fold up. It could publish what it wanted but would undoubtedly focus on issues of concern to the workplace community and the performance of the company. It would also serve as an educational tool helping the community understand the business and its relationship to society. It would be provocative, informative and an expression of the various elements within the community like any other daily newspaper.

Motorola doesn't have a newspaper of this kind but it does create work teams among its 95,000 employees and selects members from these teams to serve on steering committees at the next highest level in the company for the purpose of sharing insights and raising appropriate issues.[26] If nothing else it creates an atmosphere of openness and individuals may expect that their concerns will receive attention. This kind of program is becoming more widespread where organizations are acting upon the responsibility to communicate honestly with their employees.

3. Understand that everyone wants to do a good job and be successful. Hand-in-hand with building a trusting, open environment is recognizing that people would rather be useful than not; would rather succeed than fail; would like to help the organization than see it hurt; and, would rather take pride in their work than be ashamed of it. Few people are as naive as to think that they can succeed while the organization fails. Though some managers and owners operate an organization while disregarding its employees, a workplace community cannot. While individuals at all levels in traditional organizations can commit self-serving acts and "rip off" the company, in community they get called directly by peers to account for their actions. That kind of behavior, though, is less likely to occur in community because of the significance of the relationship one has with the organization and because of the sense of respect for the "commons" that is nurtured there.

Each person in a community contributes because his or her fortune is tied in to the performance of the company in the marketplace. When they see themselves as owners or vested in a gainsharing program, they become acutely aware of the connection between themselves and the organization's/community's success. One stunning example of the difference this fact makes is the experience Avis Rent-A-Car has had as an employee owned company. For the first six months as an employee owned company it's profits were 35 percent higher than the comparable period a year earlier under the old owners. It has remained profitable ever since and its stock has increased in value each year. One key to its success is the employee participation groups which get each person involved in company matters in a meaningful way. According to the Center for Employee Ownership in Oakland, CA, when employees get involved with decisions about their jobs the company grows on the average of 11 percent faster than when they own the company but don't get involved.[27]

The Avis story should not surprise anyone. The legacy of the Judeo-Christian ethic has been an American society committed to hard work and achievement. Some people have claimed a weakening of this ethic; that we have become hedonistic and lazy. The problem is apparently the disparity between our poor treatment on the job and our rising expectations that work should be meaningful and dignified, and that the rewards should be fair. Until now we have depended on management to learn new methods of tapping our productive abilities in ways other than the prevalent "carrot and stick" approach. The transformation now underway is witnessing a shift in this behavior to a more holistic view of motivation and an understanding of the power of sharing responsibility. This accentuates the importance of making each individual an integral part of the community.

4. People are willing to accept responsibility.   Community invalidates autocratic and arbitrary behavior, particularly that based solely on "superior" position and replaces it with competence, coordination and accountability.

Solararchy is to solacracy what hierarchy is to bureaucracy. It exists, however, not as a ranking, but as a difference in job responsibilities. The objective is to eliminate the idea that one is subordinate to another. Some tasks need to be done so others may perform their job and some people are better at doing some things than others but there is no need for a universal designation like "subordinate" which conveys inferiority and diminished value. Differences are based solely on skill, wisdom or a convincing appeal. One's proficiency at a task or recognized insight prevails in a group's endeavor. Where there is no agreement on one's superior talent or a situation boils down to preferential choices, a task team may assign coordinating and/or decisional responsibilities to an individual who will then act on the group's behalf and become accountable to the group as well as to others in interdependent teams.

Behaving much like a team leader, an individual chosen by the group coordinates or shares in the facilitation of its activities and represents it to other groups in the organization. The group may also choose to rotate the function; it is up to them. Where skill is virtually equally distributed in the group, it would tend to choose a more personable individual to coordinate its work; evidence abounds that individuals with a sense of responsibility and commitment to a group make intelligent choices—particularly if they are personally affected by their choices as, indeed they would be, as a member of the group.

People are willing to take responsibility when they are empowered to act as opposed to being delegated a task that is ultimately to meet another's approval. Criteria are either known and understood by the individual doing the job or they are worked out against a standard—a goal that the organization wishes to reach.

Where conflicts do arise, a process of managerial mediation can be undertaken either by the parties involved or with the assistance of a third party. Managerial mediation is a learned process of resolving differences that all members of an organization can quickly acquire. It will be discussed in more detail in a later chapter.

5. The individual is capable of and willing to subordinate his or her ego to the needs of the group.   The most profound change in the work force in the information era has been the internalization of many organizationally relevant values and behaviors. The professionalization of much of the work force attests to this. Organizational survival has become dependent upon group rather than individual effort alone. Teamwork is the new buzzword because it so dramatically changes the productive capacity of the organization when people are organized to work together collaboratively. But work has become so complex that there is no other way to work.

Managers as bosses add less value as knowledge, and access to knowledge, devolve to everyone. Tofler has pointed out that this dramatic power shift is occurring everywhere and is having a revolutionary effect.[28] With the advent of desktop computing and terminals connected to information networks worldwide there is little an individual will need to know that requires the direct interaction with a supervisor, as a supervisor, though there may be much interaction and mutual assistance in sharing information and insight with many people. Thus, the major assets for any manager will be either knowledge or facilitation skills. If you don't have one and can't do the other, you're in the way!

Individuals commit themselves to the success of the group and vice versa. One asks, 'What is the best solution to the problem or the effectuation of the goal?" rather than "What can I get out of this? or How can I get my own way (for its own sake)?" In an organization where power prone individuals seek to rise up a hierarchy the reward is very much related to their ego involvement; in fact their personal satisfaction in life depends on it. In community, however, the checks are ever present so that power is granted to people by virtue of their standing in the group and they are frequently held accountable to the group. Because of the community interest that is constantly evolving as part of a process of doing work as opposed to today's typical egocentered work world, ego inflation is dealt with rather expeditiously by colleagues.

6. Recreate the sense of community.   The last twenty-five years have indeed been extraordinary. This generation of Americans has witnessed an unprecedented deterioration of family, neighbor-hood, and community life which has had grave consequences for our emotional and psychological well-being. Calling for a renewed sense of community may be a requirement for sound mental health. Community means many things which have been discussed through-out this book but it must at least return a semblance of personal control and involvement to the individual seeking to be part of some-thing worthwhile. Organizations are the latest hope for doing that, as the polis is rapidly shifting from geographical community to organi-zational community. But that sense of community needs to be recreated frequently in order for it to keep pace with the change that eddies all about us.

Community is in effect an organism, not a given way of being but an evolving way of being that must be ever vigilant to meet the cur-rent needs of its members. It is therefore important that the process of connecting with one another be continuously reinforced and attended to. Not only must the work be the focus of building relationships but there must be time for celebration, for play, for refreshing one's men-tal and physical energy, and time to think, to share ideas with one another outside of the formal forums and representative bodies but still during official time. It refreshes the whole community and in its own way enables it to accomplish more when it is work focused. Some companies institute social functions and sponsor sports teams of one kind or another or seasonal get-togethers. So often they seem artificial as do the so-called beer busts (or "fruit juice follies") on Friday afternoons in Silicon Valley. Some companies have extensive facilities and organize many activities but without individuals having a genuine sense of being connected to one another, many of these activities fall short of their potential as community builders and appear more public relations related.

7. Encourage authentic personal and interpersonal behavior. One reason for the longevity of dualistic thinking, the conceptualiza-tion of management vs. labor, has been the refusal to deal authentically with people. The formal organization structure, according to organi-zation charts and job descriptions, is antiseptic. Behavior is expected to be controlled at all times regardless of the circumstances. There are no messy outbursts of frustration or hostility; that is considered "insubordination" for workers and "unprofessional" for managers. The control orientation of bureaucracy expects individuals to possess total emotional self-control. Naturally this practice reinforces the duality since real feelings must be hidden from formal superiors, lat-eral competitors for higher jobs (don't display a potential weakness) and subordinates (they'll abuse you, walk all over you, lose respect for you).

Community, and its solacratic structure, supports the individuals' full expression of themselves and strives to learn how to deal with diversity. Let no one invalidate another's thinking merely through dismissing it or through the implied power of one's position to silence another. The environment becomes an accepting one.

8. Assume that everything can be improved and that people want to do better.   "The art of progress" according to the renowned philosopher Alfred North Whitehead, "is to preserve order amid change and to preserve change amid order."

The community must be engaged in constant personal and organizational learning which means that eventually everyone learns something from everyone else and is open to do so without feeling inferior or superior. Rather each person can take the sharing of the learning experience in stride as a normal part of one's experience of the community. While there are obvious benefits to learning the skills required of others in the performance of their jobs so that each person can take over for the others in their work team when necessary, and enhance their own understanding of the organization, personal learning should be encouraged for its own sake as a way of broadening the mind and encouraging the serendipitous effects on one's personal growth. In addition, the subtleties of experiencing the interconnections of the world through learning stimulates the mind when it focuses on its work to see things anew. Therefore, a training department should evolve into an education department helping people learn what they want to know as well as what they need to know and giving people opportunities to share as well as receive knowledge in the community. To cope in a changing world is to learn. When change becomes a constant so too must learning.

Furthermore, a learning environment means that growth and improvement are a way of life; that one's role and one's competence are in a process of becoming and are not a static quality to be treated as given. Likewise, assume that the work can change and that each person doing the work can best see what can be done to improve it. Let the work in organizational community be an enjoyable puzzle that intrigues members and inspires them to be challenged in the task of meeting objectives and customer needs in new, refreshing and innovative ways.

Today there is much talk of a learning organization—the creation of a system that nourishes total learning so that each person not only adapts to changing requirements of the workplace environment but also generates new insights and understandings derived from their experience at work. "In a learning organization, leaders' roles differ dramatically from that of the charismatic decision maker. Leaders are designers, teachers and stewards These roles require new skills: the ability to build shared vision, to bring to the surface and challenge prevailing mental models, and to foster more systemic patterns of thinking. In short, leaders in learning organizations are responsible for 'building organizations' where people are continually expanding their capabilities to shape their future, that is, leaders are responsible for learning."[29]

Herman Miller, an office furniture company, Johnson and Johnson, the pharmaceutical company, Analog Devices, an electronics company in Massachusetts, and Motorola are examples of companies striving to implement these ideas. According to William Wiggenhorn of Motorola, "We are just beginning the pilot but we are already discovering how to learn as a team, number one; number two, how to hook up a team with other teams who are looking at the same issues; three, how to relay that learning to areas of the business outside of your own work area."[30] Summarizing the effort at Motorola and others, Charles Garfield reported that, "The focus of training and education in the team-based learning organization is on building relationships and developing processes rather than memorizing facts and learning set procedures . . . what is crucial to it is developing the teamwork and the creative thinking skills (i.e., the process) for identifying the tasks to be pursued and approaches to pursuing them. Motorola is coming to understand that, paradoxically, the key to solving practical problems is to focus on relationships rather than technical skills."[31]

9. No rule is sacred.   Remember that except for the essential human values which enhance individual dignity and further a healthy organizational environment, no rule is sacred.

Rules and policies are meaningless when promulgated, maintained and executed for their own sake—simply because they exist. They should only be formulated when they serve to fortify the underlying philosophy, values, and objectives of the organization. When exceptions are made or requested, the principle should be to ask "Why not?" instead of "Why?"

Through the direct and representational forums, each person can raise issues leading to a reformulation of the community's rules. Through doing one's work with others, each person may discover new ways, better ways, to meet his or her objectives and this behavior should be encouraged. The only tests should be their consistency with the purposes and philosophy of the community, and; whether or not they enhance the achievement of the goals of the workplace community in serving customer needs.

10. Assume there will be setbacks. The advent of change and progress means that problems and opportunities emerge from at least two sources—the dislocation of expectations from unwanted disruption of activity and the deliberate alteration of events. In a dynamic environment such as that facing postindustrial organizations where people are in a state of continual "process" it is impossible to expect any single state of being to remain intact for very long. Whether its alteration is a setback or another step toward improvement can only be determined by the interaction of events with the organizational processes in place to deal with them, the proactive capacity of individuals and the influence of the myriad forces emanating from within the organization and the external environment. The term solacracy symbolizes this fluidity, this organic, dynamic ever present motion of people in action in a crucible of ideas that is the post-industrial work community.

Adam Smith, the dean of capitalism, suggested, and countless economists have agreed, that in pursuing one's self interest, the quality of life for all is improved. In a material sense this has been true, to a point. After all we now enjoy the highest material standard of living the world has ever imagined. However, we have come up against the limits of the continued pursuit of self interest and have reached a point where catastrophe looms. Thus, to continue to pursue one's self interest is to do so at the direct expense of the society. Environmental deterioration today is perhaps the most obvious case of a society quickly approaching a catastrophic demise but the trail leading to this point of diminishing returns and impending catastrophe is marked at every turn by an artificial and organizational-centric technique of cost-benefit analysis that has led us to a precipice and not paradise.

We may come to a point where the values we espouse, and even those we practice, are severely tried, such as when we must act on our beliefs. Are we environmentalists? Do we think through our purchases to insure that they are consistent with our beliefs about need and waste? Do we recycle? Our behavior is the true test of each individual as it is of the organization.

Though we may weaken as individuals and sacrifice or compromise our values in the crunch, organizations may not be justified in doing so without at least allowing the entire membership to participate in the decision. At that point the community acts as one voice and yet it may, in its group deliberations, arrive at suitable alternatives to the violation of what are its sacred principles. In the case of a no lay off policy, one can imagine implementing several methods of handling the eventuality to avert the policy being reversed. For example, allow the membership to decide the criteria for disassociation. Or perhaps the company can have a development fund to finance satellite companies to draw off underutilized employees, or perhaps employees could be redeployed in some other productive manner, or everyone could consent to take a pay cut, or any number of alternatives that might be a suitable, even profitable, way of dealing with the issue.

Describing a process at Apple computer for nurturing the entrepreneurial impulse among employees that weren't satisfied with the mainline product development process, John Sculley, CEO said, "Because we believe that interdependencies—networks of smaller companies—are a major source of strength, we are spinning out from the Apple mothership new ideas, new business directions in the form of new companies."[32] He distinguished between a spinoff and a spinout: "A spinoff means 'goodbye and good luck'. It's the stripping off of assets that the corporate parent no longer has an interest in. Our spinouts will remain a vital part of the network of interdependencies around which the third-wave corporation garners its strength and flexibility. Rather than 'good bye and good luck', we're seeking a long term relationship with our spinouts because we believe they are essential to the success of the mother ship."[33] Faith in the participative process leads to unforeseen remedies and guarantees that at least people are treated with dignity and respect as they face the hard choices, together, as a community. IBM followed suit and ". . . slice(d) off a new unit to focus exclusively on developing and manufacturing PC hardware."[34] In this case the purpose was simply to free the PC unit from the IBM bureaucracy that impeded their competitiveness against faster acting rivals such as Compaq.

In a pluralistic society such as ours many companies are legitimately stymied by any social action since the diversity of values is so great at points they become contradictory. Furthermore, organizations per se, it is argued, are not the framers or disseminators of values; that task is left to religious, legislative and community bodies formed for that purpose. This has been true but is becoming invalidated as the organizational world and its impact on the society overwhelms all other institutions and their capacity to establish and maintain social consensus. Consider the vacilations of various political administrations, court decisions and public opinion. The public arena has not given a very clear picture to the corporate world of which way to go, yet one prevailing value throughout our history seems to have been the tendency to democratize our institutions.

Since you don't know what you don't know, both activities and processes must allow for innovation, clear benchmarks against which to gauge progress must be established. Resourcefulness, creativity and experimentation on all fronts are necessary to expand what one does know.

All journeys are fashioned after a dream and the ones that succeed are those which, in their prelude, develop and adhere to a body of principles which encourage everyone to behave with the knowledge that whatever happens when the dream becomes real, it becomes real for everyone and each was responsible.

MAKING IT WORK: ALIGNING STRUCTURE AND BEHAVIOR

Organizations are groups of people. Yet we attribute to them human characteristics. We can say, for example, that AT&T strives to convert its bosses into champions. But what is meant by that? What exactly is an AT&T? What entity is decreeing that bosses become champions, or design a policy about hiring minorities, or decide to move into new telephonic product manufacturing? There is a tendency to reify the people comprising the company; to objectify them as if they are something other than individuals with specific responsibilities. It is fallacious to think of the nature of a company as distinct from the people within it or that somehow, magically, AT&T decides anything while the individuals within the enterprise are powerless to influence the decisions.[35] It may be true that in conventional organizations, only a select number of people are in the decision-making arena and announce their decisions. But they are still individuals who must be held accountable for their actions. If work is bad, the relationships are bad between people; or if the rules, created by some people for others to follow, are objectionable, it is the people constituting the decision-making body who must be held accountable. For example, one must not be fooled into thinking it was an act of an entity called AT&T. All actions are perpetrated by individuals.

Mary is an operator at AT&T. Someone made up a rule that operators must raise their hand to go to the toilet, be acknowledged by their supervisor, and then return within an acceptable amount of time.[36] Is this the action of an AT&T or of Joe, Bob, Sally and others on the system's procedures team? In conventional organizational parlance it is an impersonal business decision. If AT&T could talk it might have said, "No offense Mary, but this is the most efficient way of running a business and as a human resource we need to deploy you in the most effective way possible. Pardon us for not consulting with you but, really, we know what's best and we really don't have time to discuss this with you."

There is no such person as AT&T though there is a legalism and an economic instrument of the same name. For Mary, AT&T is her boss and the rules she must follow—created by Joe in operations and Sara in personnel under pressure from Stan, a vice president for systems design. To the public AT&T is Mary getting a number for a customer, and the phone installer and a clear line to San Diego. The organization is ultimately one-on-one and an aggregate of the many relationships within the corporate entity. But what it does, it does as people making the decision to do so and we sometimes forget this and allow the corporate structure to absolve the individual from personal responsibility for the actions that are taken. Court cases resulting in convictions and low fines sometimes dismiss personal responsibility and perpetuate the myth of the corporation being distinct from people. It appears to exempt them from accountability. No organization has gone to jail (and so few corporate officers as to make criminal behavior virtually risk free); no organization has been subjected to capital punishment for the most heinous crimes against nature or mankind (marketing known carcinogens in the third world for example, or conspiring to meddle in the affairs of a sovereign government as ITT tried to do in Chile). "In Chile, where the ITT-owned utility faced nationalization, the company offered the CIA $1 million to fund a campaign to block the election of left-wing candidate Salvadore Allende for president. The offer was made by John McCone, former CIA director who happened to be a director of ITT."[37]

A community can't dismiss its responsibility. All policies, indeed all actions, are to be attributed to people or their representatives. In all cases people are accountable for actions taken in the name of the organization. Collective accountability may be required as when the business enters bankruptcy or makes a profit in which all share equally or to the extent of an agreed upon formula for the distribution of profits and losses. The perception of employee worth as represented solely by wages is changing. Employees' creativity and contribution to the bottom line is being viewed by many people as worth a proportion of sales, or profits in addition to wages. This change corresponds to the shift in perception of employees from being simply hired hands executing the wishes of management, to imaginative contributors to the bottom line in their own right.

Mary can rightly question the treatment she receives as being dehumanizing. She can rightly protest that she is diminished as a person in being considered merely a "human resource" to be deployed without being included in the process of designing her own work or the environment in which it will be conducted. She can rightly object to being considered a means to a corporate end without being treated with the slightest dignity or respect. In workplace communities that use a solacracy Mary is a vital part of the work team and participates in the process of defining her tasks and methods. She is a member of the community and is entitled to activate her membership through direct or representative means.

Workstation technology can either liberate Mary by freeing her from the supervisory tyranny of her "boss" and give her enhanced power to regulate her own work duties, or it can totally enslave her to a machine that never sleeps and has no sympathy for Mary or anyone else. Or the technology may simply replace Mary with a circuit board so she can do more interesting work for her customers.[38]

Structural Guidelines

So far we have looked at the usefulness of creating a philosophy to guide the establishment of a workplace community. It is also important to establish some guidelines for the development of an operating system and interpersonal relationships. Each of the following considerations should help provide the reader with a foundation upon which to build community.

1. Democratic behavior/expertise replaces autocratic behavior and displays of position power. Allow the group fundamental decision making prerogatives over the means to achieve their work, recruitment of new members, evaluation and assignment of each other, settling process issues among themselves and other matters particular to their work or group. Centralize those decisions which have universal application such as the value statement and also those decisions that benefit from the power of a uniform decision such as common purchases, the creation of the mission statement, and the overall strategic plans. Centralization, however, does not mean without representation from the work teams or subdivisions or that decisions made there are unquestioned. Whether or not the central authority can execute decisions, either alone or in consultation with other units, the body is accountable to the community. A board of representatives with fixed terms could meet for periodic review by the community as a whole. This is not unlike the operation of the board of directors but involves members from all parts of the community and is answerable to the community at general meetings. To centralize or not is a question of defining the work itself rather than simply a matter of assigning control to positions in a hierarchy.

This is being done at several levels. We have seen how the introduction of self-managing teams is working on the shop floor. Johnson & Johnson has decentralized its corporate structure as well to give its 166 chartered companies virtually complete independence. "Long before the rest of Corporate America made 'empowerment' a management buzzword, J&J was practicing it. . . . Because the company has been at it for more than 50 years, J&J has become a model of how to make decentralization work."[39]

In effect, consider the work group as self-managing, self optimizing, and capable of managing differences. Let compensation reflect both individual performance and group performance on a schedule that can be created for uniform application by a central accounting team or a representative body. The important point is that the group can be compensated in addition to the individuals and decide for itself how to distribute the amount or to utilize it as a group. Once again, the members themselves can determine these matters.

Infusing organizations with democratic principles is more involved than increasing the level of participation among members or guaranteeing their constitutional rights or being socially responsible, though it is all of these. It is striving to build an organization wherein participants are considered ends in themselves and where there is treatment of all stakeholders; employees, suppliers, customers, community and investors as if there was a "veil of ignorance" over us. As explained by philosopher DeGeorge[40] "behind that veil we would know that we are rational human beings and that we value our own good. But we would not know whether we are rich or poor, members of the upper or lower class, talented or untalented, handicapped or physically and mentally fit, white, black or a member of some other race, male or female, and so on. The question we are to ask ourselves is: what principles would we call just or fair if we did not know what place we would have in society? This technique is a useful one if we wish to achieve objectivity in our moral judgments." This is the kind of positive thinking underlying equal employment opportunity and diversity issues.

2. The individual is as important as the group. As in all democracies there is the threat of tyranny by the majority and for that reason voting opportunities should be carefully thought out. It may also be necessary to differentiate the kind of voting majorities required to implement changes. Quorums to determine the minimum participation in the process or particular voter percentages of one degree or another should be thought out to adequately complement the importance of the decisions to be made. On some issues it is conceivable that the individual would even have the right to veto a proposal made by the group. For example, should the group have the right to demand that everyone work overtime or regularly work on Saturday mornings? Should the group have the right to skip regular machine maintenance in order to reduce costs when operator safety may be sacrificed? One of the most controversial cases involving the right of the corporation to insist on individual compliance to a training program occurred at Pacific Bell ". . . until the state's public Utility Commission called a temporary halt to the practice—employees have been 'kroned,' indoctrinated in a mode of comprehending the world that owes its soul to the mystic Gurdjieff."[41] Finding the balance between individual autonomy and the right of a group to expect compliance will not be easy but where decisions are measured against fundamental, explicit, organizational values that have been jointly determined, fewer conflicts will arise.

For daily matters, develop consensus building skills, especially for use in the small work group teams and representational bodies. Remember consensus is not conformity it is independent assent for the good of the group. When the process runs smoothly there will be fewer and fewer divisive issues and members will feel comfortable that the group's decisions are reasonably determined.

Community building activities are necessary to bond the individuals to each other and to help them develop an underlying sense of the purpose to which they and the group are engaged. Consensus building activities depend on the strength of the individual's commitment to the group and should increase as the group evolves.

When people are considered ends in themselves—even while being instrumental for the success of the group—we develop the capacity for genuine relationships and the potential for synergy to occur. When we consider that each person is entitled to the same treatment and respect as ourselves, we open the way for a valuable source of creative input, accurate feedback and joint problem sensing-solving activity that extends our own ability to work effectively. This increases the organization's overall performance.

The individual being free to act and communicate honestly is relieved of the anxieties and fears of being wrong, displeasing others and losing face when sincerely working toward the group's objective. Relationships are collegial and collaborative rather than hierarchical by their nature and therefore they overcome the inhibitors to open creative interaction. One becomes an accepted part of a team and the burdens of building that team are shared by everyone.

To demonstrate respect for the individual include procedural rights of corporate citizenship such as the right to know and be kept informed; the opportunity to be heard and the right to appeal; the right to a community forum; also the right to be in the organization once selected, to have your needs considered and the right to help achieve the organization's goals.

Along with these rights establish due process systems to insure the individual receives a full and fair hearing regarding personal issues and disputes that reach an impasse in one's immediate workgroup. Federal Express has a system that guarantees each employee gets fair treatment. It is fittingly called GFT (Guaranteed Fair Treatment). It includes a five step process of hearings; the final panel includes the CEO.[42]

Control Data Corporation goes even further in democratizing the process. When an individual is in conflict with a policy or supervisor, he or she can appeal to an ombudsman, an independent mediator who is empowered to form a "peer panel" of Control Data employees to listen to the grievance and recommend actions to top management.[43]

3. Organizational control shifted to people with perspective of entire area of control and to task teams. Bureaucracy was a very innovative and democratizing influence in its infancy because it assured the citizenry of fair and impartial treatment from government—a virtue when applied even today. But bureaucracy is also a way of thinking that focuses on control with the mistaken belief that only rules and procedures, and not individual discretion, can facilitate the smooth operation of the system.

There is little incentive for the controllers to redesign the structure or processes of their organizations to enable a power shift to others. A power shift to self control is anathema to many people high in organizations who have sought power for its own sake and spent a career in acquiring it. Even though it is feasible to arrange and even though it will be vital to increase an organization's competitiveness in the future because decision making is faster when control is moved down the hierarchy, this shift will be resisted. As long as control is equated with power and if any alteration is perceived as a diminution of one's role in a system that has created power as a reward in its own right, resistance to fundamental change will be present.

It is not surprising that an elaborate protective control system will be imposed to protect the owner's financial interest and that it will remain in place to protect the interest of succeeding investors. And this is as it should be. We expect our financial interests to be prudently managed and protected from loss, involuntary risk and abuse by caretakers.

The broad concept of control, however, does not end with the protection of financial resources. Rather, it is a force which permeates all areas of human interaction within organizations because the very existence of people hints at a direct link between their presence and the ultimate financial performance of the organization. Hence, every aspect of the organization from decisions regarding financial allocations to procedures for operating a machine, reporting sick, applying vacation time, assigning overtime, etc., are viewed as essential owner/managerial prerogatives. In one sense that is accurate . Everything does have an influence, however obscure, on the productivity of the organization and is thus a justified concern of the guardians of the financial statements. But what had begun as a realistic safety precaution extended far beyond its usefulness to a point of diminishing returns as ever tighter and more accurate control systems began to stifle the very flexible entrepreneurial impulse which spawned the organizations in the first place.

The control function and responsibility is dispersed in solacracy; and, given the enormous power of computer technology, so too is authority. With the control process distributed throughout the organization questions arise regarding who has authority and how it is exercised. Traditionally, the control function was inseparable with the authority to carry it out. The ability to hire and fire, reprimand and penalize always rested with one's immediate boss who could, because of this power, expect obedience and loyalty.

The importance of a flexible, dispersed control system becomes evident when organizations realize that a strict harness on discretionary activity precludes effectiveness. Control through "process" at the team level is necessary for long run productivity since the process itself unlocks an individual's total abilities and creates understanding and commitment toward the group's goals and a desire to make it work.

In short, control is based on expertise and relevance to the work flow. It remains close to the teams and radiates only through the relevant network of associates that work together in the performance of their duties.

4. Means are as important as ends. Decisions affecting people are as important as those affecting profits. As the nature of work in the postindustrial age becomes more indefinite to the extent that people work with abstract information, symbols, and constructs, the process of doing work becomes replete with uncertainty and risk requiring the creative manipulation of data and the imaginative use of available resources. The process of achieving the organization's objective becomes as important, perhaps even more important, than the final product itself.

Take an insurance salesperson. Sounds simple. He or she studies the policies and sells them to potential clients on the basis of their actual benefits and perceived sense of security. But it isn't so simple. The customer has particular needs and raises numerous inquiries about exceptions. Is this item covered? What about the personal delay due to loss? Do I need to verify a loss against replacement purchasing costs or against depreciation schedules? and so on. The point is that while the salesperson might be able to answer many of these questions he or she is increasingly creating a personalized policy, even a totally new product in the case of customers with very special needs. But he or she can't do this alone. The salesperson's role, then, is linking the customer to the organization's resources. Actuaries, financial experts, assessors, special risk analyzers, marketing experts and others may all ultimately get involved. The issue for the organization then becomes not just the creation of a policy that it sends along with salespeople on their calls but developing a continuous process of meeting unique needs. When this becomes the standard way of behaving, as is increasingly the case, the process becomes as important as the product. In fact the product becomes the process.

It is this realization that propels the total quality movement. Virtually all processes, as has been pointed out by Deming, Crosby and others, focus on the flow of work and each person's contribution to the flow—the process itself.[44] The total customer service movement likewise focuses on the process for, indeed, the service is the process—and the "product" of one's efforts as in the case of the insurance salesman just mentioned.

Attention to the process of working together and meeting each others' needs in the organization on a continuous ad-hoc basis requires a totally new set of skills. Not only does one need the skill to perform his or her job but also the many skills required to work with one another cooperatively and collaboratively in the achievement of larger organizational goals. This requires attention to the processes of working together. The rapidly changing conditions of the business world make this necessary but organizations are finding they haven't been very well equipped to deal with this ability since their mental model of life in the corporate environment has been one of competitiveness, individuality and secretiveness.

One fundamental difference that sets apart traditional organizations from solacracies is that in a solacracy decisions affecting people and the process of working together are as important as those affecting the work itself. Indeed the process is the work. There is as much attention placed on process as there is on product. Getting cooperation and collaboration and working out any differences that arise in the process are crucial. Training and reinforcement with ample opportunities for thoughtful feedback become a way of doing business, not an exception.

Though "time is money" and the propensity in traditional organizations is not to "waste" time with activity that doesn't directly contribute to producing its output, the post-industrial era organization recognizes that sometimes you have to invest time to make time. Planning and deliberation are needed to assure the right courses of action and to reduce risks faced in an uncertain environment.

In addition to planning, there is also a great deal of time spent on making teams work well. Because so much of the work done in a solacracy requires sound interpersonal relationships among peers, professional colleagues and individuals on a cooperative, collaborative basis, the quality and effectiveness of the output is directly related to how well people get along with, understand and inspire one another. Cooperation takes time to develop fully and it requires the continual exchange of feedback useful to the team building process. This attention to process is the human analog to preventive maintenance and care given to machines and computers.

The functions of management are no longer solely assigned to select individuals. Coordinators and facilitators initially guide the interactions of team members toward achieving their work and each member eventually contributes to the management of the team. Without paying attention to the process, relationships are not only distant but the available personal resources and their respective talents would be unknown. With immediate or frequent interaction in working relationships, assets are fully utilized, a team can readily develop, and managerial vision becomes clear.

On a deeper level, the treatment of individuals, as individuals and not just part of a work related process, is vital. Individuals must be treated with respect, as ends in themselves. This point needs reiteration because when we are caught up in the work flow we often forget this and demand total compliance and subordination to the project; sometimes at great personal sacrifice. Tracy Kidder made this point eloquently in his dramatic account of the development of a new computer in *Soul of a New Machine*.[45] In the end the team broke under the stress as just so many particles in the production process. Who would commit or recommit to this pressure again? How can a company sustain its own growth under such circumstances? Though stress often comes with the territory and there are always moments when people are asked to give all they've got, they too need maintenance and reassurance that their role was worth it, not just for the company or work group but for themselves as well.

5. Everything is considered tentative. The processes of organizing become the organization. The processes must evolve to reflect the changes within the organization as well as to adapt the organization to new external contingencies. This is all the more true in solacracy because the boundaries of any task structure or team are not easily identified. The interaction of tasks, knowledge and people require processes that are flexible and responsive to rapid change. Hence, the admonition to consider everything tentative is to recognize that, except for the bedrock principles governing the organization, the organization should be in a position to recreate itself as needed.

To suggest that everything should be considered tentative is to remind participants in solacracy that all action must serve an identifiable purpose and that all processes, objectives and tasks should make sense; should serve to move the organization toward its goals. When it becomes apparent that rules are followed or goals pursued or processes carried out simply because they are in place, and not because of their furtherance of organizational or individual ends, they should be changed. When they no longer can be identified with furthering the group's achievements or morale, they must be abandoned.

6. Process is malleable. "Assume that there are processes which create, maintain and dissolve social collectives, that these processes constitute the work of organizing, but the ways in which these processes are continually executed are the organization."[46] The processes governing planned activities and relationships must be sufficiently elastic to account for the vagaries of actual behavior, random events and individual/group differences. This is particularly true in solacracy because "The more widely the freedom to initiate change is spread, the more difficult it becomes to control the outcome."[47] In solacracy, since teams are the basic decision making units (either independently or linked to others), the intention of processes should be to channel activity and knowledge toward appropriate goals. Keeping it malleable assures responsiveness. Remember all decision making is based on incomplete information. One can never know enough and all data is historical by its nature—it is gathered from the past about the past. No matter how much information one has, the decision itself is a step off into uncertainty—the future.

One needs therefore to develop certain intuitive powers and the confidence to use them in addition to available data. Data provides us with a tangible representation of ideas and appears to be real as in "hard data," yet we sometimes deceive ourselves since the so-called data, especially in the social sciences, aggregates human perceptions and is, thus, only a vague approximation of reality; often based on a construct which itself may be inaccurate, such as is frequently the case with survey data, public opinion data, focus group data, and projections from past behavior. Of course, it would be more helpful to develop group based intuition as well so that the task teams can get "a feel" for the direction of the group and what would constitute the best course of action. Combining best data with best feel makes a lot of sense since the more information one has to base a decision the more likely it will be to succeed.[48]

Given that workstation technology linked to information networks will put all the information one needs at their instantaneous disposal, and people will be intellectually highly capable throughout the organization, being able to use that information and to distill it becomes that much more important. It also means that managers or coordinators will need to focus their attention on deriving meaning from the vast amounts of data and develop the ability to access and share knowledge throughout the work flow process even though ubiquitous data flows directly into each workstation. The workstation becomes a node in the organizational conversation as individuals discuss the uses of the information with one another in the electronic corridors of their community.

Process of work and the flow of information/cooperation through the organization replaces the idea of an assembly line. Process is everything. It must be designed and maintained in order that the individual can routinely perform to his or her best, that the organization accomplishes its goals, that people and products/services can adapt to market needs, and that all the while the organization can learn from experience.

In this way the organization must continually recreate itself as needed in order to meet changing conditions and invigorate its interpersonal processes. This assures responsiveness to markets and employees.

7. Creativity and individual resourcefulness as a way of being replaces slavish compliance to rules and precedent. When individuals are empowered, ideas can be created and implemented as a response to a perceived opportunity and to the needs of others in the community. Decentralization and personal or task team decision-making discretion stimulate empowerment.

One may look at organizations from a variety of perspectives. Solacracy can be viewed as the product of the accumulated output of each person. Most individuals in a post-industrial organization will find a larger portion of their activity requiring creativity, initiative, and resourcefulness. Circumstances such as random and rapid change stimulate each team to develop entrepreneurial behavior. This is true since ends may sometimes be only vaguely understood while there might be a limitless number of means to achieve them. An analogy with "blind man's bluff" wouldn't be far off in describing this new environment.

8. Work is designed in complete packets.   Industrial era organizations subdivided work into its smallest units. This division of labor was an attempt to make work as efficient as possible and to reduce the level of skill needed by an organization to as low a level as possible to minimize labor costs. From a managerial point of view, the efforts were quite successful. From an employee's point of view, work became more and more unsatisfying and, eventually, alienating. This process of atomizing work proceeds from two managerial needs: First, to reduce dependence on the work force as much as possible, and; second, to control costs by being as efficient as possible. In a static system where labor is a hired hand, this made sense. In a dynamic system where labor activates its mental power and adds value in the work flow process, this doesn't make sense.

Rather than fixing a person to the smallest possible discrete task, tasks are pooled and individuals share duties. If working on a subcomponent is absolutely necessary, rotation is utilized to expose the individual to the various parts to help her or him comprehend and work on the whole. In addition, work teams are terminals or nodes of action in the work flow and become the basis of the organizational structure. Fixed job descriptions or functional departments are eliminated in favor of product or service groups or even customer response groups. It isn't important to use only one structure but the structure should facilitate the work flow process in terms of specific output objectives and not just categories of tasks. There are many examples of this today. For example, Indiana Bell "faced a ruinous turnover rate among employees who compiled the company's telephone directories. The job had been divided into 17 separate tasks, from scheduling the work to proofreading, and each worker performed a single task. Under the job enrichment program, each worker was given an entire directory to compile—and turnover plunged."[49]

In solacracy work is designed in units or packets of useful assignments to each team. The team divides work among each of its members. Jobs aren't fixed but are based on the demands of the project and eventually will be dictated by the requirements of individual customers. Individuals share and/or rotate duties according to principles of equity, skill, reward and interest. Each team determines how the specific work will be assigned. Totally undesirable tasks may be rotated equally or assigned to the week's poorest performer. Some tasks may be given as rewards or to those with the unique skill to complete them. Others may be assigned or reassigned simply to avoid boredom. The main point is teams are the basic unit necessary to complete a goal. They break down each goal into a course of action and assign each member of the team to an activity that will attain the goals.

Teams link together with others as a network and are always designed so each serves a necessary objective. It completes a task that each member can understand and identify with even though it in itself may be a sub-component of a larger entity.

The organization takes the form of a flow chart with two tracks of activity. The first is output directed ending with the product delivery or the performance of a customer service. The second track is maintenance of the organization which includes both attention to the internal needs of the organization as well as its processes required for the maintenance of stakeholder relationships. Conspicuously absent from such an organization chart is a reporting relationship based on the distance one is from the owners. Traditionally that chain of command has represented the flow and degree of power and only tangentially the accomplishment of the organization's purpose.

The overall design of the organization should be brought in line with the flow of work from resources to product or service delivery to the customer. Work teams should be formed along the route which will serve as the basis for the solacratic structure. The following chart demonstrates the relationships in a solacracy.

In solacracy, the hierarchy of power is considerably reduced as each person, as part of a team, serves either of only two possible major purposes. The interdependence of teams is managed through a negotiating process where team coordinators, or group representatives function to resolve conflict and allocate resources. The fluidity of people is exemplified by their serving in a variety of capacities in their work teams.

9. All activity of the organization is subject to stakeholder review. All stakeholders are either directly or indirectly represented at the organizational level when issues of governance arise. Ongoing representative bodies work on issues and represent the mixed constituencies providing a forum for all who wish to participate. Problem solving councils are created as the need arises to address emergent issues, future objectives.

All of the housekeeping functions of management devolve to the members themselves. An elected position such as superintendent, mayor, or director is created to organize this.

Personal problem solving opportunities may be handled by colleagues trained in mediation and process observation skills at the request of anyone at anytime. An ombudsman's office would be fruitful for this purpose. That office would also handle all organizational level conflict from any stakeholder and establish forums so the community could discuss and consider issues of organizational social responsibility, among other issues.

EXHIBIT 6–1
One Example of Solacracy

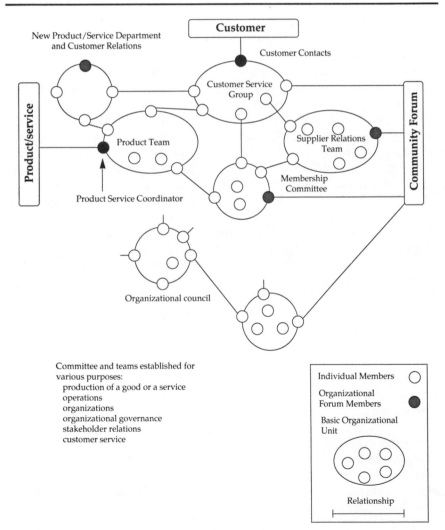

10. Establish Community Forums. When the transformation of American organizations takes place it will occur with a speed that will amaze many people but it too will be a confirmation of what has already occurred to huge numbers of people throughout the country as holistic thinking replaces the traditional orthodoxy.

Unlike fads and panaceas that come and go, solacracy is a complete revision of a system and is internally consistent making it a suitable organizational alternative compatible with the coming transformation. It represents a structure that the transformation will require to align societal changes to the organizational world.

Because it is a systemic change focusing on power sharing with built-in sustained reinforcement through continual process observation, its chances for success are higher than other management programs that depend on the benevolence of top managers. When a program depends on benevolence, it can be reversed just as easily and one's successors can undermine the program at will. Witness how companies are turned upside down as the founders retire. Thus, solacracy isn't just another transient search for excellence, it is the joint creation of excellence based on an irreversible foundation.

No matter how the transformation emerges, however, organizations will require the development of forums for the discussion of the changes that need to be implemented and how to best go about doing it. These forums of representative parties will be important to insure that all people are kept informed as well as to adequately represent the entire membership.

A fundamental aspect of the transformation is the creation of a constitutional framework that separates the governance function of the community from its commercial function. People serving in either the governance and commercial roles are, however, similarly accountable to the members of the community and the constitutional framework establishes the duties to be performed, the powers of important positions and the process of selecting and removing position holders. The constitution also establishes representative bodies to consider and mediate strategic commercial issues as they impact on the community. For example, a decision to drop one line of production or to close a plant and to purchase another facility would impact the members directly and should be dealt with in a manner that reflects the community's interests as a whole.

This principle isn't unheard of in corporate America. According to John Clancy, formerly president of McDonnell Douglas's CAD/CAM Company and now CEO of Valisys Corporation, "our management is very explicit about the decisions it makes, and as with the US Constitution, all other decisions devolve to the employees themselves."[50] Not a major structural change but the awareness is there. The transformation has reached the top of some companies.

CREATING SOLACRACY

Necessity is often the mother of invention, necessity can also cause the redistribution of power. If financial catastrophe is near companies are very receptive to instantaneous change. It is at those moments when a hostile takeover is threatened or the company is facing bankruptcy that what otherwise would be considered outlandish notions become quite reasonable. Many companies such as Weirton Steel (7,000 employees), National Steel and Shipbuilding (4,000 employees), Textileather, and Adrian Fabricators[51] have been bought by employees at times like these and solacracy would be appropriately introduced then as well. Needless to say, if you are a CEO you could begin exploring the appropriateness of solacracy for your organization now without having to wait for a calamity to occur.

Usually, the change process proceeds from the perception that there is a serious problem, that life in the organization could be better, that something is wrong. Productivity, morale, profits may be suffering. Markets may have shifted quickly, turnover may be unacceptable, new ideas are few and far between. These and other kinds of circumstances provide the motivation for change. How extensive the change will be is, of course, a function of the seriousness of the problems. As the transformation of consciousness continues apace, individuals will be seeking opportunities to make significant changes in their work lives and these kinds of problems may really turn out to be symptoms of the changing consciousness among the work force.

Once there is a sense that things could be better and people feel that they would be willing to take responsibility for making them better, there is a climate for development. Organizational surveys to discern the climate and the disparity between what exists and what people would prefer to improve the operational health of the company, could serve as the starting point for a discussion for the need to change. Exploring each person's perception of the problem and their willingness to get involved would be a fruitful beginning.

Hold work group discussions about solacracy and its implications regarding the new way of running an organization and people's willingness to become capable of working in a solacracy. Helping people to deal with their fears will be beneficial to all concerned. Safeguard all jobs. Those that are totally unwilling to participate or are unable to overcome their fears should not be forced to, but they should not be allowed to block the program either. Assignment to a job or role that respects the individual's rights but doesn't interfere with the change process would be desirable. One novel approach to dealing with employees' fear of change is to assign a tutor to individuals to help them through the process. Florida Power and Light does this for their managers who have difficulty learning new management skills and TRW ties pay and promotions to employees ability to change as an incentive to do so.[52] On occasion the removal of people may be necessary but should be done in a fashion that allows for their smooth outplacement. Fair treatment and respect are essential. Use a recommitment exercise periodically to renew the mutual commitment throughout the change process.

Current organizational structures and policies need to be examined to discover how they interfere with solacratic principles and recommendations for change need to be proposed. All employees need to be involved to the extent of their willingness and ability. Task forces should be composed of sectional representatives of all existing levels and interests.

To build on this beginning it would be useful to continue the process of gathering data and feedback from a wide cross section of the organization. The development of a solacracy follows a flexible framework to account for the interests and insights of the community and each community will have unique needs and priorities. To conduct these exploratory sessions and build toward an agenda for change is a worthwhile exercise but it must culminate in the implementation of resolutions developed by the community itself. Remember, there is nothing worse than beginning a powerful process like this and reneging on it or reversing it.

HOW DO YOU KNOW WHEN YOU'RE THERE?

Solacracy should result in simplicity, completeness (robustness, elegance), the ability to adjust to new contingencies.[53] It should also test all innovations against the total pragmatism test: does it work for individuals as well as the organization as a whole? And it should pass the communicability test: can you get people to see it, to know it, and to do it? Each community will add its own criteria such as: Do we enjoy a low stress work environment and is it fun?[54] or, How well is it implementing social service policies such as EEO or the adoption of safety standards?

In any case, have faith in the process and in the people in your organization to be willing and able to make a constructive difference in their work lives. And then begin.

NOTES

[1] B. Zablocki, *Joyful Community* (Baltimore, MD: Penguin, 1973), p. 59.

[2] F. Capra, *The Tao of Physics* (New York: Bantam, 1980).

[3] C. Garfield, *Second to None* (Homewood, IL: Business One Irwin, 1991).

[4] L. Vesio, "The Renaissance Manager," *AT&T Journal*, March 89, pp. 4–10.

[5] M. Moskowitz, R. Levering and M. Katz, *Everybody's Business* (New York: Doubleday, 1990), p. 223.

[6] *Business Systems Direction Statement* (Stamford, CT: Pitney Bowes Business Systems, 1989).

[7] Remarks by the company's founder, Rinaldo S. Brutoco as a panel member, "The Corporation as a Vehicle for Personal and Planetary Transformation in the 1990's" at the San Jose *Whole Life Expo*, September 14, 1991.

[8] See G. S. Crystal, *In Search of Excess: The Overcompensation of American Executives* (New York: Norton, 1991).

[9] M. Moskowitz, R. Levering. and M. Katz, *Everybody's Business* (New York: Doubleday, 1990), p. 470.

[10] Ibid.

[11] J. O'Toole, *Vanguard Management* (New York: Berkley, 1987), p. 88.

[12] M. Dunahee and L. Wangler, "The Psychological Contract: A Conceptual Structure for Management/Employee Relations," *Personnel Journal*, July 1974. p. 518.

[13] J. Rawls, *A Theory of Justice* (Cambridge, MA: 1971), p. 60.

[14] E. Eve, "Social Contracts: The Oral and Written Law," *Handbook for Scientific Utopianism* (San Francisco: Kerista, 1988), p. 46.

[15] J. H. Dobrzynski, "Chairman and CEO: One Hat Too Many," *Business Week*, November 18, 1991, p. 124.

[16] Levi Strauss & Co.'s Aspiration Statement as reprinted in: R. Howard, "Values Make the Company: An Interview with Robert Haas," *Harvard Business, Review* September/October 1990, pp. 133–44.

[17] *Fortune Magazine*, October 8, 1990.

[18] J. C. Hyatt, "GE Is No Place For Autocrats, Welch Decrees," *Wall Street Journal*, March 3, 1992, p. B1.

[19] A. Maslow, *Eupsychian Management: A Journal* (Homewood, IL: Richard D. Irwin, 1965).

[20] C. Barnard, *The Functions of the Executive* (Cambridge, MA: Harvard University, 1948); D. MacGregor, *The Human Side of Enterprise* (New York: McGraw-Hill, 1960); R. Likert, *The Human Organization* (New York: McGraw-Hill, 1967); P. Drucker, *The Concept of the Corporation* (New York: John Day, 1972); Herzberg, et.al., *The Motivation to Work* (New York: John Wiley & Sons, 1959); C. Argyris, *The Individual and the Organization* (New York: Harper and Row, 1957).

[21] R. Levering, M. Moskowitz and M. Katz, *The 100 Best Companies to Work for in America* (Reading, MA: Addison-Wesley, 1984), p. 145.

22 A. Maslow, *Eupsychian Management* (Homewood, IL: Dow Jones Irwin, 1965).

23 P. Bernstein, "The Trust Culture," *SAM Advanced Management Journal*, Summer 1988, p. 5.

24 R. Levering, *A Great Place To Work* (New York: Avon, 1988), p. 214.

25 J. Huey, "America's Most Successful Merchant," *Fortune*, September 23, 1991, p. 54.

26 W. Harman, and J. Hormann, *Creative Work* (Indianaplois, IN: Knowledge Systems, Inc., 1990), p. 173.

27 "How the Workers Run Avis Better," *Fortune*, December 5, 1988, p. 106.

28 A. Tofler, *Power Shift* (New York: Bantam, 1990).

29 P. Senge, *The Fifth Discipline: The Art and Practice of the Learning Organization* (New York: Doubleday/Currency, 1990). Excerpted in "The Leader's New Work: Building Learning Organizations, *Sloan Management Review*, Fall 1990, pp. 7–23.

30 C. Garfield, *Second to None* (Homewood, IL: Business One Irwin, 1992), pp. 234–35.

31 Ibid., p. 235.

32 J. Sculley, *Odyssey: Pepsi to Apple* (Glasgow, Scotland: Fontana, 1990), p. 525.

33 Ibid. p. 529.

34 "Stand Back, Big Blue—And Wish Me Luck," *Business Week*, August 17, 1992, p. 99.

35 One of the first theorists to recognize this was Karl Weick. See: K. Weick, *The Social Psychology of Organizations* (Reading, MA: Addison-Wesley Publishing, 1979).

36 This was actually the case contributing to a stress epidemic at the Bell System companies in the early 80s. See R. Howard, "Drugged, Bugged and Coming Unplugged," *Mother Jones*, August 1981, p. 41.

37 M. Moskowitz, R. Levering, and M. Katz, *Everybody's Business* (New York: Doubleday, 1990), p. 561.

38 S. Zuboff, *In The Age of the Smart Machine* (New York: Basic Books, 1988).

39 J. Weber, "A Big Company That Works," *Business Week*, May 4, 1992, p. 125.

40 DeGeorge, *Business Ethics* (Englewood Cliffs, NJ: Prentice Hall, 1981), p. 67.

41 D. L. Kirp and D. S. Rice, "Fast Forward-Styles of California Management," *Harvard Business Review*, January-February 1988, p. 81.

42 Reported by R. Levering, in: *A Great Place to Work* (New York: Avon Books, 1988), p. 64.

43 J. O'Toole, *Vanguard Management* (New York: Berkley Books, 1987), p. 128.

44 W. E. Deming, *Out of the Crisis* (Cambridge, MA: Massachusetts Institute of Technology, Center for Advanced Engineering Study, 1986); P. B. Crosby, *Quality is Free* (New York: Mentor, 1979).

45 T. Kidder, *Soul of A New Machine* (Boston: Little, 1981).

46 According to K. Weick, *The Social Psychology of Organizations* (Reading, MA: Addison-Wesley Publishing, 1979).

[47] D. Ewing, *Freedom Inside the Organization* (New York: McGraw-Hill, 1977).

[48] The use of intuition in management is gaining considerable attention. Dr. Weston H. Agor currently coordinates the Global Intutition Network headquartered in El Paso, TX. This is an outgrowth of his early work: W. Agor, *Intuituive Management* (Englewood Cliffs, NJ: Prentice Hall, 1984).

[49] D. Cordtz, "Listening to Labor," *Financial World,* September, 3, 1991, p. 46.

[50] Comments as a panel member, "The Corporation as a Vehicle for Personal and Planetary Transformation in the 1990's" at the San Jose, CA, *Whole Life Expo,* September 14, 1991.

[51] Source: National Center for Employee Ownership, Oakland, CA.

[52] M. E. McGill, *American Business and the Quick Fix* (New York: Henry Holt, 1988), p. 74.

[53] A. Low, *Zen and Creative Management* (New York: Playboy Paperbacks, 1976), p. 104.

[54] Digital Equipment Company was one of the first companies to explicity identify fun as a worthwhile corporate goal. Among other objectives their statement advocates: self-direction, growth and development, openness, taking responsibility and respect of differences.

Chapter Seven

New Organization, New Skills: Working in Community

". . . industrialists could hardly have done better at creating an antihuman work situation if they had deliberately set out to do so. Man has put himself in his own zoo. He has so simplified his life and stereotyped his responses that he might as well be in a cage."

—Edward E. Hall[1]

If we attempt to grow alone we assure that the oppressiveness of the system eventually will close in around us. If we grow together, the system itself must change.

—Melvin Gurtov[2]

The rash of mergers and acquisitions followed by divestitures and downsizing that has swept through Corporate America has been the catalyst for massive and unexpected changes in the way people work. Reorganization combined with the influences of major environmental forces already at work are propelling organizations into a postmanagerial era. And, as we have seen, that will mean a transformation of our organizations.

As organizations change, their members need to develop and practice new skills and understand the kinds of barriers that will stand in the way of fully implementing them. To that end, this chapter explains some of the fundamental skills required of all individuals in the new organization and some of the underlying assumptions about working together.

The new focus on self-coordination instead of external management control will require the political skills (in the positive sense) of negotiating, compromise, cooperation, and accurate, supportive, interpersonal communication. Thus, each person needs an opportunity to learn and practice new skills and to be organized to use them advantageously.

In the wake of corporate reorganizing and the utilization of new time-saving information technologies, we have seen the hierarchy of the industrial era give way to networks. Chaparral Steel is an example of what's happening. "To become the world's low-cost producer, (CEO Gordon Forward) focused on three ideas: the classless corporation, universal education, and freedom to act."[3] The functions of middle management are being rapidly transferred to the shop floor. As *Fortune* reported, "In return for extraordinary freedom and trust, workers are expected to take the initiative, use their heads, and get the job done."[4]

As middle management is eliminated and self-managed work teams absorb its responsibility, top management's role will be confined to external affairs, particularly environmental scanning, securing financing and liaising with regulatory bodies and investors. Management of the internal operations of the organization devolve more and more to the self-managed teams and their representative bodies.

The coming transformation isn't just a matter of restructuring our organizations nor will it simply be the result of a power struggle. There are many skills to be developed in order for the post-managerial era and community to succeed. In this chapter, several new aspects of managing people are identified and then crucial managerial skills are outlined. The individual is clearly the focus here. Everyone must be considered a manager since community and the solacratic structure require universal basic managerial competence in order to be an effective part of the new era. Workers in community become organizational citizens, each needing to have the skills necessary to live up to one's new responsibilities.

Taking a proactive role in readying the organization for the transformation can utilize the power of the evolutionary forces already at work. There is much to consider in preparing for the change. From the organizational perspective, norms, procedures, evaluation and compensation systems, the manner of hiring and promoting individuals, distributing authority, the degree of competitiveness and cooperativeness, the definition and demarcation of tasks and roles, morale, attitudes, quality of contributions, quantity of ideas, and customer satisfaction with service are all examples of organization level intangibles and they are becoming more important as the information/service era replaces the industrial era. All of these aspects of organizational behavior can be measured and used as a starting point for performance improvement.

From the individual's perspective, all experience in an organization is fraught with a personal interpretation which may be inaccurate. How do members of an organization perceive:

- their role?
- the expectations others have of them?
- the quality of their performance?
- the effectiveness of the relationships they have with others?
- the fairness of situations they face?
- the real commitment to missions, strategies and objectives?

All of these dimensions, and many others, are intangible aspects of one's workplace experience. And they are all aspects of organization life that will need concerted personal attention by everyone in the community. In order to fruitfully deal with these issues, each member will need to learn new skills as well as new ways of looking at their responsibilities.

This need is dramatized by the fact that the new, solacratic communities now emerging create a volatile personal montage of impressions, feelings and abilities as roles and responsibilities change and impact on others and the situation. We produce our own reality yet the group must deal with it, and that of others, in an aggregate fashion in order to create an effective operating team. What we perceive is largely created through interactional processes. These intangibles of our relationships at work influence both our relationships with people and the work we perform. They will play an increasingly important role in the postindustrial era simply because the nature of work itself is becoming group centered around complex tasks. This requires extraordinary efforts to maintain alignment among all participants.

There is another compelling reason to examine these issues and to prepare the organization to develop a continuous process to deal with them: the rising cost of errors, the increasing speed required to satisfy customers and the demands of a competitive marketplace all add up to enormous pressure on the individual to do more in less time. The epidemic levels of stress now sweeping the country accounts in part for the highest level of accidents at work. Northwestern National Life Insurance questioned a random sample of 600 U.S. workers. "Almost half (46%) said their jobs were highly stressful; 34% said they felt so much stress they were thinking of quitting."[5]

The major causes of stress are controllable; they stem from the workplace environment and supervisors. Once the organization is conceptualized as a singular, inclusive, community and individuals are truly empowered with the skills to deal with these issues and to confront their supervisors about their behavior, the workplace becomes more productive and less stressful. As M. Scott Peck reminds us, "It is not impractical to consider seriously changing the rules of the game when the game is clearly killing you."[6]

ESTABLISHING THE LEARNING AGENDA: EVERYONE IS A MANAGER IN THE WORKPLACE COMMUNITY

When Toto pulled the curtain on the wizard of Oz to reveal just a rather frail grandfatherly figure, the awesome bluff and bluster that scared the intrepid threesome immediately evaporated. Dorothy, the Lion, and the Tin Man, discovered that they had the powers they sought all along. Pulling the curtain was the end of dependence and fear. It was the realization that one must take responsibility for oneself in life and that most of our fears and dependencies are unnecessary.

The revelation of latent powers within, and the misplaced dependence on others showed the Lion that he already had courage and the Tin Man that he had a heart. We can achieve our goals and take responsibility for ourselves. Our cultural traditions have validated this for over three hundred years. It has been our history. It is more than mildly ironic that as we take pride in our individualism we are so ready to surrender it to others in the workplace. Of course it may be easy to do and convenient to do but over the long run it diminishes our sense of self. Once we realize our capabilities it is a small step to imagine how great our organizations could become. As organizations evolve into communities and follow the path of equitable involvement and mutual commitment, this energy will be released. Finding the power within and between each of us and the courage to understand what is in our shared best interests and to live accordingly is the challenge of cooperative action. The following issues are important for each community to grapple with. They establish the learning agenda for the skills that we will need to develop.

First, however, let's look at the power of a work team building community; it is representative of the transformation now underway. The example reported here is taking place at Lesher Communications, a printing company in Walnut Creek, California that produces four daily newspapers including the Northern California edition of the New York Times and other publications. They began a sociotechnical systems change that eventually resulted in the creation of self-managing work teams in their new printing plant. It started out simply enough. The company was keeping up with new technology and modernizing some printing processes. But they also took the opportunity to increase productivity through employee involvement.

They created a situation of which they are quite proud. Twenty-seven people are now doing what it takes almost 260 people to accomplish in their other traditionally managed plant. These numbers aren't nearly telling the whole story. What has happened is that people who performed narrow, closely supervised jobs before are now, after extensive training, taking the entire responsibility for the plant's performance. Middle managers jobs were basically eliminated as their functions were assumed by the workers at the new plant. The employees learned all the jobs necessary and decided all issues surrounding payroll, scheduling, hiring, vacations, troubleshooting production problems, mediating team process issues and deciding how they would do their work. To do this they created a continuous learning organization where each employee by taking responsibility for the plant's output willingly commits him or herself to learning all they need to know to effectively execute their responsibilities.

Some dramatic innovations are practiced by the members of this self-managing team. Besides handling all the traditional middle management functions leaving middle managers to train, facilitate, and plan, the workers themselves elect members of their hiring committee which interviews, screens, tests, and selects their colleagues. Conduct, absenteeism and discipline issues are also settled by the workers by representatives they select. And, they elect members to their own safety committee. The point here is that former hourly workers are now making all decisions related to the work of the new plant and are heavily involved in its governance processes. This is a dramatic turn about. Many of the points that follow reflect the essence of what occurred at Lesher. Each company, however, must decide for itself how to approach each step as it begins the journey toward self-managing teams and beyond them to community. Ultimately this breathes new life into organizations and facilitates the evolution of the community model of organizing. The evidence is very clear that it works; that people can and do rise to the occasion and that once they taste this kind of effectiveness there is no going back to the old mindset. Those days are fast on their way out. The task that lies ahead is to refine the process and extend it to everyone; to fully transform the entire organization to reflect the values and practices established in leading edge self-managing work teams.[7] And then move toward community.

This scenario is only the beginning of the breakthrough toward System Five and workplace community. Once these forces are set in motion they perpetuate further innovation and the evolution toward paradigm two continues apace. The issues you will grapple with include:

1. Perpetuating a vision.   Organizations need to pursue the realization of a vision or mission. Typically, a leadership function has been to formulate the vision and inspire employees to buy into it. In community, members formulate the vision and nudge one another toward its realization.

Getting people together in visioning and strategic planning exercises requires group meeting and facilitation skills in an open trusting environment. The organization must prepare for this and train members in these skills before beginning the exercises.

By jointly creating a shared vision the organization begins to establish a "psychogogic" environment—one which makes well people grow toward self-actualization; of developing an organization focused on growth needs, not deficiency needs.[8] Individuals as members of the community share in the act of creation; they establish their own sense of purpose.

2. Reward long-term and holistic thinking.   Given our extremely high rate of mobility (almost 20 percent of all households move each year) and a short-term mentality due in part to living in a hyper-stimulated society, it is unrealistic to expect that the long-term will be considered without providing an incentive. Changing compensation and reward packages may be one way to help executives focus on the long-term. Even fractional long term thinking may pay off, that is, when short-term changes are assessed against their usefulness in achieving long-term goals. In a fast paced highly competitive world it may even be contradictory, perhaps dangerous, to expect people or companies to be solely concerned with long-term objectives when immediate demands must be met creatively.

Measuring our performance in ever shorter units of time creates an obsession with the short term. This has resulted in an increasing number of demands requiring a virtually instantaneous response from us. When processes are in place to assure that we are considering long term interests, a measure of stability returns to our daily affairs. Team reviews of demands may help alleviate the stress from letting the demands constantly drive the work of the group. One way of gaining a measure of control over the temptation to focus solely on the short-term is to frequently examine long-term implications. Hewlett Packard, for example, does not pursue contracts that require hiring short-term employees because they want to assure employment to the greatest extent possible. This simple policy helps them focus on long term goals.[10]

One obvious model of a successful approach to long-term stability and short-term flexibility is the US constitution. It is a long-term document; the structure and processes of governance and individual rights are defined. But it allows for short-term influences and contingencies to be dealt with through the execution of the administrative, legislative and judicial processes. It is flexible enough to be interpreted and used in accordance with the demands of the times.

Typically, corporations have not structured themselves as well as the U.S. Constitution. Instead they have remained totally malleable with a "bias toward action" that has an apparent immediate link to the bottom line and investor interests. The bias for action, however, too frequently sacrifices employees in the name of what is good for the management and in so doing jeopardizes the future of the organization by destroying employees' will to sacrifice for the common good. So the short term often looks good at the expense of the future.

A systems analysis to determine how the organization rewards short term thinking is important to determine where change is needed. Asking how systems contribute to the mission of the organization keeps all apparent short-term tasks focused on the long-term future, the purpose of the community.

3. Leadership.   The leadership fetish that has swept this country in recent years is testament to the power of conventional organizations to keep us locked in dependency on a "superior" person; see management myths one and two. If we continue to define leadership as a personal skill that few of us have or can develop or that it is an organizational asset that requires only one or two of us to possess, we are limiting our potential. Have traditional organizations ever considered the possibility that leadership can be a shared function? A widely dispersed talent? That if we give people responsibility they can become "leaders" by virtue of executing those responsibilities?

Just as the "Santa Claus" myth survives among children, adults want to believe in a wise, visionary "leader" to guide them. When Toto pulled the curtain it was Dorothy that was thrown into a bout with Twentieth century angst. She was despondent when the power of the wizard was revealed to be just a displacement for her own personal strength. Eventually she recovered from the setback and with the human scale advice of the ex-wizard (as mentor) was able to make her way home.

It is not leadership from any one person that is required, it is an aspect of leadership each of us summons from within. In this respect, the same qualities we have sought in one person can be found distributed among many people who learn, in community, to exercise their "leadership" at appropriate moments. This occurs when people are vitally concerned about issues or when executing their responsibilities. Leadership thus becomes a rather fluid concept focusing on those behaviors which propel the work of the group forward.

Fortunately, we do distinguish among types of leaders. Churchill and Hitler were leaders but we refer to them with reference to titles such as "the bulwark of democracy" or "tyrannical megalomaniac." To use leadership as a synonym for "head" does not serve a useful purpose in distinguishing the effect one has as a pivot, spokesperson, or representative of an organization. Nor does it help us describe the individual's relationship to peers and subordinates in a modern organization.

The major flaw in our thinking is that while some companies can do well no matter what kind of leadership there is, one tends to equate organizational success with the leader. It is then assumed that the leader's style is the cause of success. If he or she is a tyrant then that's the "success" model to emulate. As long as organizations are perceived as hierarchies, and extensions of individuals at the top, then success or failure of the organization will be attributed to that individual and his or her style. This way of thinking is inappropriate in a transformed workplace. As the leadership function devolves to many, if not all individuals, and responsibility for the success or failure of the organization is clearly shared among each member of the organization, "leadership" effectiveness becomes another way of discussing personal effectiveness.

The qualities required to execute one's responsibility are the same for everyone. While no one person is given responsibility for others, everyone is responsible to the whole and each takes a pivotal role when it is appropriate to do so. The fact that one person has a particularly pivotal role or is distinguished because of special skills does not make one a leader per se and one's functioning as a leader or facilitator may be independent of such positional qualities as seniority or rank. Even the armed forces understands this when it mixes individuals of various ranks but recognizes those with superior expertise or specialized roles as the "leader" in specific circumstances due to one's competence and formal role in achieving a task.

The act of leadership as described here is the assertion of competence or the facilitative, or coaching, or spokesperson's role. It is, perhaps, enhanced by one's personality or likeability but many of the techniques may be taught to assure that the function is properly fulfilled. The charismatic part becomes less essential as responsibilities are shared and each member of the organization takes an active role in determining the success or failure of the organization. As the process of running the organization becomes a subject of concern to each person throughout the course of doing one's job, traditional expectations of charisma and personal loyalty become less important.

Because everyone is expected to take responsibility the need to rely on another's' charismatic power or force of personality diminishes.

There is no question that dealing with group interpersonal and work processes will take time but it is unavoidable as the nature of work increasingly deals with the invisibles and intangibles mentioned earlier.

Though there is a tendency to be impatient when dealing with the process side of issues because focusing on process gives the appearance of wasting time, it is wise to keep in mind the Japanese proverb that "sometimes one must waste time to save time." Planning and attention to process issues may appear to take a lot of time and be wasteful but when properly done will save time in the execution of the group's task responsibilities.

Consider an alternative American practice where "there is never enough time to do the job right the first time but there is always enough time to do it over!" We usually conceptualize activity as being either goal directed or process directed. Typically we prefer the action oriented focus, straightforward thinking about our objectives and getting the job done. As Americans we are quite proud of our practical nature and our dogged determination. In the earlier agricultural and industrial eras these were life saving virtues since the problems faced were tangible, physical challenges to survival. In addition, the social structures were more stable and more homogeneous because they were localized to family and community. That measure of stability also reinforced other values and civic behavior that served as a reliable platform for mutual understanding and cooperation. Today, that is obviously not the case. Deliberate planning and intentionally dealing with the processes involved in our work and relationships are essential if we are to be successful and create quality products and services. High levels of mobility and cultural and lifestyle diversity demands this.

In conventional organizations, the higher one climbs the less able or willing one is to take the time for process issues though one becomes immersed in company politics necessary to achieve very specific personal and organizational ends. This is easy to understand because the nature of conventional organizations ascribe ownership properties to top management. That is to say, the CEO fully expects a proprietary reign over the organization; it is an extension of his will. It responds to his thinking and desires as if it were an enlargement of himself and as if it were in reality as in his fantasy, a small family business.

There is a saying, that, "The bowl has structure but its usefulness is based on its emptiness." Thus, one must take into "account the simultaneity of structure and the sequence of process."[11] In the new solararchic organization described herein, this awareness is constantly developed among all members and accounts for the ability to share the leadership processes. One doesn't own the organization. One doesn't rule. Rather each person is an integral part of the organization and serves in a role that subjects each person to the scrutiny of the membership at appropriate intervals. Whether there is a daily, weekly, or monthly feedback session or yearly elections that serve to remove an individual from a role or validate one's performance, everyone is subject to review.

In conventional organizations, "The impact of the formal structure influences leadership behavior toward being more autocratic even when there exist informal norms emphasizing a more egalitarian climate and when the leaders consciously try to be more 'democratic'."[12] This is one of the most insidious reasons reforms continue to fail. The structure isn't changed to accommodate the new processes. Individuals gravitating toward the top and behaving consistently with the conventional reward structure and the rules for getting ahead are, in the overwhelming number of cases, inured to egalitarian reforms—even when such reforms could strengthen the bottom line. The point was first demonstrated in County Lanark in Scotland over 150 years ago when Robert Owen reformed his cotton mill along egalitarian lines only to find his successors revert to more conventional ways. The practice of simultaneously meeting the needs of workers and investors has, throughout the industrial era, usually been short lived regardless of the financial rewards because the perceived loss of power on the part of management was simply too great to accept. We have learned that egalitarian reforms must be safeguarded through structural changes as well as processual changes if they are to survive the current management.

The financial rewards for organizations that restructure into a solacratic community and embrace the idea of every member a leader, are quite strong indeed. Zenith, Polaroid, Weyerhaeuser and Deere are sometimes cited as examples of companies moving in this direction[13] In addition, as we saw earlier, circumstance are beginning to demand it. But the personal incentive for any one manager to change will be nil unless personal rewards for change efforts and executive compensation are tied in to performing in this new fashion, are established. But who will take the initiative? Those that have are still in a very elite minority. After all isn't part of the reason managers are where they are due to their having bought into the conventional structures? Haven't they sacrificed their entire careers to arrive at the pinnacle of the hierarchies they so ardently served? Besides, the current compensation madness among top executives is so intoxicating that to expect them to voluntarily dismantle that system would be a delusion of the worst sort. They have been part and parcel of the creation of a super-class compensated to a degree unimagined only a few short years ago. Take for example, Anthony O'Reilly the Chief Executive Officer of H.J. Heinz. His total compensation was $75.1 million in 1991. That included a base salary of $514,000 plus bonuses and stock options. According to *Business Week*, he may make even more next year after the award of 4 million additional stock options for signing a new five year contract.[14] By way of contrast, the President of the United States plus the Vice President of the United States plus all 14 Cabinet members plus all nine Supreme Court Members plus all 537 members of the Senate and House of Representatives plus all 50 Governors of the States *combined* earned less than $75 million in 1991![15]

In order to disperse the leadership function, the composite skills must be taught, exercised and reinforced among everyone to share the role. Meeting facilitation, self confidence, information analysis, and interpersonal skills can be taught. Indeed they must be taught if corporate America is to successfully utilize the team-based approach to work that is now sweeping the country.

4. Separate administration from task leadership. With the dispersal of leadership among many organizational members, project competence is disassociated from group maintenance activity. The leadership function is broken down into separate responsibilities and shared among the group's members. The separation of administrative functions from task leadership enables prioritization of action and different kinds of personal involvement for the membership. Inevitably there are record keeping and coordination functions that can best be routinized or accomplished outside the main work processes through permanent or temporary assignments of interested individuals (or through rotation). These kinds of issues such as scheduling personal time, administering benefits, representation of the group to others, or settling minor disputes, can be handled by setting aside a separate administrative time period.

5. Create self-development/learning groups.   An organization facing a constellation of intangibles and increasing demands must become a learning organization; an organization capable of rapid assimilation of new information and able to appropriately adjust to new realities. In the learning organization managers become teachers. In a learning solacracy each member of the community becomes a resource and tutor to colleagues.

Attention to process is itself a statement that the group is an ongoing, changing, adapting, living organism willing to accommodate new information and develop new perspectives on existing information. Examining a group's processes is itself a statement of the willingness of the participants to learn. The next step is the formation of self-development groups that influence the progress of individuals' learning and their ability to adapt to change. A self-development group is an assemblage of people that voluntarily choose to assist each other in achieving a personal growth agenda. Usually it addresses specific individual needs as those needs relate to work performance and interpersonal relationships in the organization but the focus can be broadened to include any issue an individual has identified which the group is in a position to support.

A work group becomes a self-development group by virtue of its devotion to communicate fully about work goals and processes with a problem-solving focus. The personal self-development group is distinctive in its being formed in response to personal needs of individuals and their willingness to support one another and volunteer additional time together. This is comparable to participation in professional associations with the exception that membership in a self-development group may either be interdisciplinary with a specific term and an initial agenda to get started. They are usually created because individuals experience a discomfort and identify a personal problem in one's self, the system, or within others that stimulates their desire for change. These groups are easily formed because the skills needed to operate them are learned in the course of one's work as well as through the group. The self development group may be of any duration and include any number but an optimal number seems to be between five and fifteen.

6. Work teams choose their facilitators, coaches and colleagues.   Work associates select their own facilitators and their rep-

resentatives to other parts of the organization. This is what empowerment is all about. They will also determine what tasks are necessary
for the group to accomplish, a time frame in which to accomplish
their work, an understanding of the expected standards of performance and the freedom to decide how work will be accomplished
and with whom.

7. **Work teams negotiate individual roles and their function.**
Roles are negotiated among group members given the expectations
of their group and the nature of their work. Individuals are more
concerned about being able to do what needs to be done rather than
conforming to a fixed description of their job.

It is also important to remain voluntary lest there be a tyranny of
the majority or unjust peer pressure. People can be expected to perform at a specified level to earn their pay and other benefits of community membership. But they should not be forced into extra hours
or duties unless willing to do so. Usually pay for knowledge systems
serve as an incentive for individuals to acquire and use additional
skills and sometimes additional hours are voluntarily spent in service
to the organization because one is challenged or committed. But each
person must be respected if they are not inclined to devote time
otherwise devoted to their families or other pursuits.

8. **Everyone a facilitator.** If management and coordination is
to be shared, or rotated and decided by each group, everyone must
think like a manager. The first managerial skill includes an ability to
be ego-detached. The individual use of power for achieving one's
personal goals is often an overwhelming temptation. Detachment is
the ability to focus on the task to be handled and on performing a service to one's colleagues without using the group as an instrument for
one's personal gain. There is a great deal of satisfaction in helping the
group become successful. Thus the first skill is a reorientation to
focus on the group's objective and develop a sense of caring for the
success of the group.

To accomplish this each person is taught how to execute managerial
action. That includes skills in running meetings, observing the interpersonal processes at work in the group, measuring performance
against goals, participating in work facilitation and handling one's
tasks with responsibility.

9. **Connect employee to customer (both internal and external).**
Everyone is part of a work flow process. Each input to one's work
and output from one to another is more than a symbolic representa-

tion of serving a customer and being a customer. It is a fact. We are a customer to everyone we depend on. Likewise we serve a customer in providing our work to others, whether they are external to the organization and pay us for our product or whether they are down the hall from us and need our work to do their own. The same mentality of quality service applies to all transactions and it is that simple. The satisfied customer who pays for our service is just one of many customers that need be satisfied in order for our organization to survive. Satisfied internal customers create effectiveness in meeting the needs of external customers. Naturally, people should become conscious of their impact on others and realize that the effectiveness of the organization is in part determined by the care and execution of their responsibilities.

10. Keep a sense of perspective. One danger of self-managing teams and personal involvement in the workplace is the tendency for members to so identify with their work role that they lose sight of other aspects of life and responsibilities outside the workplace.

It is important to determine the point of diminishing returns and to maintain a sense of balance, of perspective, when dealing with issues either in the work flow or that arise between individuals. Allow people to keep their personal space, privacy. Know when people are being pushed into discomfort because of the group's intense enthusiasm or when disclosure and discussion are entering danger areas for the individual. While stretching is important, it is also important to respect the individual's state of readiness and to allow the individual to move at his or her own pace.

FUNDAMENTAL INTERPERSONAL SKILLS

Setting the Stage: Learning, Learning, Learning; Process, Process, Process

There isn't always an obvious connection in people's minds between spending a lot of time on process issues and organizational success. There is still an attitude about getting on with one's job and not being bothered by what often seems like endless talking in endless meetings with nothing getting done. We really have little choice since, as separate individuals, we can't possibly know all that we need to know and don't have the ability to see our work and place in the organization as others see it. We are constantly faced with the need to create alignment, to refine our understanding of ourselves and how we meet the needs of the organization and its external customers. The need to understand our connectedness at work is becoming crucial for organizational success. It determines the quality of our relationships which determine how well we understand and can meet the needs of the market.

Working in an idea age, a world filled with intangibles, requires the free expression of thoughts, feelings, and ideas from each person in an organization. How else can you innovate? Meet unique customer needs? Solve problems? Understand each other's needs? The cluster of skills required to elicit and use the input from each person is the central requirement underlying the competencies needed for future personal and organizational success and building a workable community.

Reduce Barriers Between Individuals

Try to eliminate barriers to communication between people. Individuals must first understand what is required of them to communicate clearly and honestly with their colleagues. They must understand the elements of their job and how to articulate their needs. Personal skills in formulating and expressing ideas are essential to begin the communications process. Being creative, analytical, and informed about one's job and how it fits into the group's and organization's purpose is essential. Each person shares this responsibility.

The structure and processes in place must be audited to determine the extent they facilitate or interfere with interpersonal communication. Do people fear telling the truth? Disagreeing with bosses or the group mind? Will one face action by the organization for speaking freely or suggest ideas that seem "unusual" or counter to the conventional wisdom? Are there various opportunities for self-expression outside of formal task-oriented meetings where free reign thinking is possible? Are there rewards and recognition for creativity? Are people encouraged to develop novel ways to approach nagging problems and issues? Are there particular people that ridicule the efforts of others when bringing up new topics, issues, and approaches?

Survey individuals to gather their perceptions of the kinds and extent of the barriers they face to being open and communicative. Begin a dialog around these issues and develop a list of priorities for improving the communication climate.

Build Interpersonal Compatibility

One way to minimize the influence of the closed, resistant or obstructive individual is to have frequent opportunities for meetings, committees and rotating task forces that require everyone's involvement. Providing a variety of meaningful opportunities to participate in idea generation, discussion and evaluation reduces the negative effects of any one individual and reduces the systematic inhibition of individuals' efforts to communicate freely. When feedback skills and the use of meeting facilitation techniques are learned and each person is trained in their use, individuals are less able to obstruct the work of the group. They can not hide behind their position as in a conventional hierarchy and this behavior will be confronted. The facilitator playing a coaching role will show people the effects of their behavior. Eventually all will be able to do this as they become trained in these skills. This is a dramatic change from the usual silence that befalls groups in today's organizations because of the protocols that discourage confrontation, negative feedback and the expression of beliefs and feelings—especially "upward" in the hierarchy with all the personal and career hazards one faces as a result of speaking one's mind.

One of the most inhibiting factors in communication, perhaps more so than any formal obstruction or interfering boss, is simply the personal discomfort commonly felt in the presence of unfamiliar people. It takes a while to get used to one another and to feel comfortable in freely expressing oneself, particularly if there are status or other differences that inhibit one's willingness to communicate. Providing many opportunities to get to know one another is a form of social lubrication that allows individuals to become psychologically comfortable and willing to more freely express themselves. It is vital then, to reinforce the emotional safety factor as people get to know and work with one another. It should not be assumed that we are all able to make this effort without encouragement or organizational facilitation.

Fear or uncertainty in dealing with "strangers" at work is not uncommon and is easily remedied through frequent contact to enable people to get comfortable with one another. Then, norms are created and intentionality, behavioral agreements and commitments among work group members develop. These are requirements for succeeding at community building.

Because life in hyper mobile America pulls us away from kin and community into a career maelstrom that moves us from place to place, we depend thoroughly on strangers in our day to day lives. We must create a type of instant intimacy with our proximate citizens and fellow workers. We are expected to hit the ground running in each new location; to get along with each new set of colleagues. Working with these strangers is a challenge that is usually met in the most casual and serendipitous ways. Rarely are there substantial formal orientation, introduction and bonding rituals to help us establish our new roots whether in the organization or in the larger community.

We fend for ourselves. And this results in a patchwork of relationships each for a particular aspect of our needs. For example, in our "professional" lives, our network, provides career knowledge and stability.

Superficial relationships endanger the organization as well as individuals. With each move, or reassignment, "Our culturally determined social units have thus suddenly expanded to encompass more than just our relatives, while our biology has been especially primed for protective behavior only toward them and our close associates. Defense of these new larger units and cooperation within them have accordingly become a real problem."[16] The barriers to working with strangers also include cultural and psychological dimensions.

Conscious approaches to finding out how to work with others successfully in any environment are rarely approached systematically. It seems that each individual must discover anew, ways of operating, fitting in and finding out what's what. In establishing oneself and participating in meetings and on teams decide what you need to know, want to know, the background necessary to fill in the context of the work environment and find out what others think you should know both about the work to be done and who you will be working with

Continuous informal as well as formal socialization is an attempt to thoroughly inculcate communicative habits that lead to precise understanding of the work environment and overcomes inhibitors to free expression. It also helps create norms for openness with others in the organization with whom one may be unfamiliar, so that practicing frequent communication and sharing, in one part of the organization, will prepare individuals for openness with others in the parts of the organization that are only infrequently met.

And remember, when it comes to communicating there should be no chain of command.

Illustrate and Be Clear About Your Purpose and the Work Group's Goals

If you are a manager or facilitator, make clear how you are helping the group achieve its goals. Introduce or reintroduce the role you are playing at appropriate moments and remind the group of your strategic purpose—how you will be acting on its behalf. Make objectives concrete targets. Animate them. Create images of what the team wants to become and how you intend to facilitate this achievement. Frequently illustrate these goals and display them to all staff members. Show competitors products and services and how you are doing in comparison.

THE SKILLS

Some of the skills for implementing successful team practices and for developing teams into community begin from the same general platform from which the development of all other interpersonal and community-building skills proceeds. Some of these are discussed in the following paragraphs.

Interpersonal

Meeting facilitation skills. Meeting facilitation skills are essential since much of one's work in community will occur in meetings. Learn the various roles and how each contributes to the group's success. Some of the roles that might be allocated are: facilitator, process observer (to comment on how the meeting went, what made it effective or ineffective), wall chart note-taker, recorder, time keeper, devil's advocate, refreshment coordinator, and facilities planner.

Dispute resolution through mediation skills. Using peer supervision, process observation, role clarification and self-assessment skills, personalize the causes of high performance. These techniques show how a person's efforts fits in to others in the organization and leads to results for the group. Each is a method to gain clarity about, and focus on, one's part in the group.

Dealing with conflicts that arise between colleagues. Managerial mediation is a useful technique to apply when confronting differences and disputes. It's simple and easy to apply. The mediator supervises the process to insure that the four steps are followed:
Step 1: Disputants agree to find time to talk and to allow another person to mediate the discussion.
Step 2: Everyone agrees to a comfortable meeting place and time with no distractions.
Step 3: Each side talks, expresses appreciation of the process and with the other's willingness to work out the issue. In addition, be optimistic about finding a solution and agree not to withdraw or use force (physical or psychological) of any kind. Then state the issue and begin the dialog. Remember, don't get off track, tell jokes, scapegoat, give up, or remain silent.
Step 4: Watch for conciliatory gestures and support them and look for the breakthrough—a voluntary shift from a win lose approach to an us against the problem attitude. When the breakthrough occurs

make a deal. Be behaviorally specific, write it out and include a time line for follow up.[17]

Suspending judgment using DeBono's concept of "PO".[18] It is important for work group members and participants in any democracy to have certain general skills that also apply to solacratic organizational communities and solacracies described here: "As in a democracy, individual participation in teamwork requires personal commitment and maturity, self-discipline, flexibility, capacity for give and take, the willingness and ability to learn, basic respect for the other fellow with all of his differences, and the ability to examine oneself in relationships with other people with a degree of objectivity."[19] PO is a position beyond yes or no. It requires you to suspend your impulse to judge long enough to fully grasp a situation before you act.

Team building skills. Team building developed out of the human potential movement of the 1950s and became very popular in the 1960s and 1970s. Today the concepts of teamwork and team building have undergone a renaissance and are fast approaching buzz-word-panacea status. The intention is, of course, to help work groups operate more smoothly and effectively and to improve quality. The basic elements of teamwork haven't changed much since their introduction but what is vital to their continued practice and success is the creation of an environment that reinforces the behavior that makes teams effective. The context within which they operate is the key to their success. In creating community, organizations establish the kind of environment consistent with the operating principles necessary for effective teams. Without it teams will be short-lived, becoming just another passing fad. Remember, just because people are placed in groups doesn't make them a team.

Using survey feedback and action research is an effective way to discern the sense of the group when it is too large for meeting all at once or if there are logistical or time concerns that make it impossible to do so. Survey feedback is the ability to construct questionnaires that elicit members' perceptions of important dynamics of the group. This helps determine areas most in need of improvement and areas in which the group is doing well.

Action research is a follow up process that engages the group in the refining of their perceptions and the establishment of a specific plan to remedy ills, establish new goals, or reinforce existing practices that are working well.

Developing creative problem identification and problem solving techniques is also important. This includes using statistical data as well as creative imagery to gain and apply insights from the work processes itself.

Personal

Keep agreements. Mean what you say and say what you mean. In establishing and fulfilling agreements communicate authentically and honestly. Develop your creative thinking ability and problem solving skills.

Giving and Receiving Feedback

Feedback has become a cliché for simply talking with one another but it is much more than that. Basically it is getting to know and letting others know the impact one has on another person. It is a willingness to listen and a willingness to disclose one's feelings. More than an exchange of niceties, feedback takes two forms.

Positive feedback.   Positive feedback is conveying the satisfaction one has with the effect of another's work or behavior. When someone does a particularly good job or has executed a responsibility or been particularly insightful, telling them how they have affected you gives positive feedback. It not only lets someone know they have done well and are appreciated but helps her or him understand exactly what it was that was so effective. It encourages more of the same performance in the future. It is more than a polite "pat on the back" as well. It is a focused behavior on a specific incident; a reflection on an action someone has taken. During breaks or informal time, make a point of acknowleging how a colleague did well, helped you, or otherwise made a favorable impression.

Just being polite or conveying a generality that you liked someone's work is not particularly helpful though everyone does appreciate being acknowledged. It simply is too vague. When you take the time to be specific you assure that the individual understands and is focused on specific things he or she did that were effective. Niceties have a place, of course, but in addition to being vague generalities they have a shorter life than either accurate and focused feedback (or negative feedback) and may need to be reemphasized in order to get through the listeners social filter. The social filter accepts positive generalities in much the same way that one hears, "have a nice day" or "I'm fine" when exchanging pleasantries. In addition, positive feedback is rarely noted in one's "file" and rarely has a direct link with the organization the way negative feedback does, so we often diminish its importance; it has much less impact than it deserves, especially so when it isn't specific.

Negative feedback. Much of our lives is enveloped in the expectation that things will work properly and people will perform well. Therefore, we typically become critical when this isn't the case. We are more prone to complain than to praise others. Both actions are uncomfortable and usually are avoided except in the most noteworthy instances such as unexpectedly good service or being severely inconvenienced by bad service or expensive mistakes. Negative feedback seems more personally relevant and important because it stems from a painful experience one is immediately motivated to overcome.

Negative feedback, unlike positive feedback also implies that the individual receiving it must change to prevent the situation from arising again. It is often perceived as serious in a work context if it comes from an influential individual and carries the implicit threat that action will follow if the cause of the negative report isn't corrected. Perhaps it is recorded and lives in a personnel file long after it serves its purpose and the causes are corrected. When used this way negative feedback is rightly perceived as a control mechanism that keeps one living in fear for their career security. When used for control purposes, negative feedback insures conformity but reduces risk taking and honesty and willingness to be vulnerable about personal needs or short comings lest they be recorded, or used against the individual at some future date. By the same token when feedback is used simply as a means of control, positive feedback is less frequently used because it complicates a future case for dismissal or reassignment of an individual.

When feedback is appropriately used as a learning tool and not a control mechanism and individuals are free to communicate and take risks, performance improves for individuals resulting in a more effective work group and a more profitable organization.

Acceptance of feedback from others. Giving feedback is only part the skill in developing an open communications climate. It is also necessary to accept feedback from others. Where there is a pattern and many people give you the same feedback it would be a good idea to think about it more seriously. Test if the feedback is accurate for you and think twice if you receive the same message from differ-ent sources. In either case become receptive to others speaking frankly to you; invite helpful criticism and get in the habit of asking, as the former Mayor of New York Edward Koch used to say, "How 'm I doin'?"

It is also important to develop the ability to make a "reality check" that provides feedback on group performance, particularly when you play the role of group facilitator. Take the opportunity to assess the state and health of the organization along important dimensions such as the level of trust, morale, active participation in meetings and deci-sion making process, satisfaction with feedback processes, willing-ness to communicate, the presence of undercurrents in interpersonal relationships (are cliques forming?), and the extent of community cohesion.

This reality check may take the form of a questionnaire or a process oriented inventory of the group's working requirements and relationships. Having "How're we doing?" sessions seek to assess the condition of working relationships as well as work productivity. Regularly devoting time to this is important.

Self-disclosure. The feedback loop can only work if each member of the group is willing and able to give and receive feedback. Thus, it is necessary to be open and authentic; to present yourself to others genuinely and to express yourself naturally. The level of inti-macy in the group will be determined over time as each member assesses the authenticity of the others and they reach an understand-ing of how far the group is willing to go in being open with one another.

Ability to listen/empathize. In order to fulfill the need to give and receive feedback as well as to heighten the general commu-nication effectiveness of the group, one naturally needs to develop listening skills and the ability to empathize with the speaker. Listening requires clearing the time you spend with the individual from other distractions so that you can focus on what is being said and the context in which it is said. Show the speaker that you are lis-tening and check in with the person to determine if you have been understanding the message by reframing it as a statement or asking a question to clarify points of interest. In short listening is paying attention.

Capacity for self-reflection. The capacity for self-reflection is strangely absent among many people who seem oblivious of their effect on others and their social situation. This deficiency takes many forms from one simply being awkward to being obnoxious and instigating frequent and intense interpersonal conflicts. Even frequent silences or being a loner may indicate the hesitation on the part of others to engage in conversation or in the work process at hand. Self-reflection is an attempt to put one's behavior in interpersonal perspective by examining the influences one has on others and the impact of others behavior on oneself. It helps people determine their preferences, dislikes, biases, patterns of relating and habits that may inhibit or facilitate interpersonal relationships.

Honoring inquiry and dialog. In the world described in this book, there is little room for dogmatism, orthodoxy or immutable conventions. Remember, everything is considered tentative. Everything must be justified by performance and human need. In a fast paced changing world where ideas, creativity and innovation form the basis of most work, exploration of concepts, original thinking and openness to new ideas must be practiced by everyone. When armed with a capacity for using team building and meeting facilitation techniques, each individual is fully equipped for assuming a pivotal role in the work group when the circumstances require it.

Keeping everyone informed. The power of sharing information was demonstrated over fifty years ago during World War II when, ironically, circumstances called for conditions of utmost secrecy. During the atomic bomb project at Los Alamos no one told the unit of programmers and data entry clerks what they were doing or why. They were just supposed to input data. Richard Feynman, a renowned physicist, asked permission to tell them what they were doing and why. Once permission was granted and the unit was informed they got very excited. According to Feynman once they understood the mission, that "We're fighting a war!" a complete transformation occurred. "They began to invent better ways of doing their work. They improved the scheme. They worked at night. They didn't need supervising in the night; they didn't need anything. They understood everything; they invented several of the programs that we used.

"So my boys really came through, and all that had to be done was to tell them what it was. As a result, although they took nine months to do three problems before, we did nine problems in three months, which is nearly ten times as fast."[20]

Enhanced communications will be one of the most important issues throughout the 1990s and beyond. We are living in an information glut unlike anytime in history. It seems the number of claims on our time and the number of unwanted, uninvited distractions increases each year. The major issue at work is not simply to inform but to inform in a way that helps the individual focus on what is important and act appropriately. The idea of focusing and then acting appropriately will require incredible attention to detail, timing and appropriate channels of communicating while checking on the receivers comprehension.

When we talk of creating a vision its execution depends on its continuous reinforcement and its interpretation into individual actions on a daily basis before it becomes a viable canon for each member of the community.

Attention to focus and action is due to the number and depth of the information barriers individuals create in their lives. The organization is competing with all other experiences the individual faces—all other "to do" lists, all other personal priorities, all other needs. Focus and action are the two essential ingredients for meaningful comprehension. The intensity of the message depends on the nature of the information disseminated and the purpose to which it will be put. Routine job information is easily acted upon by each member. What isn't so easily utilized are the messages involving the context of one's role in the work group and community or that involve thinking about changes. The contextual messages help people develop the capacity to know the best course of action to follow in ambiguous situations and gives them the confidence to set appropriate priorities and take the initiative in getting the information they need. For example, a contextual statement about being self-expressive may result in early detection of design flaws in a new product because of individuals voicing specific concerns about their experience of the product.

Consensus building and mediation skills.   Open communication, access to information and a willingness to share power in order to be responsive, flexible and innovative requires skills in building consensus and in resolving conflicts. When each person is trained in these skills they can follow the processes intelligently from the perspective of a shared interest in an outcome best suited to the work to be done by the group.

Development of personal efficacy and self-confidence. When each member of the community is trained in the skills of managing; of serving as a pivot, of performing leadership functions and capable of running meetings for the group and playing other necessary roles, the sense of personal efficacy is reinforced and motivates action for the good of the community. Confidence has always stood in the way of the ill informed and uninformed and from one's taking responsibility. When information is available and communication is focused and assists in directing future action and each member of the workplace is trained in the skills requisite to taking responsibility, productivity, and efficiency are enhanced.

Process observation skills. As each person prepares for pivotal, leadership, and meeting facilitation roles it is necessary to learn to observe and interpret interpersonal dynamics while they are occurring. It is best to focus on interpersonal dynamics of others such as in a meeting where there is a formal observer present to offer the group feedback at the end of the meeting about behaviors that helped or hindered the process. It is also helpful to develop this skill to help you glimpse your own behavior and assess your impact on others and them on you in real time. This is a much more difficult skill but does develop as the general capacity for process observation is developing within the group. The more practice you have the better, of course.

This skill is important for group assessment and for understanding how each member is working with others. It helps the process itself establish a form which is manageable and uses language to describe occurrences that everyone will understand. It creates a shorthand to explain what happens when people work together.

Reducing anxiety. A major factor interfering with the achievement of long term teamwork is a widespread irrepressible anxiety. In spite of the latest buzzwords promising "empowerment" and "teamwork" that emanate from traditional organizations, the truth is that in a conventional context these are hollow slogans. As long as all work is subject to unilateral approval by a superior and that all promises can be rescinded, teamwork becomes just shared delegation. Anxiety about the fundamental relationship between employer and employee still defines the context of the employees experience. The bottom line for employees is that they still serve at the will of the boss and all major parameters of the employment contract and the team's functions are thus defined and controlled by others. Anxiety due to powerlessness remains. There is still accountability in one direction: upwards. All rewards of productive teamwork are skimmed off by the "organization" without the slightest return to the employees. Isn't that what inflames employees' anger;

especially at the annual review of executive compensation? Was it really Anthony O'Reilly, alone, who made H.J. Heinz successful? What about all the contributions of the other 34,000 employees? His salary and bonuses alone in 1991 amounted to $2206 per employee!

Inventors, marketers, customer/account service representatives, quality control supervisors, drivers, bottlers, advertising copywriters and secretaries who serve on teams, contribute to daily efficiencies, and create valuable new ideas, are rarely rewarded with the same care and concern as a few at the top. It is often a matter of respect—the lack of it, which is the basis of the continuous anxiety. They must compete for "best ideas" or "best employee". They are told that they are paid for their ideas and shouldn't expect financial rewards. They are given turkeys or a gift certificate for new successful company products. Is it any wonder that there is a withdrawal of very capable individual workers from real commitment and involvement. Isn't it ironic that their good ideas are treated with such contempt when they serve as the basis for an organization's profits.

Nothing short of a re-write of the social contract can work to reduce the major factors contributing to anxiety.[21] They are:

- inadequate support from superior
- ineffective performance by superior
- inadequate performance from subordinates
- not knowing precisely what is expected on the job
- not receiving credit/recognition when due
- inadequate information about career advancement requirements
- not being able to depend on the word or actions of managers

It seems that guaranteeing the security of one's position and providing clear expectations, which are as basic a pair of prescriptions that have ever emerged from the management literature, can reduce most anxiety and clear the way for unfettered individual contributions to the work at hand.

Self assessment.   Learn how to assess your behavior in interpersonal contexts.

In addition, the individual must check his or her attitude about authority; one's temptation to abuse or misuse power or position; the view toward apparent incompetence on the part of one's boss or one's self; and arbitrary, subjective or intimidating behavior. In other words there is inevitably a potential for a dark side. We have seen how easily one can be tempted by power, position, or privileged information to behave as an SOB: to exercise Self-Oriented Behavior.

Other skills.   There is also the need to build coalitions for support and to network beyond one's immediate work group in order to understand the resources available throughout the organization, how one's group fits in to the overall process of production, and how others in the organization can be served better.

Know when to set aside time for attending to process and other issues within the group. Create half-day or full-day think-ins as a way of keeping the team informed, of orienting new members, and building team cohesion. Professor Charles Handy mentioned the Tate Gallery in London developing think-ins for new staff as brain storming opportunities much like teach-ins during the 1960s informed academic communities of pressing social issues.[22]

Personalize pride in accomplishment, recognize good work, and encourage personal goal clarification so that everyone's efforts can be more clearly related to performance issues. Show the link between performance and goals in the organization. In other words: communicate, communicate, communicate. And think of refining what you and the work group does to improve its performance.

In Summary

Here are ten steps to personal readiness for community:

1. Have personal and organizational integrity: be true to the values, visions and policies as they develop and evolve in the group.
2. Make sure you and others understand all non-negotiable standards and expectations of membership in the group.
3. Try to understand the motives of people in the organization and the purpose of their behavior within the work context. Find out what is on others' personal agenda. Be empathetic.
4. Help reduce ambiguity, and thus anxiety, by helping to establish clear expectations of individual and group performance.
5. Enlarge your area of indifference regarding others' lifestyles and off- job behavior. Focus on essential behaviors necessary for getting the job done and for getting along with work group members.
6. Reduce interpersonal barriers created by artificial differences such as rank and status. Learn to appreciate cultural diversity and the enhanced resources in the group where there are racial, ethnic, gender, and age differences.
7. Assuage individual job-related insecurities. Help eliminate threat, ridicule, secrecy, and non job related biases from the workplace.
8. Make things happen—seek out the possible, try to say yes and always have faith in the community building process. Communities draw their strength from individuals' resourceful-

ness and their ability to seek out and manage change, new ideas, a willingness to improve their relationships, and an attitude that problems are really opportunities.

9. Join with others in a self-development group that includes aspects of your personal growth unrelated to your work. It expands your horizons, talents and sense of self.

10. Help market the organization and its mission to all members. Constantly communicate system-wide events, and community building messages. One may be able to help convert dysfunctional behaviors into constructive behaviors through re-creating a sense of purpose and a sense of belonging to the community and work group. Enhanced self-worth derives from an efficacious experience in the organization and when personal wants can be achieved through membership in the group.

"One study of sixteen thousand managers found success associated with a trusting attitude, concern for the personal fulfillment of employees, a lack of ego, willingness to listen to subordinates, risk taking, innovation, high expectations, collaboration, and the ability to integrate ideas."[23]

Remember that articulated and internalized values are one's compass. Get and keep in touch with them and try to align each individual with the group. This is a continuous aspect of managing and the processes used in community building should include many opportunities to align and realign individuals to the fundamental operating principles and the specific vision toward which everyone is working.

Conclusion

In conclusion, R.G.H. Siu offers sage advise appropriate for anyone contemplating participating in an organizational community. If you facilitate a process or mediate a conflict it would be useful to keep his words in mind:

- "Heed the context". Know the difference between an isolated incident and a trend. Watch for meta messages—the unarticulated forces that maintain the larger context which creates the status quo. Also listen for what isn't said!

- Be alert to what may emerge from an apparently dead issue. "Think not in terms of maximizing which is at the expense of something (or someone) else, but of optimizing, which accommodates all."

- "Draw others into the organizational center of gravity . . . so the entirety can move as an integrated activity and adapt to the contingencies of the environment."
- Know when to do nothing.
- Don't assume you can have all the facts.
- Deal with issues as soon as possible, e.g. when they occur.
- Don't allow distrust to fester: "The corporation is distrustful even of loyal employees, suspecting that they too are marking time for more attractive opportunities."
- "Even though a person can give a logical explanation, he will never be a genius at action until he acquires an unerring intuitive sensitivity about things."[24]

BUILDING COMMITMENT

The goal in building commitment among work group members is to develop a consciousness of ownership that links one's efforts to rewards, both material and psychic. Specifically:

- Recruitment practices should focus on individuals who share similar values and can develop a community centered view of their role while clearly identifying with the rewards that come with membership
- Personal and professional growth planning would be useful to help individuals as well as the community attempt to meet future needs. It would also ensure that the organization would maintain its focus on learning throughout its existence.
- Stabilize employment by hiring only when a long term commitment is anticipated. Otherwise hiring can be specifically offered as a fixed term contract. The hiring process should also involve the community in both its determination of need and the selection and orientation of new members. Short term hiring, however, should not be used as a way of cutting the budget or reducing a community's commitment to individuals in the manner of their treatment or the entitlements of association. Second class citizenship is not an option. Contract workers also lower the level of personal commitment to the group so they should be sparingly used.
- Have a customized benefits plan rather that a uniform plan. While each person may be allocated the same amount or percentage of

their salary as a benefit entitlement, they should determine how to utilize it.

- Review the reward and reinforcement behavior of the community at frequent intervals to insure that people and groups are being rewarded for what is desired and not inadvertently rewarded for undesirable behavior.

Actually we have been talking about these kinds of prescriptions for years. Unfortunately they simply have not been perceived to be in the best interests of top management and middle managers have been too stressed out to either practice these suggestions or to design systems to implement them. Building commitment from the middle has just not been an option. Until now. The computer assisted decision making technology that links all people in the organization coupled with their interest in networking to build a more responsive organization enable individuals to build commitment easily.

CAUTION

Could it be that we know too much? That in specializing and making a science out of the most narrow lines of inquiry that we can know much more than we could ever hope to operationalize? Might it not be that, like the original personnel policy Moses handed to humankind millennia ago, we are destined not to practice what we preach? To fall frustratingly short of being able to do what we know is right?

Are we not demanding too much from people? From ourselves? It's easy to identify myriad factors that comprise what might be considered a professional "wish list" but ignore the rather messy fact that in the real physical situation where one's natural personality and propensities; one's likes and dislikes, engulf one, while he or she is immersed in a sea of emotions—one's own and others. Should we really expect that one can truly integrate the prescriptions, skills and advice discussed here and that others will react accordingly and willingly join us in their use?

Perhaps. However, it is a fragile process and if the willing cooperation and the continuous intention is not present and reinforced, the process can break down, especially in the early stages when it is tempting simply to continue doing things the way they have always been done. Thus the process of building a cohesive community requires the constant reinforcement of the vision and constant attention to the various processes mentioned here and all the while knowing that it is being instituted among people often uncomfortable with just such a massive change in the routines of their work lives.

Furthermore, techniques fail because while they are expected to, they can not operate within the traditional system. The techniques would be crushed by the organizational immune system. They can be successful only to the extent of the willingness of organizations to make substantive changes. To superimpose them on the existing system (with the implication that they can be withdrawn) is to be artificial and avoid institutionalizing the new practices. Under these circumstances members can't trust in the process. The recent call for empowerment, for example, is not something one gives another. It requires a change in philosophy and an accompanying change in the way the system distributes and rewards the use of power. Nor can it be offered and then be withdrawn as if to disempower someone because he or she hasn't pleased a boss. Empowerment is a process that respects individuals ability to do the job they were hired to do and creates a structure and process that recognizes a continuous quality philosophy in a continuous learning environment.

In light of changes in population characteristics, technology, managerial roles and fundamental assumptions regarding the nature of work, and organizations, the interpersonal relationships within them can reflect an infinitely greater degree of personal choice. The creation of methods and goals representing the wishes of the groups' membership can be accomplished. A solacracy is an intentional organization in the sense that there is a conscious effort to meld individual, group and organizational ends by making the object and processes at work explicit through a participative process.

The traditional system is designed to encourage competition within a highly controlled environment. It is based on individualism and one's responsibility for those below. It is virtually irresistible to meddle in the affairs of subordinates, to control their outcomes, to supervise closely since one is held to account for their actions. Under these conditions it would indeed take a strong individual who could resist meddling in subordinates' work and model the behavior described herein. Given the present system, to empower others freely and still get a good night's sleep may be an impossibility or require a Herculean quality not found in many mortals.[25] The point cannot be overly emphasized: To overlay cooperative, democratic practices onto an authoritarian, competitive system is to force a breakdown. There must be alignment between the structure and the processes. The practices must reflect the intentions. One must walk the talk.

NOTES

[1] E. Hall, *Beyond Culture* (New York: Doubleday/Anchor, 1976), p. 5.

[2] Quoted in M. Ferguson, *The Aquarian Conspiracy* (Los Angeles: J. P. Tarcher, 1980), p. 191. from M. Gurtov, *Making Changes: The Politics of Self Liberation* (Oakland, CA: Harvest Moon Books, 1979).

[3] B. Dumaine, "Chaparral Steel: Unleash Workers and Cut Costs," *Fortune*, May 18, 1992, p. 88.

[4] Ibid.

[5] A. Farnham, "Who Beats Stress—And How," *Fortune*, October 7, 1991, p. 71.

[6] M. S. Peck, *The Different Drum* (New York: Touchstone, 1988), p. 18.

[7] Special appreciation is recognized to Lesher Communications and particularly to Donald Jochens' team that so beautifully presented their change program to the *Bay Area Organization Development Network*, May 28, 1992.

[8] A. Maslow, *Eupsychian Management* (Homewood, IL: Richard D. Irwin, 1965).

[9] U.S. Department of Commerce, *Statistical Abstract of the United States, 1990* (Washington, D.C.: Bureau of the Census, 1990), p. 19.

[10] R. Levering, M. Moskowitz and M. Katz, *The 100 Best Companies to Work For in America* (Reading, MA: Addison-Wesley, 1984), p. 144.

[11] A. Low, *Zen And Creative Management* (New York: Playboy Paperbacks, 1982), p. 30.

[12] C. Argyris, *Personality and Organization* (New York: Harper and Row, 1957), p. 70.

[13] J. O'Toole, *Vanguard Management* (New York: Berkley Books, 1987).

[14] M. Mallory, "Tony O'Reilly: Turning Ketchup into Big Dough," *Business Week*, March 30, 1992, p. 58.

[15] All salary figures from: *The 1992 Information Please Almanac* (Boston: Houghton Mifflin Company, 1992), pp. 41, 771-72.

[16] D. P. Barash, *The Hare and the Tortoise* (New York: Viking, 1986), p. 135.

[17] D. Dana, *Managing Differences* (Wolcott, CT: MTI Publications, 1989).

[18] E. deBono, *PO: Beyond Yes and No* (Harmondsworth, Middlesex, England: Pelican, 1976).

[19] N. Brill, *Teamwork* (Philadelphia: J. B. Lippincott), p. 30.

[20] R. Feynman, *Surely You're Joking Mr. Feynman!* (New York: Bantam, 1989), pp. 110–111.

[21] Some of these characteristrics were selected from: R. P. Hummel, *The Bureaucratic Experience*, 2nd ed. (New York: St. Martins Press 1982), p. 132—33, from an American Management Association survey.

[22] C. Handy, *The Age of Unreason* (Boston: Harvard Business School Press, 1990).

[23] M. Ferguson, *The Acquarian Conspiracy* (Los Angeles: J. P. Tarcher, 1980), pp. 348–49. This has been reconfirmed by much of the leadership literature. See, for example: B. Nanus, *The Leader's Edge* (Chicago: Contemporary Books, 1989).

[24] R. G. H. Siu, *The Master Manager* (New York: Mentor, 1980).

[25] A. Kohn, *No Contest: The Case Against Competition* (Boston: Houghton Mifflin, 1986).

Chapter Eight

Barriers to Creating Workplace Community

"There is no failure except in no longer trying."

—*Elbert Hubbard*[1]

Inevitably, weaknesses emerge to limit the prospects of a perfect organizational future. To be sure, people can be irascible, illogical, mean spirited, unscrupulous, selfish, obstinate and nasty. They may make wrong choices and fail to keep commitments. Such is life. During the industrial era people were controlled and penalized for these kinds of behaviors and most likely they will continue to be penalized for them in the future, perhaps even more so as the costs associated with these acts increase.

What is different, however, is that in community we take a closer look at why we have problems dealing with one another and we take responsibility for working out the inevitable episodic expression of unpleasant interpersonal behavior. Self managing means that we take responsibility for our actions and the success of our organizations and we deal with problems directly since they influence not only our organizational performance but our rewards.

The barriers to creating workplace community are indeed formidable but not insurmountable. And it should be kept in mind that life in organizational community does provide certain advantages to its members that do not exist elsewhere in society. First, it can create its own rules and regulations. This enables any group of individuals to fashion for itself exactly the kind of community it wants. Second, the organization can depend on people's willingness to be socialized and possessing some useful skills before they join the organization, and third, through recruitment and dismissal procedures the organization can screen out or throw out (if rehabilitation or training fails) the truly socio- or psychopathic.

Still, there are identifiable barriers that help explain why it is so difficult to improve organizations even when we know how to do it. These barriers will definitely provide the major challenge for organizational members of the solacratic communities of the future.

The changes in store for the organization and each of us must be dealt with carefully and thoughtfully. The following may seem like a catalog of insurmountable difficulties but since so many of them are powerful only because of our ignorance of them, once they are identified much of their influence dissolves and they are easily handled when dealt with authentically and directly by the group.

The skills and processes outlined in chapter seven enable work groups and organizations to overcome most of these barriers. Still, good faith, a willingness to get involved and the organization's commitment to job security are extremely helpful prerequisites.

CULTURAL BARRIERS

A Malay proverb states that: "It is better to let our children die rather than our customs." This is an example of the power of a cultural influence ruling from the grave—imposing practices that bind the future to its ways. In fact, each generation has a responsibility for creating its own rules and the culture best suited to its particular circumstances. In contrast to the Malay proverb, an American proverb might state that "Government is for the living, not for the dead." and we have been proud of how fast we can change. Thomas Paine reminded colonial America that "Every age and generation must be as free to act for itself, in all cases, as the ages and generations which preceded it. The vanity and presumption of governing beyond the grave, is the most ridiculous and insolent of all tyrannies."[2]

Sacrosanct traditions and seemingly immovable conventions, however, even in the United States, have a way of developing quickly. There is a tendency to seek stability in much that we do and to settle into the psychological comfort of established habit. In our organizational lives we accept, virtually unquestioned, the prerogatives of bosses and the rights of bosses to select who will govern us at work. We accept the decisions of a few people to hire, assign, evaluate and compensate or fire each employee. And we accept that they are unaccountable to us, as employees.

We also accept the idea that private investment can be freely made for the benefit of investors and that the public must assume the costs of dealing with its side effects. The car is the most visible product to illustrate the relationship between private good and public cost. Car manufacturers are not responsible for building roads or providing emergency crews to rescue accident victims, or set standards for the operation of their machinery, or provide police to enforce the rules of the road, or the cleaning of either air or water damaged by emitted pollutants. In fact it could be said that automobiles have driven much of the economy of this country directly or indirectly over the last 75 years. The "rescue" of Chrysler for as short a period as it was, was deemed in the public interest because of the potential domino effect on Michigan business that would have resulted had the car maker failed in the late 1970s. Yet the benefits, even of the public bailout of Chrysler, have been disproportionate to private parties. Only a small fraction of the original employees still work for Chrysler and at a sacrifice of wages and benefits. "In 1977, Chrysler had a payroll of 250,000; five years later 80,000."[3] Today it has a payroll of about 121,000.

What we accept as legitimate and "the way things are" is simply due to convention. We can alter those conventions once we are in agreement that they no longer serve our needs. But some are mighty difficult to change, such as the idea that only a board of directors and a small management cadre should make all decisions for a firm while answering solely to its own conscience.

We have also accepted the fact that "Contemporary business life allows competitive relations only in which the major emotions are anxiety, tension, loneliness, rivalry and fear."[4] This is apparently the cost of living in the late twentieth century where it is also accepted that the accumulation of money and its material representation is the primary measure of an individual's worth. The prime motivation for hard work and developing a career is, in fact, to "prove" oneself a success, a winner, as defined in terms of the money one earns.

Organizations also perpetuate a controlled, institutional violence on the individual in both psychological and economic terms. It is another cost of contemporary life. Resistance to the institutional violence is growing such as when Anita Hill and thousands of women exposed the abuse of power by some male bosses in the form of sexual harassment. That is merely the tip of the harassment iceberg, however, as all forms of intimidation and the abuse, for one's own gain, of assigned organizational powers, become widely recognized. Sexual harassment and all forms of discrimination in the workplace are just the initial attack on the more visible and reprehensible forms of corporate violence that clearly contradict current societal wisdom.

In any system where one is assigned unaccountable powers over others, abuse will be rampant. Perhaps our newfound willingness to re-examine some of the old assumptions of running businesses stems from the realization that corporations represent a new form of community nexus. In order to align organizations with our democratic cultural traditions, it is necessary to redesign the conventions and our business culture, for employees and other stakeholders, not just top management and distant investors—"for the living not the dead".

Organizational community as proposed here, is an attempt to provide the mechanism, the first social technology since bureaucracy itself, to enable orderly democratic change to occur within organizations. Organizational community is the first social artifact equipped to deal directly with the massive influences of technology upon individuals and society. It is a way of overcoming the powerlessness that people often feel in dealing with technological and social change within conventional organizations when they are treated as merely "human resources" undifferentiated from "material resources".

SOCIALIZATION INTO WORK VALUES AND CLARIFYING EXPECTATIONS OF GROUP MEMBERS

A culture, whether of a nation or an organization, provides the socialization of the individual toward work. This includes one's underlying attitude and recognition of norms such as how to behave with strangers; what professionalism means; the extent individuality will be accepted; how social issues surrounding loyalty, race relations, gender and age will be dealt with; and, when to give and how much help to render others. These are just a few examples of the underlying attitudes and behaviors conveyed through the socialization process.

We have few cultural mechanisms to help us deal with people who we have never seen before. Where our biology signals caution our culture has established rules of etiquette and manners to help determine an appropriate way of acting but this is of limited value in fully overcoming our innate hesitation to take interpersonal risks and become vulnerable to others. Ironically, with a fast changing organizational world requiring instant response to coworker and customer alike we need to develop a way of being in our organizations that reduces the cautions we rely upon while securing our standing with the group.

Achieving congruency between the group's espoused values and its actual performance is also often sought in the socialization process. At the organizational level, several issues make the socialization process extremely difficult. Values in the larger society are in a constant state of flux. Living in a multicultural, hyperstimulated society propels change in expectations as well as in values, making it very difficult for a group to reach agreement on how best to serve its members or even what constitutes membership. Setting performance standards for the group will likely fluctuate as well. Because turnover is so high and loyalty and morale are so low, the socialization process within organizations must be a deliberate and long-standing process in order to be effective in establishing shared personal behaviors.

BIOLOGICAL BARRIERS

Limits of perceptual acuity.   We simply can't "know" what is outside our own skin. We are designed to be cautious in dealing with the world and its environmental hazards, especially in dealing with other people. The purpose of our nervous system is maintaining our physical well being but it's limited to the extent of our physical ability to process data and signal appropriate responses.

Perhaps the most dysfunctional aspect of our biological propensity to protect us moment-to-moment is its general inability to deal with the future. When we complain about short-term thinking in this country, it is because that attitude is consistent with our nature. We know the present. We do not know the future. Thus, our interests are always expressed in immediate terms and our impact on others, and our impact on a future course of action is generally a secondary concern.

Any threat to our biological integrity immediately focuses our attention on the requirements of the situation. For example, when a doctor tells you there is a spot on your X-ray it immediately gets your attention, while pleas to quit smoking because of the potential damage to your lungs are easily ignored. Likewise in organizations, the immediate needs of one department or another often obscure their cooperating to meet the long term goals of the organization.

An organizational prosthesis or intervention may help overcome our inability to think far into the future and our frequent blindness to the ramifications of our immediate behavior on others.

One simple intervention could be to establish a joint decision-making body to consider the organizational investments in research and development or new plant and equipment with an eye toward the future. Perhaps a certain percentage of net income could be assigned to these functions so that their cutbacks to achieve short term, but misleading, increases in the bottom line can be avoided. As one executive reported the dilemma, "Do I do the right thing by my people? Or by the bottom line (including my bottom line)?"[5] This is especially poignant when to do right by the bottom line directly results in an executive's compensation but doesn't tell us how the bottom line was enhanced. Another organizational intervention such as total quality circles or feedback sessions can result in the development and presentation of emerging issues to be considered. It may also serve as a check on the otherwise unilateral short-term decision-making process exercised by individuals acting alone.

PSYCHOLOGICAL BARRIERS

Just as our biology tries to maintain our physical security our psychology tries to maintain our view of the world and our self concept. Our psychological defenses are especially activated when confronted by others ideas about the world that differ from our own.

False Attribution

We have a propensity to attribute motivational causation to the behavior of others. We do this in order to "explain" others behavior in terms that fit our world view and self-concept. If an individual is late to work once, we may think nothing of it; if the person is late once a week on Monday we may explain this by attributing the cause to a very active weekend social life, or assume the individual is irresponsible. Clearly these are judgments we choose to make rather than a reflection of "reality." The "true" cause for the lateness may be very different indeed such as if the person has a doctor's appointment early each Monday morning.

Transpersonal Invalidation[6]

Transpersonal invalidation occurs every time you tell your child that ghosts don't exist or tell subordinates that unions are communist inspired. In the former case if a child wakes up one night having seen ghosts, it is a real experience for the child and must be dealt with as such. In the later case if employees wish to organize a union for the benefit of having trained contract negotiators handle their wage, salary and grievance handling issues, questioning their motive at the level of an international conspiracy is invalidating the workers experience of simply seeking assistance much as their company does when hiring human resource professionals and lawyers.

This is another case where the usefulness of creating an organizational prosthesis comes in: designing an acceptable process that allows inclusion of diverse points of view while establishing a method for settling differences when rational agreement can't be reached. One such method is voting or using the entire framework of *Robert's Rules of Order* if there is a high probability of much conflict.

These devices, however, are still only as useful as the underlying good will of the participants which must first be established in order to maintain the viability of the system as a community in the first place.

There are other psychological states that influence organizational success. Issues of individual power, self-esteem, one's social comfort zone in interpersonal relationships, and in the application of competencies to assigned tasks, issues of dependency and relating to authority, trust and trustworthiness, and affection toward and being accepted by the group. Additionally, the fear of taking responsibility, of making a commitment to the community with all that that might entail, the lack of self-confidence, the lack of personal discipline and internal motivation will influence the complexion of the community.

There are also psychological defenses such as rationalization, repression, stereotyping, and projection which people use, sometimes unwittingly, to help them cope with their experience of the world. These defenses and other personality characteristics will always be operable and, in the aggregate, will affect the organizational climate in any given group. Being conscious of these dynamics enables the group to deal with them when they become dysfunctional. This is not to say the group is in a constant state of encounter, or group therapy, but these aspects of personality can affect performance in a group and can be dealt with by the group. Learning the basic skills needed to do this is a part of the training that each person receives as a member of the workplace community.

Risk Taking, Failure, and Blame Seeking

When things go wrong we want to know why. We seek a rational explanation, a reason we can understand. Though accidents do happen we struggle to understand them as if everything can be explained in an acceptable cause-effect fashion and determine who is responsible. Often this is compounded with the assignment of penalties (or rewards) because of the claim one has (or is assigned) to responsibility. Blaming someone also exonerates everyone else who is then relieved of any guilt that might be associated with the event and the burden of any penalties.

Knowing, if not blaming, also fills in the gestalt. We get a sense of completion, of filling in the whole of our understanding of events. But when blame is sought out we reflect a fundamental tenet of the old paradigm which is to establish winners and losers, failure and success. A total quality environment requires continuous universal learning and appropriate feedback about performance; not to assign blame and penalties but to correct errors and improve performance.

Frequent feedback will be necessary during the work process itself to help create the appropriate organizational response to circumstances. This will help avert truly costly mistakes and thoughtless unilateral action. The key is in the process of working with one another so that individual learning, group development, and assimilation of the intangibles takes place.

Respect for the individual also assumes that people take educated/calculated risks based on their intimate relationship with the circumstances surrounding their decisions. Individuals in solacracy should be at the center of the information necessary to do their job well.

Risk taking and experiencing momentary "failure" simply helps the individual, and thus, the organization push back the limits of its creativity, experience, capabilities. It is a natural part of the growth, learning, and adapting processes.

Inability to Transcend "isms"

Racism, sexism, and ageism are the most potent and deep seated biases we hold. They are sometimes hard to recognize and they are hard to overcome especially when they are institutionalized.

For want of a cup of coffee the organization was lost. When an executive insisted that a female subordinate prepare coffee for all meetings, his action became the basis for a sex discrimination suit that the company lost. The stereotyping of roles as well as steadfastly holding on to outmoded role perceptions can be very dangerous. In transforming a company into community one issue will be to deal with the old role differences, their associated privileges and, accordingly, their ordering of status. Where personal prerogatives once made arms and legs out of subordinates, instead of independent contributors out of colleagues and team members, the transition can be particularly difficult for the boss. Ego defenses and personal attachments to status or role can be a barrier to open communication and interpersonal trust. This has been THE major problem in situations where participative systems have been implemented without giving consideration to the existing psychological set of the managers experiencing the change.

Psychologically Flawed Individuals

Not everyone is emotionally stable and no one is perfect. All organizations function best when people are psychologically healthy. The overwhelming majority of people are. Where that is not the case, the organization can assist the individual in becoming appropriately functional in the community. If necessary, the community can remove them. Because of the group-based nature of work, dysfunctional behavior can be dealt with early and the remediation or dismissal processes can begin quickly. Unlike in traditional hierarchy where abusive superiors remain virtually unaccountable to their subordinates, in community this behavior triggers immediate attention. Where the dysfunction is limited to a certain type of interpersonal behavior which can be managed by simply reassigning the individual, this becomes a third remedy.

The conditions necessary for attaining the goal of a nontyrannical, psychologically healthy and participative corporation require that the accumulation of all powers in the same hands must be avoided and that factions may not succeed in acting adversely to the rights of other corporate citizens or the community.[7] In creating solacracy and participatory systems which hold all people accountable to the system the impact of psychologically flawed individuals is minimized because they are held accountable to the group.

An authoritarian personality

An authoritarian personality usually can't tolerate ambiguity and uncertainty. Frequent change is upsetting. The future being increasingly chaotic will threaten this type of individual. The authoritarian personality is characterized by fear and the inability to trust, to let go, to detach—an inability to being vulnerable, to be part of interdependent interpersonal relationships.

We Expect Predictability in the World

When we want or need something, from a table in a favorite restaurant, to the car running every morning to a card on our birthday, we like to assume everything will operate as expected. We know intellectually about the world of chaos, the intangibles, and the abstractions, but we would prefer that these be minimized. Being in a constant state of flexibility is to be in no state at all. It is stressful not knowing what to expect all the time; in some ways it even paralyzes us. We need to balance predictability in relations at work while dealing with customers' and clients' unpredictable demands from the outside world.

In living in a turbulent world we tend to take our pleasures for granted while the disappointments end up defining our change agenda. Perhaps instead of justifying saying "yes" to someone in our organization we should make each other justify saying "no" as 3M does in its new product development system.[8]

Intensity of Change Creates a Personal Overload

The stress one experiences in massive change processes just isn't worth it and it may not even be within one's capability to handle without severe psychological costs. Phasing in the change and providing training, and personal preparation is necessary to avoid overload and disorientation.

Self Defeat

There are a variety of ways individuals contribute to their own failure, some are controllable and, sadly, some are subconsciously deliberate. And some are simply a matter of choosing a lifestyle that emphasizes activities other than work.

Some reasons for failure, however, are also a matter of not really thinking much about one's role in the organizational environment and not trying to improve it. For example: not keeping up in one's field or not reading widely; being unwilling or unable to look at the influence of one's values on his or her behavior; having a role in a work group that is not clearly thought out; or having a win/lose attitude that pervades interpersonal dealings.

Under these circumstances one may fall into patterns resulting in blind complacency and dronelike behavior which leads to an unquestioning acceptance of the system and the conventional wisdom. One pursues his own needs based on a sense of their deficiency and gets impatient with process issues and change programs. Even thinking becomes an unwanted activity by raising too many questions or suggesting the imperfection of the system. This may give rise to a fear of change and lead to personal stress over one's job security—especially in a recession. Unfortunately there has been enough evidence with recent restructurings that, too often, change does lead to a loss of jobs.

Impatience

Finding others difficult, slow, or obstructive only because they do not share the same interests or have the capacity to move at our own rate makes one an irritant to others and conflicts are likely to emerge.

Self-Oriented Behaviors (SOBs)

SOBs can also hinder one's effectiveness particularly if the act is a misguided rationalization. For example, power oriented dominance strategies and their accompanying mind set are SOBs as are excessive pride and the need to always be right, be on top of everything, or always needing to be the most creative person in the group.

Power

One way to overcome the arrogance of leadership is through MBDL (Management By Doing Less). It is important to avoid thinking that because one is entrusted with a position or with certain organizational resources that one, by definition, knows more than others or possesses all the wisdom necessary to make decisions for others. To impose one's will on others simply by virtue of holding a position in a hierarchy is to invalidate the contributions of those closest to the specific problems they, themselves, are paid to deal with.

Caution

These and other psychological barriers interfere with the organization's potential and demotivate members. People are affected by the barriers as they create a tense and stressful environment. Dissatisfaction sets in and the temptation arises to go back to the old ways of doing things. People who can make the transition, and are willing to work toward successful change, risk being frustrated and becoming cynical when improper implementation invalidates the change process.

Transforming an organization is a difficult process and everyone's barriers arise in a self-protective manner, often subconsciously. The change program must anticipate this and plan accordingly.

Aspects of the old paradigm such as a hierarchical mentality about people at work and the allocation of compensation and perks, will linger and fade unevenly among fellow workers. Establishing the value of specific skills, jobs and roles is a very difficult process. So-called market forces alone are not enough to convince the group of fairness which will drive much of the concern members have surrounding the compensation of individuals as they measure their preparation, experience, skills and proficiencies against one another. The sophistication of each person's understanding and commitment to the new paradigm and the new processes as illustrated throughout this book will influence the selection, orientation, and development of new members. It will also influence the patience individuals and the group will have for the processes of working through the difficult early transformation. But here the disease may also be the cure in as much as continuous attention to process issues and team-building will help overcome the very difficulties these aspects of community may create in the early days of their implementation during everyone's readjustment.

ORGANIZATIONAL BARRIERS

At the organizational level there are also specific unique barriers to overcome. First is the "we've always done it this way syndrome". Where one doesn't naturally discover the need to begin the transformation there is little motivation, especially if business is profitable. Simply put, if there is no pressing need to change or if we haven't thought about it, it isn't a problem or worth worrying about. It is an attitude of the "Why fix it if it ain't broke?" school of thought.

The skills required to make the transition may be in scarce supply and the cost to begin the process may seem prohibitive but preparing for the future requires starting now.

TABOOS

The Power of the Status Quo

The status quo is powerful by virtue of its very legitimacy and because of most people' s tremendous zone of indifference. Perhaps it is best that way. Jefferson speaking through the Declaration: "Prudence indeed, will dictate that Governments long established should not be changed for light and transient Causes." Remember, it took a virtual second revolution by workingmen and women over a seventy-five-year period from the Civil War to the depression to seek out some measure of protection from an economic system prone to abuse instead of benevolence. The right to organize and form representative unions with the accompanying right to strike is a fairly recent phenomenon and even now there is a stigma attached to union activity; it being considered somehow subversive or unpatriotic. The status quo is a glacier—extremely slow in moving toward the future.

Legitimacy of Tradition

Long standing institutions, whether political, religious, or economic, develop a legitimacy simply by surviving the ages. The accepted role of a boss or an owner to acquire and dispose of one's property as he sees fit is a venerated keystone of a market economy and so permeates our society it is virtually an inviolable characteristic of the culture. Therein lies a societal dilemma. On the one hand respect for property rights is a safeguard of our personal security and freedom; it protects the fruits of our labor. It is motivational as well since one will work as long and hard for personal gain as one so chooses without fear of confiscatory taxes or other intrusions of the state. The demise of the Soviet Union is ample evidence of the debilitating power of state ownership of all property.

On the other hand we know that as a society we desperately need to limit and regulate corporate affairs for the good of the national community. The fear is of course that any limitations or regulation will lead to the destruction of the system itself by bureaucrats once the regulatory process is set in motion.

The right to own and dispose of our personal property extends to all permutations of the concept and from one's automobile, house and one's personal effects to small businesses, factories, global services and even huge enterprises such as General Motors, Exxon, Microsoft and Safeway which, under the protection of laws of incorporation, enjoy the same rights as individuals (though not always the same responsibilities). The owners of these enterprises are also entitled to the unfettered disposal of their "property" as they see fit. Of course there are regulations such as in the areas of pollution control, fiduciary responsibilities and reporting requirements, and safety and health related areas. No regulations focus on the management methods used or the internal governance systems, however, and do not recognize the corporate environment as an emergent polity.

We know something isn't right when we consider a person's home and belongings in the same context as the plant, machinery and waste of a major corporation but we are paralyzed to act when it comes to making any exception to the principle of private property. Pressing environmental issues show that our entire way of life may be in jeopardy if we tenaciously persist in living by a conservative interpretation of the right to personal property. Continued unfettered pollution alone will simply destroy our air and water and make human life in this country impossible. Or, if mergers and acquisitions, the buying and trading of businesses and employees, continues unabated individuals by the millions will be arbitrarily and capriciously dismissed from the means of maintaining their livelihood. As businesses contract and fold under a debt burden they tend to move operations offshore. Even if they remain profitable the net effect, as we have seen in the 1980s and early 90s, is that the standard of living of the workers caught in this shuffle declines and wage concessions and lower paying alternative jobs result from the reorganizations.[9]

CEOs in effect have a proprietary right over the assets of organizations including the human resources and can simply dispose of most anything at will. Thus, the supremacy of money (property) and material accumulation over national well being or nonmaterial shared values is reinforced on a tremendous scale.

Workers, even those at the highest levels, and the poor are by definition inadequate. They have no money, thus no power. People with money can simply buy the right to manage others by virtue of investing that money in wages to pay employees. Without money, one needs to prove oneself as in a professional capacity—a long validation process of earning a degree, being loyal to a company or code, and surviving organizational trials by fire. Still the process of getting the right to manage others requires no more preparation than does parenting. It is being able to buy and manage workers toward one's personal ends. Alternatively, one can earn an appointment to a managerial post to serve the owner or investors. Thus, management per se has never even been considered an act important enough to require specific training in interpersonal relations and governance as if people matter. By the same token, in our culture parenting, the most important human function, is still formally an untutored exercise lest we give rise to the cry that it is a parent's right to do with their "property" (children) what they wish!

INHIBITORS TO APPLYING THEORY

There are many difficulties in applying the new thinking even when the barriers are understood.

Sensing the Need to Change

The day-to-day work of an organization is programmed by the existing demands to provide a product or service. In meeting these demands, an organization is a boiling cauldron of individual emotions, competing self-interests and factions. This makes sensing, analyzing, and acting upon the need for change a difficult, if not an impossible, prospect without the deliberate and substantial purposefulness that only top management can bring to bear along with the irreversible commitment to the change process.

Suspicion

The existing system casts a shadow of organizational abuse and control over individuals that leads to a deep suspicion of change programs among most employees. Manipulative strategies will be rejected, as will transient programs and non participative processes. Trust and evidence of real and substantial change must be established early.

DEALING WITH DEMOCRACY

"An organization is democratic if and only if the process of arriving at . . . policy is compatible with the conditions of popular sovereignty and the condition of political equality. . . . Political equality and popular sovereignty are not absolute goals; we must ask ourselves how much leisure, privacy, consensus, stability, income, security, progress, status, and probably many other goals we are prepared to forgo for an additional increment of political equality."[10]

Until recently, the comforts of our material wealth have convinced the masses that the system was working for them; everyone was getting richer. But, ". . . stunned families are discovering that the social escalator is going down for the first time since the Great Depression."[11] The new generation is not expected to do better than its parents. In an age of mass education and mass media this is a dangerous situation. Promises won't suffice when evidence of significant change is not forthcoming. In an era of changing values and ecological danger, issues of democracy in the workplace will gain serious attention particularly as the workplace is recognized as the arena most able to influence our personal well being either through the quality of work life it establishes or the economic rewards it provides.

Perceptual Gap

But how do we create an egalitarian workplace without substantial preparation? We must first overcome the ingrained tendencies to evaluate, compete and measure everyone on both real and imagined criteria as is our national obsession to order everything around us from sports contests, grades in school, cities in which to live, investments to make, ad infinitum. The perceptual gap, then, in terms of how we see and measure each other, and the issues that arise from doing so, will need to be addressed before changes are made toward an egalitarian system. Each organization must begin to discuss these issues in depth and begin to explore appropriate first steps to reconcile the value shift occurring in the society and the way we work with one another.

The perceptual gap also includes how we see "our" responsibilities compared to "their" responsibilities. There is a constant temptation to blame "them" while "we" take credit for our circumstances. There must be a realignment of our perceptions to accept the organization as "us" and to take the necessary share of the responsibility for its welfare; its successes and failures. Community helps us do this.

Tyranny of the Majority

What about the creative or intelligent individual who clearly has a better idea and gets lost in the group or overruled by it? In democracy, is the painting reduced to separate colors? The house to just a box? How do you maintain the support of the group when you are trying to create something as an individual? Some things can't be done and shouldn't be done in committee.

Being democratic and participative, however, doesn't mean everything is done by a committee. This should be emphasized. And it is also possible to nurture a group's wisdom. The danger is allowing a tyranny of the group to develop. It isn't inevitable.

There are innumerable options in establishing the rules for group decision making and behavior. Remember, everything is tentative. We can choose the system that works best for us and amend it when necessary. We can even assign decisions randomly to individuals to propose a course of action to the group. That person must then seek out the ideas and opinions of the best minds within and outside the group before presenting his or her work to the group for approval. Once again, this is just one option.

And there are unlimited possibilities in structuring a participative process from choosing direct or representational groups, rotating responsibilities, creating individual terms of office, subgroup assignments or ad hoc individual assignments, and even establishing a process for personal bidding for responsibilities within the group based on credits earned through previous job performance or service to the group. These are just a few options to balance individual accountability to group responsibilities.

Perhaps having individuals accountable for the actions of the group could also be used to prevent people from hiding behind the facade of committee decision making. This would make it a personal versus an anonymous process.

RULES OF THUMB FOR IMPLEMENTING CHANGE

Change should proceed after an examination of the entire system—
not just a segment of it. Regarding innovation remember:

- Innovation enters an organization faster at the top (especially in command and control hierarchical bureaucracies)
- Innovation is accepted faster in small packages
- Some persons will accept no innovation at all
- Too many innovations at one time will slow each other down
- If alienated, conservative or bureaucratic managers do not destroy an innovation, the side effects of the change may
- People will accept change faster after it has been accepted or advocated by one of their own
- A highly unified organization is capable of both massive resistance and rapid change
- People accept change faster when they have had a chance to talk about it.
- The chances of change by written directive are near zero.[12]

The real danger in the minefield of barriers and inhibitors is to think they are insurmountable. One may be overwhelmed by their potential to obstruct fundamental change and be tempted to revert to the old paradigm. And it is so easy to do. It might even be irresistibly appealing. Don't.

As Polaroid's vice president of human resources has said, ". . . there will be times when the company gets clobbered for slipping into the old paradigm." But Polaroid isn't going back. He says, "We're resolved that we're going to change."[13]

Do not compromise good management practices in bad times. Until the transformation is complete and the system is fully integrating the new concepts there may still be opportunities to renege on the changes by top managers. They should not violate the trust of community members. If nothing else it would precipitate a crisis the organization might never recover from.

Good practice isn't a luxury, it is a requirement of doing business in the contemporary world. There simply is no going back. The organization needs people to pull together the most in bad times. To undermine them is to commit a slow organizational suicide.

Good practice simply can't be considered an arbitrary luxury dependent on the moods of a single individual or faction. It must be guaranteed, preferably through a constitution or bylaws developed through a democratic process among community members. And it should be binding upon all in the community until they are amended by the community.

In spite of the barriers, the direction is clear. New paradigm consciousness is rising; it is advocated by the professional class and a growing number of middle managers. The new paradigm cuts through the barriers. Aligning organizations with the new paradigm is also the right thing to do in order to turn back a deteriorating quality of work life engulfing the vast majority of Americans.

NOTES

[1] Quoted in: Laurence J. Peter, *Peter's Quotations* (New York: Bantam, 1979), p. 178.

[2] T. Paine, *The Rights of Man* (Baltimore, MD: Pelican, 1969), pp. 63–64.

[3] M. Moskowitz, R. Levering and M. Katz, *Everybody's Business* (New York: Doubleday, 1990), p. 242.

[4] R. Bly, *Iron John* (Reading, MA: Addison-Wesley, 1990), p.133.

[5] Quoted in: J. Patterson and P. Kim, *The Day America Told the Truth* (New York: Prentice Hall), 1991, p. 149.

[6] See: R. D. Laing, *The Politics of Experience* (New York: Ballantine, 1971).

[7] Paraphrased from R. A. Dahl, *A Preface to Democratic Theory* (Chicago: The University of Chicago Press, 1956), p. 11.

[8] T. Peters and R. Waterman, *In Search of Excellence* (New York: Harper & Row, 1982), p. 227.

[9] D. L. Barlett and J. B. Steele, *America: What Went Wrong?* (Kansas City: Andrews and McMeel, 1992).

[10] R. A. Dahl, *A Preface to Democratic Theory* (Chicago: The University of Chicago Press, 1956), pp. 37, 51.

[11] "Downward Mobility," *Business Week*, March 23, 1992, p. 57.

[12] C. A. Dailey, *Entrepreneurial Management* (New York: McGraw-Hill, 1971), pp. 44–46.

[13] C. Cox, "The Third Annual Business Ethics Awards for Excellence in Ethics," *Business Ethics*, November/December 1991, p. 21.

Chapter Nine

An Agenda for Monday Morning: Making It Happen

"Not to dream more boldly may turn out to be, in view of present realities, simply irresponsible."

—*George Leonard*[1]

Now we're heading home and we are on a journey of a different sort, this time inward bound. We will look more closely at the personal responsibilities and actions necessary to make the transformation a success. In this chapter, we will focus on some actions that we can literally take on "Monday morning" to begin taking control over the transformation of our organizations and our work lives. Turning our organizations around and realigning them with the historical imperative of our democratic traditions is an exciting prospect. And it will be especially satisfying as we witness the most hedonistic, self-indulgent, CEO-centric period in our nation's history come to an end. Let's take the steps necessary to make the change a permanent one and not an optional exercise of a CEO's benevolence. After 150 years of human resource management experiments and proselytizing, it is about time.

For the first time, as teams of workers are themselves nurtured to assume the duties of middle management, and as new computer technology is brought on line, middle managers and professionals become viewed as disposable. Clearly this is a de-skilling that forebodes another round of "trimming the fat" before the reorganization and deindustrialization of American business is complete. Middle managers are beginning to see the writing on the wall; their security is threatened and top management expects them to sink with the ship as companies downsize, fold up, or move off-shore. The perks begin to ring hollow given the debasement, frustration and exploitation large numbers of professionals are now feeling. Sacrifice and loyalty to the organization have become meaningless words to employees disillusioned by the regular massive unceremonious dismissals of their colleagues. Now, as they become willing to act and if they follow through "Monday morning," they will have a profound effect on the future of the American workplace and will witness the remission of the corporate cancer that is critically weakening our system.

Personal networking alone—readying ourselves for the moment when contacts lead to an escape into another job in another organization—will no longer save professionals from spoliation by old-style management and the collapse of the system. There is simply no place to hide. The cancer of the old paradigm is too widespread, but as I have pointed out there is reason for hope.

A great psychological advantage will be ours when we begin taking the initiative for leading the change effort by focusing attention on the internal organizational structure and processes. Understand that it will take some time but have faith in the process because with determination, and a sense of the value of the journey you are about to take, you will immediately begin to feel a renewed vigor at work and a refreshed sense of purpose. There is indeed something heroic in individuals who decide to make a difference in their lives and to help others do the same, so keep at it. We need more local heroes, not messiahs.

We need not wait for CEOs to deign to empower us. It is not for them to do so. We know we are bright, responsible and earnest. We are trained, committed professionals. And we are ready to embrace self-management in building workplace community so that it reflects the full use of our talents in an equitable, responsive, and caring fashion. We have already shown this by our involvement in professional associations. Today, millions of people sacrifice their private time to improve their personal skills and their job performance to meet the exigencies of their jobs and to network with professional colleagues. We will empower ourselves! We begin by recognizing that organizations are entities serving all stakeholders. We recognize that as professionals with extensive training in, and commitment to, making organizations work we are perfectly situated to make the changes required to align our organizations to the new reality. We can bring them back on track and recommit ourselves to the promise of the American dream. So now, instead of waiting for instructions and permission from the CEO, we'll simply do it ourselves. Why else have we spent so many years studying, networking, and developing professionally? It is time we use our talents for positive change to facilitate the transformational process.

ROADS TO REFORM

There are basically three roads to reforming organizations. First, the conventional approach assumes all programs for change will be initiated from the top of the organization and disseminated, under the auspices of the CEO, throughout the organization. This is most likely the avenue top managers feel comfortable with. It was also the avenue most understood by middle management who dedicated themselves to the faithful execution of top management's policy as they strove to be partners with, then replace, top management. Today the search for excellence, for example, or total quality, or quality circles, or even self-managed teams in some cases, are the kinds of interventions that are often (though not exclusively) introduced under direction from the top of the organization. Books on management predominantly look at this avenue. And it is the easiest road to take.

A second avenue for reform often originates outside the organization. External bodies such as consultants, regulatory agencies, legislatures, and courts frequently introduce new organizational practices. Equal employment opportunity is an example, as are the copious regulations concerning safety and health, pollution control, rules for union organizing, and many other acts promulgating social policy that emanate from outside sources.

The third avenue for reform springs from the bottom up. Infrequently used since unions won their battles in the 1930s and 1940s, the potential of this approach is a sleeping giant that is, ironically, only now reawakening, just as we find unions in disfavor and decline! There are two reasons for this. First, unions themselves will either align with the transformation occurring in the workplace or they will become totally irrelevant. If they take on a facilitative role for organizational change and don't just push for monetary benefits for their members, they could once again become a very powerful force. One way for them to do this is to transform into professional or guild associations that help their members learn new skills, find jobs industrywide (or in new industries!), advocate quality of work life reforms and protect their members from dismissal for whistleblowing or activity surrounding the changes we have discussed. If unions change in this manner they will be joined by professionals and other white-collar workers now very receptive to reform.

It is also quite possible that there will be a convergence of techniques and goals used by professional associations and unons that attract most middle managers, professionals and skilled labor, if they both take an active leadership role in quality of work life reforms and the coming transformation. Together a hybrid organization, an alliance, or a panoply of organizations, can support their members in personal initiatives taken to reform the organization and achieve an orderly, secure, transition into workplace community.

The second and potentially most potent reason why community will be introduced into organizations is that the popularity of teams and self-managed groups is a fire starter of reform that may just turn out to be the final preparatory step before the onset of the transformation. Oddly enough it was middle management that finally brought self-management into organizations. And though it ultimately will undermine much of what traditional middle managers do, it may also liberate those that are flexible, creative and adaptable to recreate their own roles and to choose a new path for personal and professional development.

By devolving responsibilities to the work groups themselves and empowering teams to act independently, organizations are setting in motion a force that will not be easily redirected from its imperative of power sharing and infusing democratic practices back into the organization as a whole. It was largely middle management and the professional staff that achieved this incredible structural breakthrough now spreading through large organizations. It is in this very redesign that their salvation resides. When self-managed teams are implemented, they will replace or embrace professionals and middle managers or lead to a redesign of the professional's role. The choice is largely their own. Those that have been made truly redundant have usually been eliminated from the organization, as we have seen, but the corporate imagination has not even begun to think about utilizing people in new ways. Its penchant for hiring and firing as needed dies hard even in light of the logic that retraining and reassignment not only expands an organization's skill pool but builds morale and motivation; both are essential for establishing and maintaining a high level of commitment to work and the organization.

The irony is that while top management has generally been occupied with strategic and financial issues, a very sophisticated training effort has evolved to imbue the work force at all operational levels with very humanistic, cooperative, positive values—particularly openness in communication and building teamwork, trust, harmony and quality-relevant norms. In doing this, management sets the stage for workers to want complete synchronicity between the way they work with one another and the way the "organization", that is, the structures, policies and norms dictated by upper management, treats them. The dissonance between the stated objectives and the reality of personal treatment creates cynicism and may defeat the intentions of the various training programs, but it is obvious that the training programs consistently reflect the new paradigm, the ethic of involvement and cooperation. Manipulative techniques and more programs by top management done "to" instead of "with" employees as members of a community will gain appreciably smaller, even negative returns, unless they are backed up with institutionalization of a structure that guarantees democratic rights to all members and acknowledges their legitimate stake in the enterprise.

Rebellion only occurs when awareness is achieved and conditions show signs of improving. If professionalization and known best practice are widely understood at the operative level, as is rapidly becoming the case, it will only be a short time before everyone demands the development of real community—a social technology that enables the transformation to succeed.

HOW CAN YOU INFLUENCE THE FUTURE?

When one person decides to act, it is remarkable what can happen. Ralph Nader taking on GM was a classic case of a modern David and Goliath showdown. Ross Perot taking on the two-party system is another example of how extraordinary commitment can be demonstrated. There are infinitely more ways of expressing your commitment in a meaningful way even if it isn't taking on GM or the political establishment. Ralph Nader was a lone crusader who eventually accumulated an extensive stable of "raiders." And Ross Perot, was a billionaire who ignited a populist revolt.

When we look inside organizations for the champions of change, they are often quietly at work exercising their brilliance in what they do and how they present themselves to colleagues. You can observe their style and energy at routine meetings and in their day-to-day commitment to high integrity and taking the initiative to live their beliefs. They have an agenda. They are focused. They respond to their environments with a consistent view of what needs to be done and where they stand on major change issues. In that sense they are centered, have clear values, and see how their objectives can be realized through their career within the organization.

To my knowledge, there are no books that discuss how an individual other than the boss can begin the process of taking responsibility for organizational reform. There are no books that assist the individual in stemming the abuses and the powerlessness one feels at work except law books that help individuals bring suit against their employers. Some books appear to offer individuals a way to change their work lives but treat the reader like a victim or advocate an atmosphere of resistance rather than the assertion of creative, organizationally sustaining actions that will actually keep the group's goal in mind.

Through the deliberate use of personal power in the course of conducting their affairs at work, an individual can exert a very strong influence on the nature and direction of events in the workplace. By having a clear personal agenda for improving the processes at work such as the way meetings are conducted, one can assert his or her recommendations in a positive way likely to be accepted by the organization. For example, simply requesting that a pre-meeting notice be sent to each participant with an itemization of topics and times allocated and the role each individual is expected to play, infinitely increases the efficiency of a meeting.

In everything you do, when you are clear about intentions such as to keep everyone informed and to encourage all relevant participation, there will be abundant, almost daily, opportunities to institute incremental improvements. One powerful opportunity is created when you sit down with an important work associate, and initiate a discussion about how you both work together, in order to clarify goals and develop or refresh a common understanding of each other's role and a new appreciation for the other's efforts. This small invitation to cooperation and acknowledgment of past help, whether to a colleague, boss or subordinate, so positively focuses attention on the relationship that it opens new avenues for inspired effort in the future. It helps refine and fuse an important relationship. This single initiative, though at first awkward, emotionally risky, and fraught with personal apprehension, because it may be out of the usual mode of behaving at work, is guaranteed to stimulate the development of a higher level of closeness that will instantly make the workplace less stressful.

These are but two examples of how, by living your new awareness and demonstrating your renewed commitment, you can begin a major change in the consciousness of those around you. They will perceive you differently, with added respect. They will also begin their own consciousness raising experience as they perceive new possibilities and the benefits of workplace community in which they can become a more authentic communicator, less stressed, less prone to negative politics and destructive game playing and more at ease with their colleagues. In another sense this is modeling the potential of formal and large systems change through personal example that shows others the results of a new way of being.

Personal growth and its expression in the workplace must be contextualized, however, to avoid the pitfall of any zealot who lacks a sense of proportion and overwhelms those around him or her. We have seen all too much of that in recent times. Thus, it is important to maintain a balance and a mindfulness of the readiness of those around you to understand and act upon the new attitudes and behaviors you'll be modeling. A frustrating disappointment of the personal growth movement has been an almost exclusive focus on the individual, ignoring the fact that people live in a web of relationships. Thus, ironically, while individuals have sought personal satisfaction or self-actualization independent of one another and outside of the workplace, their very self-centeredness during this pursuit makes it difficult to develop mutually satisfying relationships within groups and/or organizations. Thus the personal growth devotee has been accused of the ultimate escape from personal social responsibility—a complete turning away from the group as being a lost cause, or becoming disillusioned, surrendering to solely egocentric needs. Personal growth efforts have, ironically, often involved a mind set that pushes people apart and makes relationships even more difficult due to the insistence of like mindedness among all associates. As a result, many organizations in the recent past have become hopelessly undermined by interpersonal struggles for individual gain at all levels, or staffed with the defeated who have reverted to virtually an anomic existence. In your efforts to model reforms, take on a coaching, facilitative, patient and respectful demeanor as you show others the power of personal change.

These ideas are gathering enormous force and traditional organizations, like the proverbial camel before the last straw, seem blind to the impending transformation. What shall be the catalyst? The last straw? Your new behavior.

The smartest, most capable, most resourceful group of people in the world inhabit corporate America. And you are one of them. Don't squander your potential as we have squandered our other natural resources. As you keep a keen eye on the areas in need of change and begin discussing these ideas with your network of colleagues, you will be able to bring about much change—especially since it is the middle management professional class that is designing and operationalizing organizational policies in the first place. Once their consciousness has been raised and they embrace the possibilities of the emergent paradigm and its implications for creating community, together you can make it happen.

WHAT CAN BE DONE: FIRST GET READY

"In and through community lies the salvation of the world."[2]

—*M. Scott Peck*

The strategies outlined here are designed to help professionals and middle managers and each person in an organizational setting ease the transformational process now under way.

The following catalog of suggestions is designed to help you immediately prepare yourself and your organization for the changes ahead. The suggestions are centered in four domains: first, the individual domain is explored and suggestions are made to help you keep informed and personally meet the challenge. The second domain centers around your role in an existing group or one that you will help form for the purpose of thinking about and stimulating change in your organization. The third domain centers on social actions you can take from your position in a supportive professional network. The fourth domain centers on those activities that engage the larger external community in creating change in your organization or the industry in which it is embedded. See Figure 9-1 for an illustration of how actions in the domains are interrelated and influence organizational change.

THE INDIVIDUAL DOMAIN

A Self Appraisal

First, one needs to ask: Do I really want to help make this happen? Am I personally willing to practice the tenets discussed here? Am I willing to develop the qualities to help me improve my behavior? Am I committed to taking responsibility for the transformation?

Keep Learning

Recognize that new conditions require new behaviors. Make learning a continuous process that enables you to deal with the new structures and demands of your job. It should also focus on building the appropriate employer-employee relationships best suited to the new work environment. Get ready to master the coming change by learning the skills outlined in Chapter Seven. Focus on process issues. Remember the increase in meetings and conferencing, either face to face or through electronic groupware, will require a new cooperative social technology. Meeting facilitation and process observation skills will be essential for each individual in the organizations of tomorrow. Make this an immediate part of your personal agenda for professional growth; especially if you are to take the initiative in establishing the kind of change network for your organization that will be discussed shortly.

EXHIBIT 9–1
Transforming Organizations

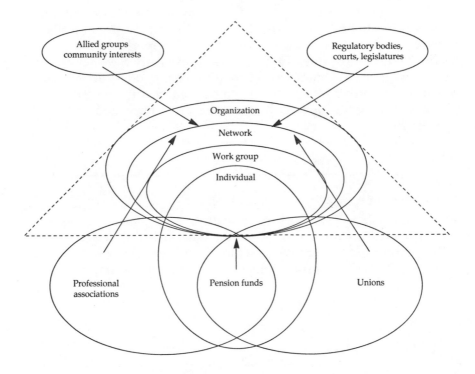

The Domains of Action

TAKING THE INITIATIVE: SPECIFIC STEPS

Build Networks, Get Allies

Don't pass the buck and don't profit at another's expense. The CEO can intimidate an organization because everyone feels vulnerable and beholden to him or her. Too many people are satisfied if they remain while others are laid off, or if they get a raise and others do not. Few people are willing to risk their jobs for the cause of justice or to stand up for other people. Most would like to but feel alone, powerless to do anything fearing they have no allies and that they would merely be another sacrifice to a lost cause. We see this behavior all the time. Personal fear is the driving force. Why fire me? Betty's newer, younger, not as good, etc., etc. Unions were broken in their early years in part because of individuals' fear of loss and sacrifice if they acted. If alliances and networks come to agreement about not accepting arbitrary and capricious behavior and resisting the unjust because it is unjust, they will force organizations to back down in the face of demands for change. You can't do it alone but someone has to start. There is only strength in numbers. The wisdom in first developing a network is that it is a way for you to gauge and develop support so you can know you are not alone. It is a risk-free way of starting the process. What would happen if the work force wouldn't accept layoffs without participative due process? If everyone supported one another? That grisly practice of suddenly decimating the work force would come to an immediate halt and the layoff process would be redesigned. Several unions, like the UAW, have been able to secure generous severance packages that include up to a year's salary or some combination of salary and benefits for workers faced with a plant closing. When GM closed its plant in Van Nuys, California last year it came as no surprise, the workers learned about it the year before and were kept on the payroll until the end of their contract in the fall of 1993.[3] That approach certainly eases the impact and auto workers have been treated well, but on occasion legislative initiatives are considered to cover everyone affected by a plant closure or part of a massive layoff. Some plans would require up to two-years advanced notice of plant closings or extensive layoffs. While this provides a measure of economic safety to those who lose their jobs, wouldn't getting them creatively involved in saving their jobs be a more positive productive first step?

Where you are a manager, begin taking the initiative in your area of influence. Begin raising the consciousness of your colleagues to see the organization as a holistic system and each employee as a stakeholder with equal standing.

Also, suggest the codification of those policies that are consistent with the new paradigm. Developing policy is better than merely practicing the new behaviors as an individual since it moves others to behave similarly. Clearly it expands the domain of personal influence.

Analyze Existing Roles

Conduct a role analysis to determine each other's expectations and perceived strengths and weaknesses. It helps the immediate work-group form more balanced relationships. It clarifies roles but also helps each person establish an agenda for professional growth.

Find out what's separating people. Are there different perks when they really ought to be the same for everyone? Are some people hourly and other's salaried; why? Where and why do norms differ? Are individuals forced to compete in situations requiring coopera-tion? How is one group pitted against another? What do you or your group think should be done? What could be done now? Later?

Renew Social Bonds

Reestablish a sense of caring and respect for one another. Develop more opportunities to mingle informally by taking common breaks or having lunch together or starting a community involvement project together or in any of a number of ways begin to appreciate each other as complete human beings. The better you know one another, the bet-ter you communicate; the better you understand each other; the bet-ter you work with one another the easier it is to participate in the change process.

Establish a Variety of Means to Communicate With One Another

Keep each other informed about transformational topics of the day as well as industry in general and your organization.

- Newsletters, bulletin boards for notes and announcements, E-mail exchanges, breakfast, breaks and lunch meetings, work meetings (each should have a definite social component even if for only a few minutes), or occasional issue update memos or newsletters are a few examples of common methods for keeping in touch. Begin to solicit people's needs and match them with talents already within the group; create an education exchange where people teach each other and share resources and don't wait for an official training program to be organized by the personnel department.

- Building friendships at work through social clubs, teams, ride sharing, lunches, and on-going socialization programs that include deliberate attention to organizational issues as they involve individuals are ways of relaxing socially with one another. Don't hesitate to initiate informal gatherings, meetings, support groups, and interest groups as the need arises.

- Work space can be rearranged to be more expressive of yourself and others, and facilitative of communications between individuals.

- Seek out and promote new work relevant skill training and exposure to lateral interests that keep you mentally stimulated and enthused. This can be literally anything of interest. Here the point is to further one's creative potential and mental acuity.

- Sponsor a lunch-time speaker or activity of a personal growth nature. Listen to a poetry reading or classical music during lunch. Create ways for enjoying the workplace more.

- Urge a resolution of those things that bug people out of proportion to their true significance. These are usually environmental issues at work ranging from smokers rights and handicapped access, to cleanliness of facilities, to location of vending machines, to the spreading of rumors, to the distribution of equipment and resources. Have community sessions to deal with these and other housekeeping chores. Select an unofficial ombudsmen if an official one doesn't already exist. Make that individual the "mayor" of your company or section and allow him or her to represent you on these issues.

- Learn managerial mediation skills and teach them to others. Offer your services to those around you to mediate for colleagues in conflict.

- Be a mentor to a junior person. Welcome newcomers into established groups and into ongoing activities.

- Sponsor a "think-in" or "do-in" on a persistent work-relevant problem. Would that be any more unusual than the many meetings now focused on issues defined by top management or mandated by regulatory changes? Middle managers in human resource management in Silicon Valley have established a Diversity Round Table to deal candidly with ways of promoting diversity consciousness throughout representatives' organizations. They meet irregularly to share resources. In a rather unique fashion during introductions they begin to list the resources each member is willing to share and later compare these with needs that have been expressed by other members. This completely volunteer group of professionals is leading a major change effort in the organizations they represent. They are clearly raising the awareness level of their organizations regarding the richness of the multi-cultural and multi-lifestyle environments they have become and how they can tap into this new found resource.

- Do not let anyone get away with abusiveness. Get like-minded individuals to discover how to detect its manifestation and then to commit themselves to challenging its systemic or personal roots. The vivid demonstration of the insidiousness of sexual harassment in the workplace by Anita Hill was only the tip of the organizational harassment iceberg. Abusiveness takes many forms and serves many purposes—usually, however, these are all utilized by individuals more powerful than their victims and almost always for personal gain. In some cases institutional harassment exists and it too must be recognized and challenged. Demands for excessive and routine overtime, for example, can be a form of institutionalized harassment when the organization or an individual insists on additional unpaid service without the willing consent of the individual involved.

- Develop group activities and social events to involve as many people as possible from different departments to sensitize them to the diversity of the work force and to teach teamwork skills. It is important for individuals to have the opportunity to mix with, work with, and play with, members of different professions, and from different organizational locations and levels, as well as with people of other races, cultures and lifestyles. Increasing the comfort zones of individuals is important to overcome both unconscious and conscious barriers that interfere with people working together.

Get a Personal Ally

Changing an organization isn't easy when you try to do so from the bottom or the middle, especially if you are trying to alter the very culture of the organization in ways it may resist. Doing so alone is to invite endless frustration. If for no other reason, getting an ally will reassure you that your efforts are worthwhile and serve as a reality check when times get tough.

Document your attempts to change, to discuss, to suggest new ideas. This is an artifact of self protective behavior of the old paradigm, but it may become important if the organization responds with familiar hardball tactics. It will also be useful when apprising colleagues in the network or a professional organization of your efforts. If dismissal ever becomes a reality, your record will be the basis for developing your defense and it will also remind you of the support you do have.

Always be open with ideas but try to develop compatriots in your network who will support their expression at meetings. It also helps to air these ideas because they encourage others, establish the legitimacy of their existence within a conventional setting and may inspire amendments and assistance from others either immediately or in the future. Networking among those who share your ideas is important, even critical. It is also important to begin establishing the agenda and to set in motion an understanding of the issues that need to be dealt with in the presence of a body of interested professionals willing to make a difference. Future allies will arise from these seeds planted early Monday morning.

Diagnosing Your Organization

In more innocent times people interested in change were admonished to "work within the system." There was the implicit notion that the system could be changed, and would in fact be amenable to change, if you simply worked your way into the old boys network. We have seen the fallacy of this position demonstrated over and over again. The bureaucratic antibodies are simply too effective. And even if you made it to the inner sanctums your urge to change the system would have been neutered by the years of waiting.

Typically, once you begin to raise difficult questions from the inside, you are branded a maverick, disloyal, an ingrate. In short, you become an intolerable threat and the system discards or discredits you. Whistleblowers are a prime example of this phenomenon. Even when they attempt to quietly inform the powers that be that a major problem exists and needs to be dealt with—a problem that has major direct legal or financial consequences for the organization—the individual is treated as a pariah, not a savior. Professor David Ewing of Harvard in a recent survey of the corporate due process system says: "A would-be whistleblower finds it difficult to use the company tribunal to, say, advance his or her claim that an ingredient the company is putting into a product should be banned. I ran into cases in which a fired employee claimed that such a belief was the real reason he or she was fired, discharged or demoted. In no company, however, did I find that the tribunal or ombudspersons were forums for whistleblowers before some act was taken against them."[4]

The real horror of this situation is not even the defensiveness of the system, we have come to expect that, but the irrational fear and loathing spewing from colleagues who sense you are also in some way threatening them. Some of the fear of a whistleblower stems from the "no ratting" ethic. One simply doesn't challenge (undermine?) the organization, no matter what—even when it is to the organization's advantage!

The difference today is that the paradigm shift has raised the consciousness of a growing number of people who, together, are beginning to ask the tough questions and who are ready to behave differently in organizations. This is partly due to the fact that no one is safe anymore, no matter how loyal, no matter how productive, no matter how creative. The effort to transform an organization is an effort to align it with new paradigm thinking and it will now be welcomed. Under these circumstances, change itself promises a measure of stability in a very chaotic organizational world.

Therefore, the first task you face is to determine just where your organization stands regarding the issues and themes in this book and its readiness to change. Look at all current practices and how management seeks and uses individuals' contributions to improve the effectiveness of the organization and the workplace climate. Is the organization receptive to ideas? Will those in traditional power centers be open to change? Are they willing to respond to questions regarding employee empowerment, restructuring and organizational transformation into community?

Review Existing Policies

New organizational forms will require new ways to motivate and compensate individuals. Be sure to review your organization's readiness for the new business environment by assuring an alignment between associated policies and the new operating procedures and objectives. Ask questions, catalog problems. Begin to establish an agenda of priorities important to working with one another. Know how your organization must change; know where it can change now and be able to itemize each area of policy and procedures that either interferes with or facilitates the evolution of a solacratic community.

Ask:

- Is evaluation and training continuous? Are the skills necessary to build community taught to everyone?
- Is there accountability to subordinates? How much weight do they have in the selection and evaluation of leaders, managers, peers? Can a peer review or a subordinate review process be developed?
- Is everyone routinely included on a meaningful committee or asked to attend governance meetings or representative forums? Is everyone involved in or represented on policy development committees?

- How are grievances handled? Is there a system in place to deal with them to everyone's satisfaction? Is the process owned by the participants or is it a game played between the organization and the individual?
- What are feedback procedures to raise issues of community formation? Are they available to everyone and does the organization utilize these procedures frequently?

Determining the organization's readiness to change is important. It will give you an idea of the obstacles you will face, the degree of preparation you will need and the appropriate strategy you and your allies must adopt in order to succeed. Unlike a whistleblower or a maverick, you are not alone. The first element of your strategy is to develop commitment within your network to proceed. Once the network has developed a clear picture of what the transformation will mean when applied to your organization, its first effort should be to expand. Get as many people as possible fired up about the potential of your ideas. Make the network a truly irrepressible force for change.

Build an Action Agenda

Eventually seek permanent adoption by the organization of policies and other changes your group develops. Bring the formal leaders into the process when your ideas are well thought out and your group's size is sufficient to warrant top management's participation. Make it nonthreatening to the individuals involved. At every opportunity, show how the transformation of your organization benefits the organization. Once management "gets it" the results can be quite remarkable. Digital Equipment Company (DEC) got the message several years ago when their Atlanta-based U.S. Customer Support Center was known as the low performer. Their performance was so bad it was ridiculed by other divisions and customers complained that service amounted to calling 1-800-DEC HOLD. They instituted a major change program which, based on the complete reevaluation of their values, realigned the organization's practices to their goals. In two and one-half years they were able to document $31 million in savings. These kinds of results are compelling reasons for any organization to reexamine the way it is working and to embrace the principles of the transformation.[5]

The benefits of change should be apparent to the organization because they stem from opportunities perceived by your group to solve problems you are facing. The reason you are changing the organization is because it is out of alignment. Once aligned it will become more effective in reaching its goals. In light of your recommendations put forth as solutions to existing problems, a rational management should be accepting for obvious reasons. By the time you have created a network that supports the basic thrust of the new changes, it may be impossible for upper management to resist. In essence your network's program may constitute a fait accompli since the support is already widespread, but the crucial issues surrounding institutionalizing long term structural changes or the adoption of a new social contract and constitution remain to be dealt with.

Phase in your steps. Remember, the transformation isn't an all-or-nothing proposition—nothing in this book should be construed as needing immediate adoption if your particular organization or group is unprepared to change instantaneously. That would only invite disaster. Inevitably there will be a variety of states of readiness among organizations. Take steps toward the objectives from the position of the current level of readiness experienced by your organization. If, for example, there is no trust, you can not expect that tomorrow everyone will be trusted. Individual acts of trustworthiness must be identified, reinforced, and acknowledged. Policies must be reversed if they are based on mistrust and replaced with more neutral ones. (Does everyone need to bring a note from a doctor after an illness?)

Discussions with others should precede the specific steps. Democracy as applied in the selection of managers or leaders can be phased in. Start with selecting representatives of work groups meeting to discuss the existing state of readiness, the policies most in need of change, the forums most in need of representation, and the positions most in need of accountability. Let this body identify the current state of affairs and needs and inform their respective groups. Discuss next steps with them.

Begin to develop a plan of small achievable steps as soon as possible within departments or work groups as a trial of some of the concepts. See what helps or hurts. With process facilitators, begin to understand the kinds of skills that need to be developed by individuals. Identify the kinds of information needed by the group to make decisions intelligently and create avenues for the dissemination of that information. Have representatives return to the group frequently at first, perhaps less so later, for revalidation and feedback. Have the representatives first experience and serve as models for the democratization of group processes and information sharing. Then move toward main stream activities as appropriate. Terms of office can be established as well as the manner of selection. The criteria for selection and all the mechanics of the choice process (including how the candidates will be put before the group and how the group will choose them) can also be determined by the group when the structure is being determined. Be specific about expectations for the position, criteria for success, and the kinds of decisions one can make for the group and those one must return to the group for advice or approval.

Once the network matures to the action stage it can select a steering committee to decide these matters and go back to the group for amendment and approval at timely intervals.

The point is that change need not happen all at once, though sometimes that is essential. In human systems and interpersonal affairs, sudden change is usually undesirable because of the history of expectations and the agreements already understood by the individuals. It is a good idea to prepare for the change, discuss its exact nature, implement it on a small scale, analyze the trial, adjust it, retry it, enlarge the base, and eventually repeat the process until it is fully operational with its own built-in processes for continuous ongoing feedback and change as needed.

On the other hand, when conditions so deteriorate that chaos and breakdown is endemic, then dramatic, sudden change is indeed feasible and recommended. If bankruptcy looms or a single event so dramatizes a potentially fatal danger faced by an organization, sudden change is essential. The assumption of this chapter is that your organization is simply feeling the stress epidemic, that it may be in decline but in a nondramatic way. It may sense that conditions are always reversible even though in reality they may not be, that the breakdown is inspiring more desperate acts for real change. You are in effect starting a guerrilla movement to save the organization while converting it into community.

Using Meetings

Use the full potential of all meetings you hold to explore these concepts. It is appropriate for you as a member of any group that conducts meetings to share ideas, make decisions or plan events to introduce some of the concepts discussed here. It is likely that some of your allies will be at these meetings and they provide a great opportunity for you to begin a subtle change process. Even agreeing to structure meetings so that they reflect the openness suggested here can be a vast improvement. Asking for agendas in the future, including time to discuss procedural issues or to put community building items on the agenda is to make a great deal of progress in transforming the business-as-usual routines of scheduled meetings.

Use the power of meeting with others to share experiences, focus goals reinforce intentions. Begin to call your own meetings either face-to-face or via electronic groupware or E-mail for the purpose of inventing ways to implement community-building ideas and democratic procedures.

The Association for Innovative Management in Walnut Creek, California, has introduced a new technique for gathering feedback and for evaluating meetings. At the end of their presentations they ask the audience to conduct a "harvesting." This involves asking how the presentation was useful, what could have been done differently, what actions or "next steps" can be taken, what words were most instructive, emotive, thought provoking, etc. The idea is to focus attention and reflection on the time spent together to make it a useful and productive experience. The harvesting, recorded on a few flip chart pages, then serves as a summary of the meeting just concluded. The purpose of the process is to focus, review, and inform both the participants and the discussants. It increases productivity of the meeting as well as encourage a free flow of ideas and impressions from the participants.

Caution

It would serve us well to remember Maslow's warning that ". . . perfectionism . . . is a danger. . . . A common sequence here . . . is perfectionism or unreasonable expectations leading to inevitable failure leading to disillusionment, leading to apathy, discouragement, or active hostility to all ideals and all normative hopes and efforts."[6] And never expect complaints to go away; new one's always emerge. Keep a sense of proportion and perspective about them.

Remember, too, that skepticism about the effectiveness of these ideas is a testament to the depth of the need for change. It may also be indicative of the depth of the resistance you will face. There is no doubt that the organization can resist internal "bottom up" change efforts and in some cases have done so by mercilessly destroying the careers of too vocal advocates of change. Be sure you are sensitive to the change environment and choose the methods that promise the most likelihood of success. Therefore, when you start out, be sure to build and maintain a network of committed and trusted allies and assess each step carefully.

Sooner or later, as you experience change and develop a sense of community aborning you'll overcome your fear (knowing that your base of support is widespread and allies are placed throughout the organization) and will refuse to participate in decisions that contradict community-building principles because doing so won't make sense anymore. You will be making every choice, every decision on the basis of its consistency with the kind of workplace you want to work in; a workplace which will be necessary for the company's very survival as well as your own psychological and emotional well-being.

THE ORGANIZATIONAL GROUP-CENTERED DOMAIN

"If you plant enough seeds you'll soon be walking in a garden."

—*Margaret Hogan, AVLP*

Create a Personal Network Within Your Organization

On Monday morning call five people at work whom you feel are receptive to these ideas. Disregard rank or location in the organization. The more inclusive and widespread the involvement, the better. Arrange brown bag lunch sessions and keep a mailing list of others willing to stay connected. When the group gets large enough, think about a newsletter or electronic messaging to keep the network informed. This is getting ahead of ourselves, however. For now, begin a weekly group to discuss your refinement of these ideas and how you can together best influence the organization. Look at various practices and begin to see how they might be altered to bring them into alignment with these ideas in a way suited to the individuals involved and your particular organization's culture. Grow the network by inviting others to participate. Develop personal agreements about how you will work with one another. While discussion and support are vital, don't let the network bog down in endless rehashing. Take steps no matter how small to change personal behavior and practice the skills itemized in chapter seven.

Transforming the Organization: When You Are The Leader

Apply team building and action research technologies to the groups you now manage. Using these technologies, begin to align their specific practices with the goals of the change process: building community. Skill building and getting used to new responsibilities and processes may need to precede any further organizational change or at least be developed simultaneously.

Team Building

Almost 20 years ago Reilly and Jones cited ten goals of team building that still deserve your attention today as you establish your personal agenda for involvement Monday morning. They can help guide your efforts to build community in your organization. Teams become community when each member recognizes these goals as their own. They are: To create

1. a better understanding of each member's role in the group
2. a better understanding of the team's purpose in the organization and its role as a subunit of the larger organization
3. increased communication among team members about issues that affect the efficiency of the group
4. greater personal support among group members
5. a clearer understanding of group processes
6. more effective ways of working through problems inherent in the team
7. the ability to use conflict in a positive way
8. greater collaboration among team members
9. an ability to collaborate with other teams in the organization
10. a sense of interdependence among team members.[7]

When these goals are sought and refined by the group to include aspects of community mentioned by M. Scott Peck,[8] team building becomes community building. It happens when the process stresses inclusivity, consensus building, continuous self-evaluation, trust, respect and the creation of a safe environment where individuals are allowed to be vulnerable.

Action Research

If you ever experienced one of the barriers discussed earlier, or want to follow through on a change process developed by your community building network, an action research methodology could provide a great deal of help. Action research is a data-based continuous process of gathering information about the state of an organization, analyzing the information and determining the best way to develop and implement a change effort. One of its most remarkable features is the direct involvement of all those affected by the change. And because of this the action research process is a very powerful diagnostic tool. It is a methodology that itself builds community simply by employing it.

Furthermore, the process systematically overcomes resistance to change and the various barriers to implementing new ideas. It also establishes a method of creating and sustaining continuous improvement. The process consists of the following steps outlined by French and Bell:[9]

Step 1: You have determined that community building (or a more specific issue relevant to your group) is an issue in need of further exploration. If the members of your group haven't been a part of your community building efforts thus far it is good at this point to remind yourself of some of the possible responses to change. And remember that unless people are part of the process they may react in several dysfunctional ways. Members of your group may experience a disturbance or become upset when they are asked to join you in a transformational change. They may also try to make some personal sense of it or even attempt to take advantage of it, but outright total acceptance to an invitation to change is rare—unless, of course, the change is an immediate benefit.

Try to involve as many people as possible in the change process right from the beginning and move on to the next step.

Step 2: Formulate a comprehensive definition of your intentions and determine the kinds of data you'll need to understand the impact community building will have on other parts of the organization.

Step 3: Now gather a small sample of data either through questionnaires, interviews or open meetings and see if it provides a meaningful picture of the conditions faced by the others in the work group as you originally perceived them. The data helps you determine the accuracy of your perceptions and helps make any necessary refinements to the problem definition. It also helps the group focus its attention. Be prepared for some of the unanticipated consequences of the process. For example, given the chance to look at the issue of building community in your group, some individuals will make it an opportunity to raise personal and other issues that may not be appropriate now. Be sure you are committed to the process because momentum will be building for substantive change at this point.

Step 4: Together, the group will clarify the nature of the community building process from their perspective. It validates and helps you develop an appropriate strategy at this point and establishes a benchmark. Members of the group now begin taking ownership of the process themselves. Be ready for this; detach your ego from personally owning the change effort.

Step 5: This is a joint action planning phase. Because the group is fully engaged in creating community, many of the barriers and sources of resistance to change are either overcome or dealt with directly. Keep an eye out for any remaining areas of resistance. You can tell if skepticism is still present or if silence has replaced enthusiasm, or if there is excessive maneuvering to avoid taking one's fair share of the responsibility for the change program. This step concludes when objectives and means of reaching them are formalized and agreed upon.

Step 6: Begin implementing some of the ideas the group developed.

Step 7: Now gather feedback to be sure that the process is working. Problems of, or resulting from, implementation are dealt with as the action research methodology recycles through the steps.

The action research process is best performed when the interpersonal skills such as those outlined in Chapter 7 are used. Remember: the process has as much of a message to convey to work group members as any other factor about your intentions, sincerity, and willingness to improve the group's effectiveness and the personal satisfaction of its members.

As an ongoing process, action research and community building efforts ultimately lead to a continuous cycle of improvement because of the deliberate attempt to face and overcome issues as they arise.

It helps the group deal directly with resistance, as well as with unanticipated aspects of facilitating the transformation of your organization, because of the fully participative nature of the process. It is one methodology that is perfectly aligned with the principles of the transformation itself.

THE NETWORK-BASED DOMAIN

Network Like Crazy Outside Your Organization

Recognize that changes are already taking place in some large organizations and that they will spread with the dissemination of computer and communications technology. The very forces propelling the structural changes in organizations should awaken middle managers and professionals to see the threat to their current role. This provides an opportunity as well as a danger since the potential for a more imaginative and facilitative middle management role emerges. Obviously, before anyone changes they must experience and become fully conscious of the need to change.

Examine the implications of the new structures that are emerging. Consider how your organization will use information and communications technology so that the inevitable transformation of the organization occurs smoothly. In your estimation, based on your company's past experience, how will your organization respond to these changes? If your job appears threatened, begin to think about what you can do to redesign your own role before it is eliminated. How can you add value either to the information computers will make available (that is in the analysis, interpretation and utilization of information), or in order to expedite the work flow process? Not to change in the face of the realization of its necessity will result in a slow nagging discomfort that eventually leads to one's professional obsolescence. Networking helps expose you to changes in your profession and informs you of the extent and speed of the change process in your industry. It is also a powerful way of discovering career possibilities and challenges elsewhere.

Connect with Professional Associations

After activating their already finely honed networks developed for professional growth and career security, middle managers will begin to utilize their professional associations for more actively pursuing standards of "best practice" and codes of ethics to implement within their organization. When accrediting, certification or licensing bodies begin to demand conformity to standards they set, individuals have little choice but to practice these standards of behavior inside their organization. This can have a dramatic affect on the change process. Indeed it could have an immediate and profound effect if professional bodies began to take this initiative in the areas of organizational development, human resource management and total quality control. This kind of action would not only institute immediate and widespread change but would offer a great deal of security to change agents at the leading edge of the transformation—the early adopters.

Professional groups will be expected to protect individual members and perhaps represent or insure them against capricious retaliations by companies when they institute professional standards of best practices or by seeking to avert layoffs of their members. Professionals will join with their blue-collar colleagues in quality circles, self-managed teams and other joint endeavors and forge a measure of common interest in stabilizing the work environment. Since the transformation's focus on quality and the processes of work bring these two groups together as colleagues, the idea of their eventual organizing around shared interests is a likely development.

The combined energy of individual commitment and support from professional associations will overwhelm the bureaucratic mind. No longer will acceptance of firings, harassment of any kind, or unilateral management treatment of subordinates without due process be acknowledged as legitimate. Professional bodies using publicity, boycotting and "career watch" forums will quickly serve notice to organizations that fail to become user friendly. (Career-watch forums will become the protective arm of the implementation of best practice standards.)

In developing professional organizations that become active in supporting the transformation, it may be helpful to create separate membership categories: one for those that will commit to action and another for the traditional networkers and interested, but not action oriented, members. Give different responsibilities and powers to each group. Active membership should carry with it certain requirements to perform duties for the group or to take initiatives in one's workplace. Members that commit to action, work and responsibilities within the group would have full voting and office-holding privileges while the others hold auxiliary membership.

Remember the power of assembly, of meeting, is unmatched when there is direction, a sense of purpose and the promise of meaningful action. Getting together to discuss issues on an agenda and to share support is incredibly powerful and fun. But it is not enough to change our workplaces; widespread involvement is necessary. Create a workplace cross-functional general management professional association to focus on specific issues within your organization.

Form an advocacy section in your professional organizations and outside networks to actively support members working for change—particularly for the adoption of professional standards within the association and within representative organizations. Develop interest groups to enact and promote codes of best practice. Advertise organizations that support the standards and encourage other organizations to adopt the best practice guidelines. One group very active in this strategy is Computer Professionals for Social Responsibility. They are actively working on codes of ethics and an employee bill of rights that in part focuses on privacy issues surrounding new computer technology. LAN technology, for example, has the capability to monitor and record 100 percent of an employees' communication.

Once a professional body establishes a code of ethics or best practice and requires its adoption by applicants for either certification, membership or access to its network, it is possible for them to become a major influence for organizational change. Such an organization can even move to become an accrediting body that carries weight in the application of uniform best practice industrywide. One item in the employers' code of ethics recommended by the American Civil Liberties Union requires the protection of whistleblowers; another the employees' right to privacy of voice, paper and electronic mail. These efforts, when adopted by organizations, begin to significantly alter traditional practice and redefine the social contract. Ultimately, as these issues are raised in professional associations and brought back to one's organization, they stimulate major structural changes.

Create professional committees of correspondence to assemble and disseminate information about efforts to change behavior and policy by members in their organizations, and to discuss specific barriers uncovered along the way. Give vignettes of successes and failures; discuss new techniques that could be applied and generally keep members informed of efforts to build community. This could be the basis for an addition to the association newsletter or an additional newsletter taken upon the employees themselves or contracted out to a third party, useful if there is an extreme level of fear in the organization to discourage one from being identified with the paper.

In creating awareness of issues among bosses, CEOs or others, it could be useful to begin a letter writing campaign, either sponsored by a network or an individual or as anonymous efforts to at least inform management of the agenda that is beginning to take shape and indicate the kind of support for change that is growing in the organization. This is as much of a change effort as an educational one, and though it is less dramatic than confronting issues in meetings, it does raise the issues.

THE PUBLIC ACTION DOMAIN

Outside Help

Do a community and stakeholder audit. Look at all aspects of the organization's relationships as measured against the standards for community that you have set as a goal. Invite colleagues from other businesses, your network, and your professional associations to join you in the effort. The goal here is to assess your organization in the larger, total stakeholder context and to determine the kinds of outside interest groups that would be supportive of the kinds of changes you wish to make. They might also have ideas about how to do it in light of their own experience. Investors customers, suppliers, and the local community usually have the most at stake so their commitment will be real. They can even become allies in the change program around those aspects that directly involve them. One area, for example, in supplier relations, is the new concept of single sourcing. This fundamentally shifts the paradigm from having multiple suppliers compete with one another to developing a single supplier who works intimately with your organization to insure it meets your needs.

Another way is to seek endorsement from the new socially responsible investor community. For example, talk to the Parnassus Fund in San Francisco. It is a mutual fund that selects equities for its portfolio from companies that demonstrate "enlightened and progressive" management. Or, call Working Assets, a money market investment fund, also in San Francisco, that invests in "socially responsible" companies to see if your organization meets its criteria and to learn about strategies for applying investor pressure on the organization that will result in community building efforts.

Outside support may come in many forms. Customer and supplier feedback is central. Community feedback is also important. The most powerful may turn out to be state and local regulatory bodies and legislatures. In matters of equal opportunity, health and safety, these outside agencies have been instrumental in dealing with workplace reform. In matters of healthcare and pensions, government agencies will play an increasingly important role as corporations cut back their coverage or undermine existing plans. Frequently, pension plans have been plundered prior to, or just after, a takeover to finance the debt to pay for the purchase! In some cases when the corporation was unable to survive the debt and filed for bankruptcy workers lost virtually all of their retirement plans. "Corporations removed $21 billion from their employees' pension plans during the 1980's; overall, nearly 2,000 corporations dipped into employee pension funds for at least $1 million each. . . ."[10] Getting representation on employee pension funds will become a priority and the funds, when used to reinvest in the corporation, could leverage their financial clout with substantial demands for quality of work life changes and community- building policies within the organization.

There is a new war between the states as they, and cities, compete for new plants. Low wage incentives in nonunionized areas and waivers on taxes, utilities and road construction, tax-paid employee training, state or city bonuses for each job created, and utility rebates are all components of packages offered to companies to relocate to, or expand an existing facility within, a state.[11] The new North American Free Trade Zone is putting even more downward pressure on wages and is now rightly being viewed as a way of black mailing current employees to accept cuts or lose their jobs. "So far, Philips has shifted 900 jobs to Juarez. The threat of moving more enabled it to win union concessions."[12] After the state and city bidding, though jobs are created in one area, they may be lost in another. The most intense downward pressure on wages comes from the appeal of Mexican incentives which far and away outstrip what the states have to offer;

you just can't beat $2-a-day wages! As expected there has been a massive migration to border towns along the Rio Grande. General Motors, Fisher-Price, Trico, Parker-Hannifin, Xerox, Ford, Kimberly-Clark, IBM, Samsonite, General Electric, and Rockwell, are some of the Fortune 500 companies now operating there.[13] And, if the jobs are ultimately going off shore or just south of the U.S.-Mexican border, this certainly does not serve the national interest. It only forces wages down and damages the quality of life in those communities being vacated. Along with jobs go tax revenues. The bottom line, then, has now become a strictly private affair with no positive impact on the overall quality of life here.

States may eventually redirect corporations to serve the public purpose for which they were originally established. Through corporate law, states, until there is federal chartering, can leverage change through establishing social policy and tax rules that influence the quality of life in the workplace.

One legislative avenue that would quickly lead to sensible organizational change would be the prohibition of mergers and acquisitions without the consent of employees. This isn't as far fetched as it sounds. In 1987 when Dayton Hudson faced a possible takeover attempt, "The Minnesota Legislature, called into special session . . . promptly passed a tough antitakeover bill, requiring, among other things, that an acquiring company be barred for five years from selling off any company assets acquired."[14] Other companies pass "poison pill" measures to discourage acquisitions and takeovers. The poison is the requirement that the acquiring company pay a premium for current employees laid off as a result of the purchase and it protects the pension plan from dismemberment by the new buyer. Where unemployment runs high, there is labor sentiment in state legislatures, or pressure mounts from unions, states might be forced to consider providing a voice to labor's concerns in a merger or buyout.

Employees themselves are becoming active in checking management buyouts and are making their reservations known to the public and to current investors. As reported in *Fortune*, workers at Cone Mills, "To the astonishment of Wall Street . . . invaded the financial district to seek support from anyone who would listen to their objections to the company's plan to go public." The plan would bring a windfall to management. One union representative said, "We don't mind if management gets rich. We just wish they'd cut us in on it."[15]

Ultimately, if corporations don't act on their own volition, states may begin requiring them to adopt employee constitutions that follow the same guidelines that states themselves follow for adoption, amendment and adjudication of fundamental operating policies.

Just Vote No: Using the Pension Funds

Monitor the board of directors. Attend meetings and raise issues that need to be addressed by the board to institutionalize best practice. The board may be the only body that can institutionalize an employee bill of rights, for example, and given the sensitivity of such a proposal it would be wise to plan a strategy carefully. You may need to line up the employee pension fund management to vote employee shares or, if a large enough block, to simply require board action on matters that will contribute to institutionalizing the community concepts mentioned here. Calpers (California Public Employees Retirement System with $68 billion in its portfolio) is one pension fund that swings a lot of weight. ". . . Calpers uses its clout as shareholders to push for change. This year it has chosen 12 companies to work on: four paid their executives too much, four have too few directors, and four had resisted discussions with shareholders."[16] It is evident that the clout is there. The funds, however, have generally not been pushed by employees to become a vehicle for major internal change. It is only a matter of time before employee representatives on pension funds push their custodians to stand up at board meetings and stockholder's meetings to require institutionalization of best practice and even employee constitutions. On Monday morning find out your pension fund's governing structure and how to get represented. If there is no avenue for representation, put that issue on your network's agenda.

Publicize internally, and to the press, the actions or denials of the board when it comes to institutionalizing best practices in your organization. Let all know what is happening. Dislodge the cloak of secrecy and silence that boards have been luxuriously enjoying. Reveal their actions to the local communities and investors. Begin a newsletter to investors from the employees perspective. Get support from the public and investors.

Public Relations/Public Action

When conditions deteriorate to out and out rape of the organization, such as when Russell Isaacs ran successful Heck's Department stores with more than 120 outlets into bankruptcy, leaving thousands of employees out of work, more drastic measures may be necessary to institute a transformational process. Isaacs, ". . . his managers and those who followed him received millions of dollars, collectively, in generous compensation packages, pensions and severance contracts."[17] To supervise the coup de grâce John Isaac was hired at $360,000 a year and, along with "four associates . . . managed the final dismantling of the company, collected more than $1.5 million in severance pay."[18]

In cases such as these when financial manipulation, asset stripping and mismanagement clearly threaten the organization's existence in the short run, public, legal, legislative, union, professional association and internal protests must be launched immediately. Throughout the 1980's the employees' voice has been a virtual silent scream when their livelihoods were unceremoniously wiped out through technical and financial manipulations. As a group they have quietly driven into the sunset as they bade farewell to their friends to suffer the outrage and pain alone at home. The same people who thought it would never happen to them had to face unemployment with little prospect of ever regaining the wages and benefits they once took for granted. The same employees who looked upon unions and collective action with growing disfavor throughout the go-go years of the '80's, who believed unquestioningly that the system wouldn't let injustice and abuse prevail, are now rethinking their position. This has the potential of awakening the sleeping giant of employee activism that, as mentioned earlier, will make the workplace the next political frontier.

While managing may be a game to the MBAs and financiers who play with assets as so many tokens on a life-size monopoly board, employees have had no margins when it comes to the dismantling of the organizations that provide their livelihood. The vigilant monitoring of the management process, the board of directors, the stock offerings and attempts at diversification and divestitures must now become the stuff of lunchtime conversations in the employee cafeteria. Employees will need their own intelligence gathering apparatus to keep them informed of current managerial behavior in order to take self-protective measures. Employees will need to create their own newspapers and hire their own consultants to look after their interests and interpret their options. The stakes are simply too high for employees to remain ignorant of what management is doing. Organizations that resist the transformation and see employees as the enemy, or a necessary evil, require the active vigilance of the employees in safeguarding their own future as well as current interests in building a better workplace community.

Alliances between unions and professional associations will become practical and quite sensible once all perceive the organization as a community, a unitary entity, under life threatening circumstances such as a slide into bankruptcy and the looting of the organization by raiders.

Exhibit 9–2 summarizes the actions suggested for all domains.

EXHIBIT 9–2
An Action Agenda for Monday Morning

Individual Domain

Conduct a self appraisal of your readiness to work for change.

Take personal responsibility for doing something.

Talk about issues with coworkers, begin consciousness raising around the idea of holistic systems (ecological model) and new definitions of organization and of management, e.g., inclusive entity with obligation to each in an efficacious role; management as developing relationships.

Initiate meetings and discussions, invite others to participate.

Learn new behaviors and intergroup skills.

Model new behaviors and demonstrate your new attitudes.

Maintain continuous personal growth.

The Organizational Group-Centered Domain

Establish many informal opportunities to get to know one another and facilitate communication/understanding of diverse perspectives about organizational community and current needs.

Establish or join a self-development group.

Do an organizational analysis/audit.

Develop positions on issues and pledge mutual support to each other.

Prepare an action agenda and prioritize your goals.

The Network-Based Domain

Develop a personal network.

Join or develop a professional network; urge professional associations to develop codes of best practice and ethics.

Urge protection of whistleblowers.

Insure against retaliatory dismissal.

Redesign your own job in line with likely changes due to technological/structural changes to affect the organization.

Establish committees of correspondence between professional groups and between organizational members and management.

Create a network newsletter to chart progress and new ideas for action; getting the attention of decision makers and becoming convincing in your arguments.

When network gets large enough or issues pressing enough invite top managers to forums that you sponsor.

Develop capability of refusing to comply with Paradigm 1 type demands or decisions made by the organization. Decisions without involvement that affect one's livelihood are a good place to start, e.g., layoffs.

Demand collaboration with boss and others and to be invited to policy-making decision centers. Start by demanding that minutes to all executive decision-making meetings be made public.

Public Action Domain

Use pension plan leverage on board of directors to seek employee representation and to create or adopt an employee/stakeholder constitution and bill of rights?

EXHIBIT 9–2 (Concluded)
An Action Agenda for Monday Morning

Request inclusion on board's agenda for employee issues.

Monitor legislative committees of industry and commerce.

Monitor trade associations.

Monitor labor organizations in industry.

Monitor Wall Street activity in industry and your own organization's financing.

Use regulatory bodies as leverage to affect change and know the procedures for making complaints, amending regulations, etc.

KNOWING THAT COMMUNITY IS BEING BUILT: POSITIVE SIGNS

In the world at large, consciousness is being raised regarding consumer, environmental, and human rights issues. In addition a renewed concern for public service and major reforms are all hopeful signs of the paradigm shift taking effect.

Likewise a managerial responsiveness, innovation and change would be positive signs of movement toward a workplace community. When they occur these events and successes should be publicized and nurtured. Start now. Build interest. Hold additional social gatherings coinciding with signs of change in the organization. Seek out additional individuals of like mind and follow up on efforts leading toward community and democratization.

The suggestions made here will work because of a fundamental truth: in its manifest practicality, business adapts to its environment very quickly because in a competitive market with demanding customers, the only way of maintaining business is to change, to improve, adapt, respond to the customer and societal environment. In order to survive business must be prepared to act quickly. Because time is a diminishing resource, solacracy and workplace community become a necessity; it is the only system that constantly reinforces its adaptive behavior through examining the process of facing up to the challenges of the environment! The collection of empowered, committed people able to respond effectively to changes makes this so. As the most adaptive of all institutions in our culture business will pioneer the development of living organizations and the fundamental elements of the new paradigm.

If we don't turn organizations around soon, voices from the under-side will get even louder. One such voice asserts that "It is difficult to imagine why anyone would want to have more direct control over essentially useless work, except perhaps to put an end to it."[19]

NOTES

[1] G. Leonard, *The Transformation* (Los Angeles: J. P. Tarcher, 1972), p. 13.

[2] M. S. Peck, *The Different Drum* (New York: Touchstone, 1988), p. 17.

[3] M. Nauman, "End of An Era," *San Jose Mercury News*, August 17, 1992, p. 74.

[4] D. W. Ewing, *Justice On The Job* (Cambridge, MA: Harvard University Press, 1989), p. 97.

[5] Digital Equipment Corporation, *The Healing Forest: Managing Cultural Change*, 4 Part Video Series (Maynard, MA: DEC Corporate Headquarters, 1991).

[6] A. Maslow, *The Farther Reaches of Human Nature* (New York: The Viking Press, 1971), p. 217.

[7] A. J. Reilly and J. E. Jones, "Team Building"; *The 1974 Annual Handbook for Group Facilitators* (San Diego: University Associates, 1974), p. 227.

[8] M. S. Peck, *The Different Drum* (New York: Touchstone, 1988).

[9] W. L. French and C. H. Bell, Jr.; *Organization Development*, 4th ed. (Englewood-Cliffs, NJ: Prentice Hall, 1990).

[10] D. L. Barlett and J. B. Steele, *America: What Went Wrong*, 1992, p. 193.

[11] K. Barrett and R. Greene, "The New War Between the States," *Financial World*, September 3, 1991, p. 34.

[12] "The Global Economy: Who Gets Hurt," *Business Week*, August 10, 1992, p. 51.

[13] D. L. Barlett and J. B. Steele, *America: What Went Wrong*, p. 35.

[14] M. Moskowitz, R. Levering and M. Katz, *Everybody's Business* (New York: Doubleday, 1990), p. 206.

[15] A. B. Fisher, "Workers in ESOP: 'We're Screwed'," *Fortune*, June 29, 1992, p. 14.

[16] "A Wobbly Californian Giant," *The Economist*, May 30, 1992, p. 75.

[17] D. L. Barlett and J. B. Steele, *America: What Went Wrong*, p. 136.

[18] Ibid. p. 141.

[19] C. Carlsson and M. Leger, *Bad Attitude: The Processed World Anthology* (New York: Verso, 1990), p. 145.

Chapter Ten

Afterword: The Challenge of a Lifetime

To try to live in the past, to pretend we can continue with business as usual, is to support the myths of management which serve a very small elite and their dysfunctional, perverse ethos of domination and control for the sake of themselves and a myopic Wall Street. To choose the future is to reinvigorate the organization and to harness its human energy, to rebuild, even to recreate, the planet and to do so in a way that fosters human growth and dignity in the workplace and in all of our organized endeavors. This is the choice we must make.

To scoff at the seriousness of the situation is in effect to choose the rapid destruction of our ecosystem and to foist further psychological misery on vast numbers of people. It is in effect to watch the richest nation in the history of this world choose to self-destruct.

Two stories, on the same news broadcast not too long ago, illustrate the formidable difficulty we will have in making this choice. But they demonstrate the very real consequences of choosing to act versus choosing to live a self-destructive fantasy.

The stories were about flood victims. The first was an artist who survived a Northern California mud slide and flood. She had lost everything—her house and its contents, including her professional studio with all but one of her paintings. To add insult to injury, the IRS wouldn't allow her to deduct the market value of her paintings even though the value had been established long before the flood. So here we watched a conversation with a women in mid-life who had just seen all the fruits of her life's labors literally washed away telling the TV interviewer that she "found friends she didn't know she had." The community had pulled together in this crisis, she said; each person helping others. She was clearly touched by the empathy, compassion and friendliness she found in the experience.

Her husband, standing next to her, also told of his own home-based business that was washed away. Neither one of them was insured. It was a total material loss. He told the interviewer that the experience was an "enormous personal challenge and an opportunity for growth." Here was a couple in the midst of their greatest personal crisis. Yet, they remained optimistic and actually saw opportunities in the situation—new friends and a chance for personal growth! They were clearly prepared for the future.

In that same news broadcast about other flood victims, we were shown a vast area of Missouri that was not only under flood waters but was threatened with an unchecked spread of dioxin contamination because of the damage done to a nearby hazardous waste dump during the flood. Again, a couple was recounting the tragedy of seeing their home and its contents destroyed by the overflowing river. To compound the horror, the entire residential area including the local water supply was totally contaminated with dioxin. The danger to life was real. To stay there was literally to commit suicide, the toxicity was so high.

Yet, the couple being interviewed, the pain and uncertainty showing in their expressions and quite evident in their voices, flatly stated that they would not leave their home. They simply said that they "did not believe the warnings from the EPA." To them the situation was not hazardous or a threat. If they died, too bad; they were not relocating. Apparently the thought of relocating was so inherently unfathomable that these particular flood victims became psychologically paralyzed. Facts, indeed disaster, did not convince them of the need to change their expectations. They believed that the threat of poisoning from the contaminated water was not real. Was this just another case of a momentary psychological defense mechanism protecting the couple from the full impact of the calamity? Was their reaction just an attempt to maintain some semblance of equilibrium in their lives? Was it simply a consequence of the overwhelming shock of the destruction all around them and the total material loss they suffered? Perhaps so. But for many people such defiance in the face of such an obvious and overwhelming situation is to be in a state of denial and to desperately hold on to a past that has been destroyed.

The reaction of the two couples is a study in contrasts that illustrates the very real differences among individuals when the environment creates the need for an immediate change in perceptions and consequent behavior. This difference among individuals is due to their different personalities, values, beliefs, and experiences, of course. But when disaster strikes the more adaptive survive, while the others perish, victims of their fantasies and delusions.

Organizations behave in much the same way. When an Exxon tanker ran aground in Prince William Sound, the company responded in defensive foot dragging and legal maneuvering trying to execute a policy of damage control—not of the environment, but of Exxon public relations. The company struggled for years with environmentalists, state agencies and federal agencies over the responsibilities of the accident and the extent of the damage. By way of contrast, when an Occidental Petroleum offshore platform explosion and fire raged in the North Sea, in the summer of 1988, Armand Hammer, the 90 year old CEO, immediately ordered a program to compensate the families of the dead, care for the survivors, keep the public informed, and plan for repair. He personally took charge of the effort. That was a lightening fast, appropriate and well-respected response. Here too we see that even multinational organizations are not immune to the vagaries of emotional paralysis in crisis. Some people in a pathological fashion strategically take the position of resistance to the future and to one's corporate social responsibilities as a way of doing business, while some respond with the same openness and goodwill as neighbors in a local crisis.

In a very real sense our organizations in general and American business in particular are also victims of a flood of recent changes from the confluence of societal and technological developments that demand our immediate attention. Much like the victims of the California mud slide and flood, we need desperately to develop the resilience to make the experience one of personal growth where we can indeed "find friends we didn't know we had" and thus turn the current crisis into opportunity. Or, much like the victims of the Missouri flood and dioxin contamination, we can block out the need to adjust and believe there is no danger and desperately hold on to a past shattered right before our eyes.

As a nation we have frequently been faced with this kind of choice and we seem to have been very resilient indeed. And now we must decide yet again. Shall we chose to hold on to the past? Or shall we chose the future and face it squarely "with friends we didn't know we had." We must proceed to face the future sensibly or we will perish in the coming crisis.

Clearly, to conduct business as usual, is to conduct business in decline. It's time for business as unusual: managing as if people matter.

Index